GWYNNE'S KINGS AND QUEENS

ABOUT THE AUTHOR

Formerly a successful businessman, N. M. Gwynne has for many years been teaching just about every sort of subject to just about every sort of pupil in just about every sort of circumstance – English, Latin, Greek, French, German, mathematics, history, classical philosophy, natural medicine, the elements of music and 'How to start up and run your own business' – in lecture halls, large classrooms, small classrooms and homes – to pupils aged from three years old to over seventy – of many different nationalities and in several different countries – and since 2007 'face to face' over the Internet. His teaching methods are very much in accordance with the traditional, common-sense ones, refined over the centuries, that were used almost everywhere until they were abolished worldwide in the 1960s and subsequently. His teaching has been considered sufficiently remarkable – both in its unusualness in today's world and in its genuinely speedy effectiveness – to have featured in newspaper and magazine articles and on television and radio programmes.

Also by N. M. Gwynne

Gwynne's Grammar
Gwynne's Latin

GWYNNE'S KINGS AND QUEENS

THE INDISPENSABLE HISTORY OF ENGLAND
AND HER MONARCHS

N. M. Gwynne, M. A. (Oxon)

EBURY
PRESS

1 3 5 7 9 10 8 6 4 2

Ebury Press, an imprint of Ebury Publishing,
20 Vauxhall Bridge Road,
London SW1V 2SA

Ebury Press is part of the Penguin Random House group of companies whose
addresses can be found at global.penguinrandomhouse.com

Penguin
Random House
UK

First published by Ebury Press in 2018

www.penguin.co.uk

A CIP catalogue record for this book is available from the British Library

ISBN 9781785037849

Typeset in India by Integra Software Services Pvt. Ltd, Pondicherry

Printed and bound in Great Britain by Clays Ltd, St Ives PLC

To the Family that today represents the subject-matter of this book.

CONTENTS

PART V

BEFORE THE REFORMATION:
KINGS OF ENGLAND ONLY

PART VI

BEFORE THE REFORMATION:
KINGS OF ENGLAND AND DUKES OF
NORMANDY

PART VII

THE REFORMATION: KINGS AND QUEENS
OF ENGLAND, WALES AND IRELAND

PART VIII

AFTER THE REFORMATION: KINGS OF ENGLAND, WALES, IRELAND, SCOTLAND AND ELSEWHERE

PART IX

NO KINGS, AND THEN THE KINGS OF ENGLAND, WALES, IRELAND, SCOTLAND AND ELSEWHERE AGAIN

PART X

KINGS OF ENGLAND, WALES, NORTHERN IRELAND, SCOTLAND AND ELSEWHERE

PART XI

MONARCHS OF ENGLAND, WALES, NORTHERN IRELAND, SCOTLAND AND ELSEWHERE, AND EMPERORS OF INDIA

PART XII

Preface

THIS BOOK IS intended to be useful for everyone, of whatever age and intellectual status: for children emerging from infancy at the age of about five, though only chapter 3 for them; for schoolchildren as a standard textbook; for adults in general; some of it – I dare to hope – even for the erudite.

It is intended, too, as a much more serious, and also more interesting, work on history than its size and appearance might suggest. Certainly, I have taken with the utmost seriousness the task of putting it together, and I believe for good reason. The reality is that our country's history is a *fundamental* part of what we actually *are*. The society we live in and its institutions that affect us are the result of our country's history up to this point of time. To know our history, therefore, is to help us to know ourselves, as well as much else besides.

For a society's members to know its history is also important to that society, and therefore to its members. As the great nineteenth-century French scholar Gaston Paris put it, 'There is no better measure of a people's civilisation than its interest in its own history.'

Acquiring an adequate knowledge of the history that is part of us is therefore something that we should certainly do. This does involve considerable effort, but, in the case of England's history, there is the compensating factor that, consistently, it is history that is absorbingly interesting. Indeed I doubt whether any other country anywhere has a history more remarkable in every way than ours.

We can now readily appreciate why the teaching of history always used to be considered an important part of education, and almost from infancy.

~

Regrettably, in the 'child-centred' atmosphere that dominates all education today, acquiring a thorough and orderly knowledge of English history is no longer considered practical or even appropriate. What is made to count overwhelmingly today is no longer whether knowledge of history is *important*, but whether children will find studying it interesting and enjoyable.

The result has been unfortunate, even tragic. As I know from my considerable experience as a teacher, the knowledge of history acquired by children by the time they leave school is, and has been for some decades, almost invariably minimal – only a very small percentage of what everyone used to know.

It is against that background that the position taken in this book is that the basics of the entirety of English history should be taught systematically and in reasonable depth. In the case of children, moreover, whether or not they enjoy the learning should be considered irrelevant. Ordinary common sense dictates that what is of overriding importance for children is *not* their immediate gratification but their *long-term* benefit; and that is something that responsible adults are obviously far better able to assess on their behalf than are the inexperienced human beings that children inevitably are.

~

But ...

Even the best-motivated teachers and students of history are faced with a problem that they will not read about in the great majority of books dealing with general history. It is a controversial one, and I shall therefore introduce it with the help of three prominent historical figures of the past.

My first witness is the 'founding father' of the mass-produced motorcar, Mr. Henry Ford, in 1921:

'History is bunk.'

My second quotation, usually attributed to Sir Winston Churchill, explains why:

'History is written by the victors.'

In consequence, according to a third expert on the subject, the Emperor Napoleon Bonaparte, writing during the period when he was confined as a prisoner on the island of St. Helena in the closing years of his life:

'History is nothing but the lies that are no longer disputed.'

What follows from what those three knowledgeable authorities are telling us is that history is an *exceptionally* interesting subject.

~

How, though, are we ordinary folk going to acquire the ability to recognise *real* history, which means, amongst other things, identifying errors of any significance where they exist?

We need at least the following: enthusiasm; good judgement, which comes from sound reasoning and plenty of practice; and the skills – which we need painstakingly to acquire if we do not already possess them – of a reasonably competent professional detective.

The most difficult of those three requirements is the last one. Let us ask ourselves, therefore: what is it that detectives *principally* look for in cases where there is no direct evidence?

Identifying *motivation*, whether the motivation of historians themselves or of the compilers of the sources they use, is an obvious starting point. If, for instance, a particular author were to take a position on a historical subject that is significantly contrary to the positions of other authors, and especially recognised authorities, on that subject, it would be as well to search for evidence that could indicate *why*, on the one hand, that author has taken up his position and why, on the other hand, the generality of other authors have taken theirs.

Further, if an otherwise credible author taking a position in opposition to that of most other authors has, in consequence, been subjected to scornful attacks damaging to his reputation, we can consider it likely that his love of truth and sense of justice were such that he was impelled even to make sacrifices on behalf of truth and justice.

I do not suggest that evidence of good faith needs to be as dramatic as indifference to assaults on an author's reputation, in order to earn our interest. Perfectly adequate would be evidence that a writer had noticed that a gap existed in the arena of historical knowledge that he thought it worth filling or a distortion that he thought it worth correcting. What is fundamental in every such case is that a serious author has thought it worth taking a lonely or relatively lonely stand, even, if necessary, in defiance of experts.

~

Against the background of this introduction to researching history, a practical question arises. How can the history of England best be presented in order to achieve the ambitious goal of a book that is both useful and, in the manner of its presentation, suitable for everyone? – and, as indicated earlier, I really do mean *everyone*. The following are the principles governing what I am including in this book and how I am organising it. Although the results of applying them conscientiously will sometimes prove to be controversial, I believe that the principles themselves can be seen to be a matter of common sense as soon as stated.

1. I am strictly confining the content to *recorded* history, rather than what might be called *deduced* history. Standard textbooks often open with chapters titled 'The Neolithic Revolution', 'The Bronze Age' and 'The Iron Age', and similar. What is included under such headings can, however, only be based on deduction, rather than on written records, because of course there *are* no written records, and therefore it cannot feature here.
2. In the very early part of England's recorded history, there is scarcely ever a problem of rival sets of written records. Indeed for the most part there is in fact a single purported recorded series of events, and what is disputable is whether or not that record is authentic. There, I shall give *both* the commonly held view *and* the more controversial one, examining the case on both sides, and, after some discussion, point the reader in what I believe to be the right direction and leave the final decision to him.
3. From the time of Julius Caesar's invasions to the time of the Norman Conquest in AD 1066, the political history of the country is for the most part relatively straightforward and uncontroversial.

4. From 1066 onwards, distortions, suppressions and other kinds of falsification become the continuing feature of recorded history that Ford, Churchill and Bonaparte have told us we should be wise to expect. From then on, the system in this book of presenting history therefore changes in reflection of that. This is how a chapter will be typically constructed:

- First, the main events of the reign and their dates are listed. This will be all that is needed by children at the very outset, and will be the basic background for all other readers, whatever the level of their historical knowledge.
- Secondly, a treatment of that reign labelled 'Of special interest' is given. This will include a discussion of any matters of historical controversy together with the conclusion I myself have arrived at and why. This 'secondly' is arguably this book's most important feature.

~

Normally, and justifiably, historians of the English monarchy devote approximately the same amount of space to each monarch. This would be my own preference, all other things being equal, but the nature of this book makes it impractical. Where what I say is in contradiction to other historians, it would be unreasonable to expect my readers to accept it on my authority alone. Following the principle *audi alteram partem* – 'hear the other side' – they have a right to expect any such position to be adequately defended, which in turn means defended at whatever length is needed in order to carry conviction. The treatment of some monarchs, in consequence, inevitably takes up more space than the treatment of others, and sometimes considerably more space.

~

By the time I had brought this book to the verge of completion, I had reached the conclusion that it is unlikely that there is any more difficult kind of book to put together on any subject than one dealing with an extended period of history.

First, there is the factor already mentioned and indeed – with the help of Ford, Churchill and Napoleon – stressed: the continual falsifications of history by some historians and the frequent failure by at least many other historians to recognise most such falsifications.

Secondly, there is the sheer quantity of facts that need to be identified and weighed up, both as to whether they are indeed facts and also as to whether they are important enough to justify inclusion. Thirdly, and far from least, the history of any period needs to be looked at under a number of very different headings: for instance, succession-of-events history, political history, religious history and social history. What falls under each such heading needs to be taken *fully* into account, since an inadequate or mistaken knowledge of even only one of them can easily lead to a representation of history that is gravely wrong.

Yes, compiling a book such as this is a demanding task. And it is against the background of this reality that I say that, although I and several people who have assisted me have laboured to make sure that there are no errors in what follows, I cannot guarantee complete freedom from error. As in the case of my two previous books published by Ebury Press, therefore, readers who have any queries to put, corrections to make or criticisms to offer are welcome to contact me, and even, with important ones, urged to do so.

N. M. Gwynne,
nmgwynne@eircom.net
www.gwynneteaching.com

May 2018

PART I

INTRODUCTORY

CHAPTER ONE

The Mystery of Monarchy

THE CONCEPT OF hereditary monarchy is mysterious.

What is mysterious is the concept of a family whose members are *set apart from the rest of us* as eligible to be king or queen. Rather extraordinarily, in today's egalitarian climate, there are those who favour the preservation of hereditary monarchy in our country and those, still a relatively small minority, who oppose it, but what is unimaginable on *both* sides is the notion of a *non*-royal family starting up a *new* Royal Family. At least in England and other countries where the House of Windsor reigns, such an idea would be thought ridiculous in a way that continuation of the existing Royal Family is not.

At this point, religion must force its way into the foreground of our discussion, even though, in our present age, which is easily the most non-religious era in history, religion tends to be kept well in the background in any discussion of England's history.

As even the most cursory investigation will show, it is a clear fact that, from the dawn of recorded history, virtually every sizeable group of people everywhere in the world has had kings from the outset.

No less clear is that it was claimed by and on behalf of at least most of these kings, with the acceptance of their subjects, that they had some divine connection in their origins. Sometimes the kings have been said to have been directly appointed by God, sometimes they have been said to have been descended from gods, sometimes they have even been recognised *as* gods. Always, however, there has been a supernatural element.

Just a few out of many examples:

- The Bible's Books of Kings record several kings of the Israelites of that time as being directly appointed by God.
- In ancient Egypt the monarchy was based entirely on the concept that the king was an embodiment of a god.
- Homer refers to his kings in Greece as divine.
- In India, the works of Manu and the two great Epic poems, *Ramayana* and *Mahabharata*, clearly state the theory of divine kingship.

And so on in Asia Minor, Malaya, Japan, the countless islands everywhere in the Pacific Ocean, the Native American tribes of North and South America.

When, starting in the fourth century AD, Christianity became the official religion throughout Europe, monarchy not only continued but became much more precise in its meaning and implications. There officially arose an institution recognised as a 'Royal Family', a family intrinsically different from all other families in the world – so different indeed that, in every country on the continent of Europe, members of its Royal Family were legally allowed to marry only members of other Royal Families.

~

The mystery is twofold:

1. How did this general concept of kingship come about in the first place?
2. Specifically in the case of the English monarchy, the subject-matter of this book, how can the following facts be explained?

   - The concept of the divine establishment of monarchy *still survives*, at least instinctively.
   - Even though the Queen of England is no longer ruling as well as reigning, she is still *technically* the fount of law.
   - Much more so than any mere president of a republic, she is still above the law in the sense that the laws of England do not apply to her as they do to the rest of us.

- Indeed even today she, uniquely, cannot be prosecuted for any crime whatsoever. This is of course logical. Since she is the fount of justice, prosecutions are necessarily made in her name and, in a sense, *by* her; and for her to, in effect, prosecute herself would be self-contradictory.
- When we go to war, we still fight 'for Queen and country' *in that order*, while it would, for instance, never occur to Americans to fight for 'President and country'.
- The National Anthem, despite attacks on it by people favouring republicanism and others, is still 'God Save the *Queen*', rather than anything resembling 'God Save our Country'.
- The wording of the National Anthem is mysterious throughout. 'Send *her* victorious, happy and glorious ... Confound *her* enemies, and make them fall' (my emphases, of course) is an extraordinarily roundabout way to wish *ourselves* victory in warfare. Nor indeed would it occur to people living in republican countries to sing anything similar about their head of state.
- On the side of our coins carrying the Queen's portrait, we see her name immediately followed by the abbreviation of, Latinised, 'By the grace of God' – 'DG' for *Dei gratia*.
- Members of both Houses of Parliament, on taking their seats, swear an oath of allegiance expressly to the Queen and her heirs and successors.
- So too do the Lord Chancellor, the Lord Privy Seal, the Lord Chamberlain, the President of the Board of Trade, all Secretaries of State, all judges, all police officers, everyone enlisting in the British Army, the Royal Navy and the Royal Air Force, and people becoming naturalised citizens of England.

The further we look into the mystery, the more it deepens. When a practice is the result of pressure and superstition, it can easily be exposed by anyone who is intelligent and independent-minded; and as soon as it is exposed, it soon 'feels' wrong to everyone. This has never happened to any significant extent to the concept of monarchy and of a family which is *intrinsically* different in many respects from any other family in a kingdom. To those of us who are monarchists, which is still most of us although the increasing weight of counter-propaganda during recent times has been reducing our number, this concept of such a family is good, wholesome, romantic, tastefully glamorous, and in every way appealing and attractive, and quite independently of the personal qualities of the royal persons in question. This is so much so that many countries that have become independent from what was the British Empire have retained the Queen as their head of state, with their officials and citizens pledging allegiance to her in much the same way as the British ones do; and this is despite insistent republican arguments to the effect that countries that have at last become 'grown-up' are being demeaned by having as their head of state someone who does not live there.

And all this is clearly contrary to what would be expected of an institution that originally came into existence through power-grabbing.

Then, too, there is the way in which we conduct ourselves in the presence of the Queen, as also do foreigners who meet her. We bow or curtsy, according to our sex, both when we meet her and when we depart. We address her as Your Majesty and subsequently Ma'am, never by any name. We refrain from touching her person other than her hand at the greeting. If we write to her, we do so, not directly, but to her Private Secretary.

Perhaps even more remarkably, much of this applies also to other members of the Royal Family, to whom, for instance, we also bow or curtsy, and whom we also address only indirectly in correspondence.

~

Even a single one of the details given above would make monarchy a mystery of extraordinary interest, let alone all of them in their accumulation. The subject will be further examined when we come to the reign of King James I, when the nature and rights and duties of monarchs became a topic of urgent discussion.

PART II

TACKLING THE LEARNING OF HISTORY

CHAPTER TWO

Basic Principles

IN TODAY'S WORLD, a book setting out to be a useful contribution to the acquisition of valuable historical knowledge would hardly be complete without the inclusion of some traditional education philosophy of the kind that seems now to be needed, however seldom included, in any book on education intended to be helpful.

Earlier in these pages, I dwelt on the importance of history as a part of education. I now emphasise that the purpose of learning it is *not* fulfilled by simply reading about it or being talked to about it. Starting as early as possible, and preferably even before it is possible for the child to understand fully what is being learnt, the main outlines – the essential framework – of what in due course will be tackled in gradually increasing detail should be *learnt by heart*.

Please note the term 'learning by heart'. What those three words imply is that what is thus learnt becomes a *part* of us, just about as much a part of us as our own bodily organs, and scarcely less irreversibly.

Along with so much else in education that has changed in the last five or six decades, this wording has changed as well. 'Learning by heart', which speaks to the soul, has been replaced by 'rote-learning' and 'learning by rote', which are disparaging and off-putting terms that have the effect of making memorising into a matter of using the brain as a piece of machinery. I really beg parents and teachers to oppose this term whenever they hear it, which will undoubtedly be often, and always to insist on the traditional one.

CHAPTER THREE

Starting to Put the Principles into Practice

HERE ARE THREE examples of what the generality of English children used to know by heart and still should. For preference, the learning should start as soon they are capable of understanding clearly what it is that they are learning.

1. The traditional mnemonic for learning the order of the Royal Houses that have reigned over England since the Norman Conquest in 1066: 'No plan like yours to study history wisely.' (That represents: Norman – Plantagenet – Lancaster – York – Tudor – Stuart – Hanover – Windsor. For those who believe, as I do, that the Royal Houses should begin with the House of Wessex, immediately before the House of Norman, that mnemonic could be expanded to 'Well, no plan like yours to study history wisely.')

2. The following traditional piece of doggerel for learning the order of the kings and queens from the Norman Conquest onwards, and which I give even though I shall in due course be arguing that it is by no means certain that King Richard III is deserving of the title 'Dick the Bad':

> Willy, Willy, Harry, Ste,
> Harry, Dick, John, Harry three,
> One, two, three Neds, Richard two,
> Henries four, five, six – then who?
> Edwards four, five, Dick the bad,
> Harries twain and Ned the lad,

Mary, Bessie, James the vain,
Charlie, Charlie, James again,
William and Mary, Anna Gloria,
Four Georges, William and Victoria,
Edward, George, then Ned the eighth
Quickly goes and abdicat'th,
Leaving George, then Liz the second,
And with Charlie next it's reckoned.

... unless the present heir to the throne adopts a different name when he succeeds, as several monarchs have done in the past.

3. Lastly, the names and dates of the kings and queens in the list that now follows. I recommend that the starting-point for these names and dates is *not* William I and 1066, even though that is what is traditional. Logically, the very latest starting-point should be King Offa, who, as we shall be seeing, was the first of the 'modern' kings of all England.

For our immediate purpose at this point, however, we shall open, as many other books do, with the invasions of Julius Caesar. And let the learning-by-heart begin wherever the student or teacher thinks best.

British history; that is to say, pre-English history	*Dates*
Julius Caesar	
First Roman invasion of Britain.	55 BC
Second Roman invasion of Britain.	54 BC
Emperor Claudius	
Invasion of Britain.	AD 43
Suetonius Paulinus	
Became the Roman governor of Britain. During his reign, Queen Boudicca (Boadicea), Queen of the Iceni, rebelled. At first she was successful: three towns, including Londinium (present-day London) and Verulamium (present-day St. Albans), were invaded and burnt, and 70,000 Romans were massacred. Eventually she was defeated with 80,000 Britons killed, and ended her life with poison. This resulted in the recall of Suetonius by the Emperor Nero.	61

Julius Agricola completed the conquest of Britain.	78
Emperor Hadrian visited Britain.	119
Hadrian built the wall, made of stone, that is known to this day as Hadrian's Wall.	122
Emperor Severus arrived in Britain. He made many attempts to subdue the Caledonians but failed in all of them.	208
Count Carausius, a Saxon, after first representing Rome, dramatically threw off his allegiance to Rome and declared himself **Emperor Carausius** of Britain.	286–289

~

During this third century AD, Rome became progressively weaker. Its borders in the south of present-day Europe were invaded by hordes of barbarians, and the time came when the Roman legions were unable to withstand them.

As time went on, some of the barbarians invaded Britain, namely:

- The Caledonians or Picts ('painted men').
- The Scots ('tattooed men'), who, having conquered northern Ireland, invaded the western shores of Britain.
- A tribe of Germans sometimes called the Angles, sometimes the Saxons and sometimes the Anglo-Saxons – the terms are used interchangeably, even though the Angles and Saxons are of different origin – which harassed the eastern coast of Britain.

As we shall be seeing, in AD 597 a monk, Augustine, was sent to England by Pope Gregory the Great and converted King Ethelbert of Kent and most of his subjects.

The records of Caledonian, Scots and regional Saxon invasions are insufficiently reliable for it to be worth setting down any dates. From this point on, however, the dates are certain and worth memorising.

Early Kings in England

House and Ruler	Dates
House of Mercia	
Offa	757–796
House of Wessex	
Egbert	802–839
Ethelwulf	839–856
Ethelbald	856–860
Ethelbert	860–868
Ethelred	868–871
Alfred the Great	871–899
Edward the Elder	899–924
Ethelstan	925–939
Edmund	939–946
Edred	946–955
Edwy	955–959
Edgar the Peaceful	959–975
Edward the Martyr	975–978
Ethelred II the Unready	978–1013
House of Denmark	
Swein	1013–1014
House of Wessex	
Ethelred II the Unready (restored)	1014–1016
Edmund Ironside	1016
House of Denmark	
Canute (Cnut) the Great	1016–1035
Harold I Harefoot	1035–1040
Hardicanute (Harthacanut)	1040–1042

House of Wessex	
Edward the Confessor	1042–1066
Harold II	1066
House of Normandy	
William I	1066–1087
William II ('Rufus')	1087–1100
Henry I	1100–1135
House of Blois	
Stephen	1135–1141 and 1141–1154
Matilda	1141
House of Angevin	
Henry II	1154–1189
Richard I	1189–1199
John	1199–1216
Henry III	1216–1272

Kings of England and Wales

House of Plantagenet	
Edward I	1272–1307
Edward II	1307–1327
Edward III	1327–1377
Richard II	1377–1399
House of Lancaster	
Henry IV	1399–1413
Henry V	1413–1422
Henry VI	1422–1461 and 1470–1471
House of York	
Edward IV	1461–1470 and 1471–1483
Edward V	1483
Richard III	1483–1485
House of Tudor	
Henry VII	1485–1509

Kings and Queens of England, Wales and Ireland

House of Tudor	
Henry VIII	1509–1547
Edward VI	1547–1553
Jane Grey	1553
Mary I	1553–1558
Elizabeth I	1558–1603

Kings of England, Wales, Scotland and Ireland

House of Stuart	
James I	1603–1625
as James VI	1567–1625 (King of Scotland)
Charles I	1625–1649
Commonwealth	
Commonwealth	1649–1653
The Protectorate	
Oliver Cromwell (Lord Protector)	1653–1658
Richard Cromwell (Lord Protector)	1658–1659
House of Stuart	
Charles II	1660–1685
James II, and James VII of Scotland	1685–1688
James III	1688–1766
House of Orange	
William III of Orange and Mary II (jointly)	1689–1694
William III (alone)	1694–1702

Kings and Queens of Great Britain and Ireland

House of Stuart	
Anne	1702–1714
House of Hanover	
George I	1714–1727
George II	1727–1760
George III	1760–1820 (Elector, 1760–1815, and King, 1815–20, of Hanover)
George IV	1820–1830
William IV	1830–1837 (King of Hanover)
Victoria	1837–1901 (Empress of India 1876–1901)

Kings of Great Britain and Ireland and Emperors of India

House of Saxe-Coburg-Gotha	
Edward VII	1901–1910
House of Windsor	
George V	1910–1936
Edward VIII	1936
George VI	1936–1952

Queen of Great Britain and Northern Ireland, and Head of the Commonwealth of Nations

House of Windsor	
Elizabeth II	1952–

All that having been learnt by heart, the next step is to examine each individual reign in sufficient detail to learn its effect on our history. Before we make a start with the reign of King Offa, however, there is much else of great interest for us to look at.

PART III

EARLY BRITAIN?

CHAPTER FOUR

Introducing Geoffrey of Monmouth and His *Historia*

Almost every general treatment of English history opens with the invasion of Britain by Julius Caesar in 54 BC. The first British name mentioned is Cassivellaunus, who was the leader of the military opposition to Julius Caesar in Caesar's second invasion in 54 BC. Strangely, and not typically of ancient European nations, the list of English kings starts some *900 years* later than 54 BC, in the AD 800s.

During most of the period stretching from the Norman Conquest in 1066 up until the present day, English historians held a different position about when England's recorded history started. What they believed was based on a literary work put together by a learned cleric, Geoffrey of Monmouth, who was born about two generations after the Norman Conquest and lived in Oxford for much of his life. The work in question, purporting to be a work of history, was originally called *De gestis Britonum* and is usually referred to in modern times as *History of the Kings of Britain*, or simply the *Historia*.

In this work Geoffrey included two prefaces by himself. In the first, he said that he had long been pondering over the mystery that, in various excellent works of history that existed in his day, there appeared to be no records *either* of the kings of the period *before* Christ or of those of some centuries *after* Christ, when he was presented by a certain Walter – the Archdeacon of Oxford at the time – with a very ancient book written in Welsh. He went on to set out, in the form of a consecutive and orderly narrative, the names and deeds of those missing kings, from Brutus, the first King of the Britons, onwards. And at Walter's request he had taken the trouble to translate this book into Latin.

In a second preface, which he put in the middle of his book, Geoffrey added that, while he was in the process of doing this, he was asked by many of his contemporaries to translate into Latin a book, called *Prophecies of Merlin*, which had recently been generating much interest. He was now inserting the prophecies featuring in that book into the *Historia* where they naturally belonged chronologically, while making it clear that they were not part of the original book that he had been translating for Walter of Oxford.

The two books of which the final book is made up are very different from each other in nature, and even without the second preface there would be little difficulty in distinguishing between them. The *Historia* presents itself as a work of history, and is punctilious in its attention to practical detail. The Merlin insertions are 'other-worldly' throughout.

A truly dramatic feature of the *Historia* is that it traces the earliest settlers in the British Isles back, generation by generation, to someone whom it claims to have been Britain's very first king, King Brutus, and then further back still to his great-grandfather, Aeneas. And this Aeneas was none other than the Aeneas who is the titular hero of Virgil's *Aeneid*. Important for our purpose in a history of England's royal families, Aeneas was of royal blood, related to King Priam of Troy, and one of the few nobly born survivors of the disaster that had taken place after the Greeks, at the end of a ten-year siege of Troy, had built a huge wooden horse, concealed a force of soldiers inside it, and pretended to sail away abandoning the siege. Deceived, the Trojans then brought the horse into their city as a victory trophy, a decision which, when the soldiers hidden inside it emerged during the night, at last brought about the end of the war together with the complete destruction of Troy – all as described by Homer in *The Iliad*.

~

How much credence is Geoffrey's *History of the Kings of Britain* – apparently dealing with *well over half* of the entirety of British history, about 1,900 years and ninety-nine monarchs – entitled to?

According to any academic today and most general historians during the last 150 years and more, the *Historia* has no connection at all with real history and at least very much the greater part of it is pure fiction. Interestingly, when such historians move from that to more detailed discussion, they often disagree with each other. Some say that Geoffrey partly lifted his material from three sources well known today – *The Ruin and Conquest of Britain* by Gildas, a British monk writing in the sixth century, *The Ecclesiastical History of the English People* by St. Bede of Jarrow, an English monk writing in the eighth century, and *The History of the Britons* by Nennius, a Welsh monk writing in the ninth century, all of whom are referred to in the text – and invented the rest in its entirety. Others think that Geoffrey did indeed borrow from those three sources but in addition drew sometimes on genuine Welsh oral or literary sources, which he was well able to do because of having been brought up on the border of Wales and England. There are other variations as well.

Should we be satisfied with these judgements?

In this book's Preface, I argued that we should always be ready to adopt the mental attitude of a professional detective. What should certainly at once put us on the alert in this particular instance is that the *Historia* has not in fact been *completely* without defenders – and, by any reasonable standards, *credible* defenders – during the last two centuries.

In 1718, for instance, a Mr. Aaron Thompson undertook the first translation of the Latin into English, and included with it a lengthy preface in which he firmly defended the authenticity of the history given in that book. That preface had little effect on his contemporaries, however.

In 1917, Professor Flinders Petrie, who in 1923 was to become Professor Sir Flinders Petrie, exposed something that he considered shocking: that a large body of historical documents that were evidently important sources of material was being, perhaps wilfully, overlooked by modern historians. Further, with particular reference to an ancient document that obviously sheds light on it, and is still available for examination in the Bodleian Library in Oxford today, he maintained that Geoffrey of Monmouth's *History of the Kings of Britain* had by then for a long time been *wrongly* disparaged.[1]

Petrie was the leading and best-known archaeologist and Egyptologist of his time, and by any standards a deeply learned man. Even though the subject-matter of this topic that he addressed was outside his specialist field, no one was more worthy than he of the respectful attention of his fellow scientists. Nevertheless, his address and article were slammed as worthless by the few contemporary critics who even made mention of them, and otherwise ignored as completely as if they had never existed.

Twelve years later, in 1929, the gist of what Petrie had said was taken up by another impressive scholar, Acton Griscom. In a book titled *The Historia Regum Britanniae of Geoffrey of Monmouth*, he mounted by far the most complete defence of Geoffrey's *Historia* as authentic history ever to have been published in English. Part I of it consists of 216 closely argued pages in which Griscom deals in the minutest detail with every aspect of the Geoffrey of Monmouth dispute, and:

(a) concluded that the *Historia* is unquestionably genuine in both of its aspects that matter: in what Geoffrey claimed the *Historia* to be, and in what the *Historia* recounts; and

(b) *repeatedly* marvelled at the lack of interest among the scholars of his day, an attitude that Professor Petrie's important contributions had done nothing to change, and *not* because of mere indifference – 'The prevalent attitude towards Geoffrey is dogmatic and hostile.'

Let it be granted that this 'dogmatic and hostile' opposition is not without good reasons to support it. Do we not, even so, owe it to Thompson, Petrie and Griscom to give open-minded consideration to the arguments put forward by them?

Relevant to this question is what a leading academic *opponent* of the *Historia*'s authenticity, Dr. J. S. P. Tatlock, in his 545-page book on *The Legendary History of Britain* published in 1950, had to say about it:

'Geoffrey of Monmouth's *Historia* is one of the most influential books ever written.'

Yes, '*ever* written', by *anyone*, ever.

Tatlock had good reason to say that. The *Historia* had been respected by everyone across the whole of Western Europe. It had been consistently treated as a decisive authority to authenticate claims for kingship in England, with both the Tudor and the Stuart dynasties using it to justify their succession to the throne. It was the single most popular book in the Middle Ages, and indeed, aside from books on religious matters, the very first best-seller since classical times. It continued to feature with some prominence in every relevant piece of writing on British history right up to the eighteenth century. Moreover, it was respected just as much overseas as in England, for instance being used as a decisive authority in Rome in a controversy involving King Edward I for which the reigning Pope was asked to act as arbiter.

In the light of the effect of Geoffrey's *Historia*, politically, culturally, socially and in other ways, not to give it its evident due, and, in a general work of English history, to omit to represent it as deserving of further investigation by any serious-minded reader, would, I submit, be to leave a gaping hole in history's mission of recording the reality of the past.

It is worth remembering too that many distant legends of the past thought to be fictitious have subsequently been found by scholars to be firmly based on reality. Examples are the biblical city of Jericho, the remains of which have been unearthed by archaeologists of relatively recent times, and the city of Troy, the site of which was established in the second half of the nineteenth century by Heinrich Schliemann, who was a firm believer that Homer's *Iliad* and Virgil's *Aeneid* reflect historical events, as many scholars now agree.

~

One important consequence of what has emerged in this chapter, and also of what will be following in the next chapter, is that it can be argued that the list of kings and queens given on pages 13 to 16 is incomplete, indeed very incomplete. This is remedied on pages 318 to 323, where is given a family tree starting with Britain's very first king and ending with Queen Elizabeth II, and showing how the various monarchs are related to each other.

CHAPTER FIVE

1104–55 BC

As related by Nennius and Geoffrey of Monmouth

What now follows is a summary taken from two sources. The main source is Geoffrey of Monmouth's *Historia* published in AD 1139. The other is Nennius's *The History of the Britons*, published, as already mentioned, some 300 years earlier, in around 830, and which, unlike Geoffrey's book, gives the same origin of Britain as one of two alternatives rather than as definite. The two overlap at the very beginning: both give descriptions of the foundation of Britain by Brutus, called Britto by Nennius; both record the ancestry of Brutus as far back as Aeneas; and both explain how it came about that Brutus finally arrived on the island that was then named Britannia after him. Moreover, wherever the two books overlap, they confirm each other, though with enough small variations of detail to show that, contrary to what is often claimed, Geoffrey did not use Nennius directly as a source.

I do stress that the summary just given is only a very bare one, intended to include what is likely to be of most interest to readers.

Because the facts outlined in this chapter and the next three chapters are more in number and less in familiarity than those given everywhere else in this book, I am, in these four chapters only, highlighting in bold print at least the first mention of any person or place of any significance.

~

1104–1081 BC. The Trojan prince, **Aeneas**, after fleeing from the burning ruins of Troy with his son **Ascanius**, eventually arrived on the west coast of what is now Italy and settled on the banks of the River Tiber, where **Rome** was later to be built. There he was honourably received by the local king, **Latinus**, whose name was to be memorialised as that of the language of the Romans. He married King Latinus's daughter, **Princess Lavinia**, and with her had a second son, **Aeneas Silvius**, who thus was the half-brother of Ascanius.

Aeneas's marriage to Lavinia provoked the envy of another king in Italy, **Turnus**, king of a local tribe called the **Rutuli**, and war resulted. Victorious, Aeneas became King of Latium.

On the death of Aeneas, his son Ascanius was elected King. Ascanius's son Silvius married a niece of Lavinia's, and this niece, Silvius's wife, gave birth to a son, Brutus. Brutus was thus the great-grandson of Aeneas: Aeneas – Ascanius – Silvius (*not* Aeneas Silvius) – Brutus.

Brutus

Two tragic features marred Brutus's early life and drastically affected his future life. First, his mother, unnamed in the *Historia*, died when giving birth to him. Secondly, fifteen years later, he had the misfortune to kill Silvius, his father, in an accident while they were out hunting together. Since he was in a sense responsible for the death of both of his parents, even though only indirectly in the case of his mother and innocently in the case of his father, his relations expelled him from his homeland, with long-term effects that are still with us today.

His journey in exile took him first of all to Greece, where he came across descendants of Trojan soldiers who had fought against Greece in the thirteenth century BC and had been enslaved by

Pyrrhus, in vengeance for the death of Pyrrhus's father **Achilles,** the greatest of the Greek warriors that featured in Homer's *Iliad*. Learning that Brutus was descended from their own ancient kings, and in awe at his military skills, the Trojan slaves successfully begged him to be their leader, and under his command successfully rose up against their captors, whose leader, **Pandrasus,** was descended from one of the Greek royal families. During the process of overthrowing their captors, they took Pandrasus prisoner.

After debating among themselves what the future of Pandrasus should be, the Trojans ended up offering him his life if he would give his daughter, **Ignoge,** to Brutus to wed, together with as much gold and corn as they would all need to travel elsewhere to start up a new life. This the royally born Pandrasus was delighted to do, and Brutus and the victorious Trojans, led by Brutus with his future wife Ignoge, then set sail in search of a land in which to settle peacefully and in freedom.

After leaving the Mediterranean through the Pillars of Hercules, the present-day Straits of Gibraltar, and after undergoing many adventures, Brutus and his new companions met other Trojans escaping from their captors, under the leadership of **Corineus.** The two groups combined forces, with Brutus being acclaimed as king of all of them, and in due course landed in **Gaul,** present-day France, in the part then and now known as **Aquitaine.** There they fought and won two battles and then set sail again, finally arriving at an island called **Albion,** our Britain.

They came ashore just south of what is today Exeter in Devonshire. There Brutus solemnly named the exact place where he landed 'Totnes', the word 'tot' meaning 'sacred mound' and the word 'ness' or 'naess' meaning 'promontory' or 'headland'. Totnes is still there today, now a thriving town with the same name; and set into the pavement of its street called Fore Street is a small granite boulder called the 'Brutus Stone', onto which, according to local legend, Brutus first stepped from his ship, declaiming as he did so: 'Here I stand and here I rest. And this town shall be called Totnes.'

Finding the island inhabited only by a small number of giants, whom they drove off into mountain caves, Brutus and Corineus, the original leader of the Trojans, divided Albion up between them. Brutus, wishing to perpetuate his name, called the whole island after himself and called his companions **Britons**; and, some time after his death, the language they spoke was renamed **British**, having until then been known as Trojan, or 'Crooked Greek'.

As soon as Brutus had gained control of his new kingdom, he looked for somewhere to found a city. A particular part of the main river in the south appealed to him as especially suitable, and thus came into existence, on what would in due course be named the River Thames, what was to become, as of course it still is, one of the greatest cities there have ever been. He called it New Troy.

The *Historia* at this point interrupts itself to mention that a later king, **King Lud**, the brother of **King Cassivellaunus**, would in due course rename New Troy as *Kaer*lud, or **Lud's City**, whence eventually came the name **London**. That was far into the future, however. The new city was to keep the name New Troy for some ten centuries.

'Kaer', meaning city, incidentally, is attached to the names of most of the cities of the Britons.

Shortly after their arrival in what was to be their new and permanent home, Brutus wedded **Ignoge**, the daughter of King Pandrasus, and she bore him three sons, **Locrinus**, **Kamber** and **Albanactus**. As we have seen, these sons were of royal Trojan descent on their father's side and of royal Greek descent on their mother's side, and were therefore as nobly born as anyone in history. If we believe Geoffrey, Britain is indeed 'special'.

Upon the death of Brutus, the island was divided up into four parts.

Corineus chose to remain in **Cornwall**, which is so called either as a corrupt form of his name or because derived from the Latin word 'cornu' meaning 'horn', representing the horn of Britain. Brutus's eldest son, **Locrinus**, inherited England as it would be today without Cornwall. He took the title 'King of Loegria', naming that part of the island after his own name, and in Wales today England is still is sometimes known as 'Lloegr'. Brutus's second son, **Kamber**, inherited Wales, whence the present-day name for Welsh or Welshmen, 'Cambrian', that is to be found in English dictionaries. His youngest son, **Albanactus**, inherited Scotland, whence the present-day 'Albanian' meaning 'a native of Scotland'.

Thus, according to the *Historia*, the origin of the division of Britain into four separate countries. And we may note that reminders of it still endure. England and Scotland were two separate kingdoms until 1707, and even now Scotland retains much more independence than any mere province; Wales is a distinct principality, hence the title 'Prince of Wales' that is customarily bestowed upon the monarch's eldest son when he comes of age; and Cornwall is a separate duchy, hence the dukedom of it that has been automatically inherited by the monarch's eldest son as his first title.

~

From there, Geoffrey takes British history, step by step, through to the seventh century AD, where he closes his account of it. In what follows, I am selecting some of the most memorable of the events that he recounts.

Still in the eleventh century BC. At the insistence of Corineus, Locrinus married Corineus's daughter **Gwendolen**. Locrinus had, however, already fallen in love with the daughter of the king of Germany, **Estrildis**, the most beautiful woman of her time, and very soon after the death of his father-in-law Corineus seven years later, Locrinus deserted Gwendolen and made Estrildis his queen.

A worthy daughter of her father, Gwendolen went to Cornwall, where she raised an army. In a battle that ensued, Locrinus was killed, whereupon Gwendolen took control of Loegria, and had Estrildis and her daughter Habren thrown into a river and drowned. She then published an edict throughout Britain that this river, the longest in Britain, should be called by the daughter's name Habren, which was its Welsh name right up to Geoffrey's day, although by then a corruption of speech had rendered it 'Sabrina' in other languages. In due course, the name Sabrina mutated into the present-day 'Severn', while of course 'Sabrina', thus derived, survives as a woman's name.

996–957 BC. **King Ebraucus** was remarkable for having twenty wives and being the father of twenty sons and thirty daughters. During his reign, he invaded Gaul, and sacked many of its cities. Back in Britain, he founded the city named after him, **Kaerbrauc**, the City of Ebraucus, which the Romans were subsequently to latinise as Eboracum, later to be anglicised as York.

945–920 BC. King Leil founded the city of *Kaer*leil, named after himself and which still bears his name: Carlisle. His reign ended in ruin and civil war.

861–801 BC. King Leir (more often spelt Lear by later writers), the son of **King Bladud**, founded the city of *Kaer*leir (Leicester).

920–881 BC. King Hudibras, son of King Leil, founded the cities of *Kaer*reint (Canterbury), *Kaer*guenit (Winchester) and Paladur (Shaftesbury).

881–861 BC. King Bladud, son of King Hudibras, founded the city of *Kaer*badum (Bath), the hot springs of which were thought to restore health to the sick, as of course they still are.

794–761 BC. King Cunedagius was the grandson of King Leir. It was during this period that, according to Roman tradition, Rome was founded by the two brothers Romulus and Remus.

663–643 BC. King Gorboduc was the last king to reign over the Britons who was of the royal line of Brutus. He had two sons, Ferrex and Porrex, who quarrelled about who should succeed their father, which resulted in civil war that lasted for more than two centuries. No records of the kings or queens during this period have survived.

420–380 BC. King Dunvallo Molmutius, the third of the kings to be named following the unrecorded period of civil war, first conquered the whole island and then had a glorious forty-year reign. He codified what were to be the famed and revered Molmutine Laws, a copy of which still survives. It is generally claimed that this document was in fact forged by a remarkable and widely respected scholar, Edward Williams, but the evidence that Williams was guilty of this forgery is far from conclusive.

380–374 BC. King Belinus, the eldest son of King Dunvallo, sometimes called Belinus the Great, was, of the kings that feature in the *Historia*, second only to King Arthur in importance. For the first five years he ruled jointly with his brother **King Brennius**. At one point both brothers invaded Italy and succeeded in conquering and sacking Rome, after which Brennius remained in Italy, and Belinus returned to rule all Britain. The *Historia* tells us that Belinus ratified and perfected the laws established by his father, 'which the historian Gildas translated from Welsh into Latin, and which King Alfred [the Great] later rewrote in the English language'. King Belinus was a magnificent builder, and one of his most important constructions was a gateway into New Troy, which the citizens called Billingsgate, as it is still called today.

374–369 BC. King Gurguit Barbtruc, the son of King Belinus. In his reign a British population was established in Ireland for the first time.

369–363 BC. King Guithelin, the son of King Gurguit, was another good and popular ruler. His wife, **Queen Marcia**, was exceptionally intelligent and talented, and one of her several remarkable achievements was a new code of law, which the Britons were to call *Lex Martiana*, the Marcian Laws.

363–358 BC. Queen Marcia. When King Guithelin died, Sisillius, their son, was a minor. Queen Marcia, therefore, ruled Britain for some five years, until her own death.

From this point until the accession of **King Heli**, thirty-one reigns later, we have no indication in the *Historia* of any dates, which possibly reflects a long period of political turmoil during which records were either not kept or lost.

113–73 BC. King Heli, the son of **King Digueillus**, ruled for forty years, and one of his sons was **King Cassivellaunus**, who, as already noted, was the possessor of the first name to be recorded in almost all books that include any dealings with early British history. King Heli had two other sons, **Lud**, the eldest of the three, and **Nennius**. All three were to play important parts in Britain's history.

73–58 BC. King Lud was the eldest son of King Heli, and, in his long-term influence, one of the most important of all the early kings. Famous in his day and afterwards for his town planning and construction, one of his many achievements was to rebuild completely the walls of New Troy and to surround the city with a vast number of towers. At his death he was buried in the entrance to the city, Ludgate, that still bears his name.

Even more momentous: in consequence of all this, New Troy soon afterwards was renamed after him as *Kaer*lud, the city of Lud, whereafter, the *Historia* continues, corruptions of language (some of them caused by conquest by overseas invaders) led to *Kaer*lundein, which the Romans took up as Londinium, which in turn became London to the locals, and Lundres and then Londres to the French-speaking Normans who conquered England in AD 1066.

Thus the second important step, after the original foundation by King Brutus, in the history of the city which was to be for a long time much the greatest city in the world, and indeed is arguably *still* the world's greatest city, just ahead of its nearest rivals New York and Paris.

58–38 BC. King Cassivellaunus. He became king because King Lud's two sons, **Androgeus** and **Tenvantius**, were too young to govern the kingdom when he died, and Cassivellaunus, King Lud's brother and their uncle, was chosen in their place. He gained a reputation for uprightness and generosity which spread far outside Britain, and, as soon as his nephews were old enough, he assigned a large part of his kingdom to them: the city of New Troy and the dukedom of Kent to Androgeus and the dukedom of Cornwall to Tenvantius.

55 BC. Three years after **King Cassivellaunus** had come to the throne, the first invasion by **Julius Caesar** took place.

From this point on, the *Historia* proceeds side-by-side with the history that we read in our other history books, although what is related in the *Historia* is by no means identical in every respect with what we can learn from the other history books, which of course is what we should expect if the two sources of information are genuinely different.

Where both sources are in complete agreement is that Caesar's second invasion in 54 BC resulted in: the victory of Caesar over King Cassivellaunus; Britain being brought into Rome's sphere of political influence; and Caesar failing to make any permanent conquests.

CHAPTER SIX

55 BC–AD 633. As Related by Nennius, Gildas, Geoffrey of Monmouth and Bede, though Not Always in Complete Agreement with Each Other

SIX YEARS AFTER his defeat by Caesar in AD 54, King Cassivellaunus died, to be succeeded by ...

38–18 BC. King Tenvantius, who governed his realm diligently and well. He was followed by his son and heir ...

18 BC–AD 12. King Cymbeline, known to the Romans as *Cunobelinus*, who, as in the case of King Leir, was to be immortalised in one of the plays attributed, rightly or wrongly, to William Shakespeare (from now on referred to as 'Shakespeare' in recognition of the long-running controversy attached to that author's identity). Prior to his accession to the throne, Cymbeline had received a Roman upbringing in the household of no less a figure than Rome's first Emperor, Caesar Augustus. After he had ruled Britain for ten years, he became the father of two sons. Near the end of his life, he handed the government of Britain to his eldest son **King Guiderius**.

It was during the reign of **King Cymbeline** that arguably the most momentous event in the entirety of history, the birth of **Jesus Christ**, took place in Bethlehem in Judaea, on 25 December of the year 1 BC, according to ancient tradition, though that exact dating has of course been disputed by many scholars since. That year is of course still the very basis of the dating system used by most of the world today, with the years before 1 BC going backwards and the years subsequent to it going forwards, right up to today.

AD 12–43. **King Guiderius**, after reigning for some thirty years, refused to pay tribute to Rome, which quickly resulted in the invasion of Britain by the **Emperor Claudius** in the year AD 43. With the help of unscrupulous cunning, Claudius's chief of staff, Lelius Hamo, managed to get close to the unsuspecting King Guiderius and to kill him, whereupon King Guiderius's brother, **Arvirargus**, at once took charge of the British forces, and led them with such skill that the Romans finally accepted defeat and Claudius returned to his ships for safety. Arvirargus pursued Lelius Hamo from place to place, finally reaching him in a port, 'a haven', where he killed him; and, the *Historia* tells us, 'from that day to this, that haven has been called Southampton'.

43–57. King Arvirargus. Returning to the attack, Emperor Claudius soon gained the upper hand. He ended the war by proposing peace and offering to give King Arvirargus his daughter if the King would recognise Britain as being tributary to Rome. King Arvirargus agreed, and Claudius's daughter **Genvissa** was sent for from Rome.

Finding Genvissa to be a girl of exceptional beauty, and filled with admiration for her, King Arvirargus suggested to Emperor Claudius that the two of them should found a city to give a mark of distinction to the place where they were wedded. To this Claudius readily agreed, and ordered that a city be built which should be called *Kaer*Glou (the name 'Glou' being derived from 'Claudius'), or Gloucester. Once the city was built, Claudius returned to Rome, leaving the governorship of Britain in the hands of Arvirargus, acting on his behalf as a puppet-king. On his death King Arvirargus was interred at Gloucester, to be succeeded by his son **King Marius**.

57–97. King Marius, 'a man of great prudence and wisdom', fostered justice and peace, and enjoyed friendly relations with Rome. During his reign, he defeated and killed Soderic, King of the Picts ('painted men'), who inhabited Scotland, in a great battle. The present county of Westmorland was so named in King Marius's honour because of the battle.

It was during the reign of King Marius that the eventually unsuccessful rebellion by **Queen Boudicca** (Boadicea) against the Roman governor of Britain that has been outlined in chapter 3 took place.

122. During the reign of the Roman Emperor Hadrian, the building of the seventy-three-mile-long wall known as Hadrian's Wall was started. Stretching from Carlisle to Newcastle, it was built to keep back the Caledonians who were constantly invading Britain from Scotland. This marked the northern limit of the Roman Empire and was designed to defend Roman Britain from those north of it. Some of the wall has survived.

137–186. King Lucius. According to St. Bede of Jarrow (who is traditionally referred to as the Venerable Bede), in the year 156 King Lucius wrote to the Pope in Rome asking that he might be received into the Christian faith. The Pope sent two learned men, Faganus and Duvianus, to Britain, and it was not long before paganism had come to an end throughout almost the whole island.

King Lucius left no heir, which brought about dissension and the weakening of Rome's power in Britain. The Senate sent a delegate, **Severus**, to restore Roman authority. Severus succeeded in conquering most of the Britons, though some escaped into Albany, as the part of Scotland lying north of the River Forth was then called.

221–256. King Bassanius. During his reign a Briton of humble birth, **Carausius** by name, deceived the Roman Senate with attractive promises into providing him with a fleet of ships with which to invade Britain, which Carausius then did. King Bassanius was killed in battle, with Carausius emerging victorious and forcing the Britons to acknowledge him as king, whereupon he at once gave his allies, the Picts, a large tract of land in Albany. There the Picts settled and were to remain for centuries to come, gradually integrating with the Britons.

256. The Roman Senators considered that King Carausius had usurped the British throne and sent a delegate, Allectus, to bring about the restoration of Britain to Rome by military force if necessary. In yet another battle, King Carausius was killed, and Allectus was victorious. Then, however, Allectus behaved so ruthlessly that the Britons rebelled against him, and appointed **Asclepiodotus**, at that time the Duke of Cornwall, to the kingship. Forced by Asclepiodotus to flee, Allectus ended up losing his life. After engaging successfully in further battles in which he triumphed over the Romans, King-elect Asclepiodotus took the crown of the kingdom and placed it on his own head. Once again, a Briton held the throne.

We now have arrived at what Acton Griscom, the author of *The Historia Regum Britanniae of Geoffrey of Monmouth*, considered to be the most solid evidence of all in favour of Geoffrey's *Historia* as authentic history.

When, after the victory of Asclepiodotus, a fellow officer of the now-dead Allectus, **Livius Gallius**, retreated with those Romans who had survived into London, Asclepiodotus at once laid siege to the city and begged all the British leaders for help in trying to rid Britain completely of the Romans. Their combined forces succeeded in tearing down the walls of the city, and although the Romans surrendered and offered to depart in exchange for their lives and Asclepiodotus himself was prepared to be merciful, some of the allies of Asclepiodotus went so far as to decapitate all of the Roman soldiers and to throw them into a brook that ran beside the city, which, from the name of the leader of the Romans, was for ever afterwards called **Nantgallum**, or **Galobroc** in Saxon. In the sixteenth century a road was built over it, which today, under the name of **Walbrook**, is one of the most important streets in the part of London known as the City.

And, as Griscom points out on pages 211 to 216 in his book, in the 1860s a large number of skulls, *without bodies*, were excavated from the bed of the Walbrook before it was built over. The right objects, and very unusual objects – and especially in such quantity – in *exactly* the right place, are further confirmation of the authenticity of the *Historia*.

296–306. King Asclepiodotus governed justly and peacefully for ten years. In 303, however, the Roman **Emperor Diocletian** set in process in Rome one of the greatest of all the persecutions of that era, and this extended as far as Britain, where, up until then, the Christian faith had remained respected and untouched everywhere since the time of King Lucius.

Diocletian sent over his general, **Maximanius Herculius**, who had all the churches knocked down, all the copies of the Holy Scriptures burnt, and all the priests butchered side-by-side. This was the time of the heroic martyrdom of **St. Alban** before Alban had even been formally received into the Church – to be memorialised by the city called St. Albans, about twenty miles north of London, where the martyrdom took place, and by a large abbey built there in the eleventh century, which became a cathedral in the nineteenth century.

306–309. King Coel. Soon after he became king, the Roman Senate sent one of their senators, **Constantius**, to bring Britain back into the Roman Empire. Knowing that he had no prospect of success against the might of Rome, King Coel at once sued for peace, promising submission on the understanding that he could remain King. To this, Constantius agreed, but within a month of the signing of the peace treaty Coel fell ill and died, later to be immortalised in the nursery rhyme 'Old King Cole'. He was replaced by the senator himself, Constantius, who seized the crown.

309–312. King Constantius added to the legitimacy of his claim by marrying the daughter of King Coel, **Helen**, who was to become a canonised saint. On his death, he was succeeded by his son **Constantine**.

312–337. King Constantine I was one of the most remarkable kings there have ever been anywhere. After first ruling his country justly and courageously for several years, he then went to Rome at the request of many Romans to rescue it from the appalling tyranny of **Maxentius**, who had seized dictatorial power. Capturing the city and being appointed its overlord, he went on to become one of the most famous of all Rome's emperors, the **Emperor Constantine**, who, after Rome had persecuted Christianity for three centuries, finally legalised it there.

It is his mother, St. Helen, moreover, who is traditionally believed to have made a pilgrimage to Palestine with her son's encouragement; to have visited Jerusalem, which was in the process of being rebuilt after it had been destroyed and even its name lost; and to have discovered there the cross on which Jesus Christ had been crucified.

Back in Britain, a revolt had been led by a local duke, **Octavius**, who in due course seized the royal throne …

330–335 and 335–348. King Octavius. Constantine, still officially King of Britain as well as Emperor of all the known world, sent Queen St. Helen's uncle Trahern to restore Britain to Rome's sovereignty. At first Trahern was successful and Octavius had to flee from Britain and was deposed. Trahern was then assassinated, however, and Octavius returned, scattered the Roman forces, regained the throne, and then became a popular king, ruling over a contented kingdom. Just before his death, some complicated politics arose, with the final result that he was succeeded by a nephew of King Coel, **Maximianus**.

348–362. King Maximianus obtained the crown by virtue of that relationship. One of many results of the very eventful reign of this king was that, as already mentioned, the name Brutus was memorialised in perpetuity in yet another part of the world, present-day Brittany, situated in the north-west corner of France. As may be remembered, King Maximianus, both a Roman and, on his mother's side, of royal British blood, was chosen as king by his predecessor, King Octavius, even though Octavius's nephew, **Conan Meriadoc**, had a more obvious claim to the throne. Once on the throne, however, King Maximianus quickly developed an uncontrollable lust for power. This led him to invade Armorica, present-day Brittany, first conquering it and then killing every single male inhabitant.

Becoming even more ambitious, and wanting to move on to conquer the whole of Gaul, King Maximianus issued an order that a hundred thousand ordinary men and women should be imported from Britain to 're-stock' the part of Gaul that he had just conquered, thus in effect creating a second Britain. He then gave his new territory to Conan Meriadoc, hoping that this would end the rivalry between them.

Back in Armorica, **King Conan** defended the new kingdom that King Maximianus had just given him against several attacks with great courage and skill. Brittany in effect became a sister country to Britain itself, and the two countries from then on kept close links with each other.

375–389. King Gracianus, without any legitimate claim to the throne, seized it, and ruled so tyrannically that some of his subjects eventually banded together and assassinated him. This did not improve the situation. 'The abominable Picts and Huns', as the *Historia* calls them, invaded the country, as did Scots from Ireland, and Norwegians and Danes, and they all ravaged it to such an extent that those who survived begged Rome for help, promising perpetual submission if their enemies could be driven away.

Help was duly given. After freeing the English, however, the Romans announced to Britain that they were no longer prepared to be so greatly inconvenienced 'for the sake of a cowardly pack of vagabond freebooters', as Geoffrey put it, and then left Britain for ever.

Alas, no sooner had they gone than the Picts, Scots, Norwegians and Danes returned, and seized the whole of Albany down to the newly built wall and further. Cities were abandoned, as was even Hadrian's Wall. Those who survived begged for further help from the Romans, but in vain.

402–420. King Constantine II. After several years of a happy reign, King Constantine was treacherously stabbed to death by a Pict who had been in his service. By then he had three sons: **Constans, Aurelius** and **Uther Pendragon**. There was considerable argument about who should succeed him. Before the matter was decided, there appeared on the scene **Vortigern**, leader of the Gewissei. Vortigern then opened negotiations with Constans, who had earlier decided against becoming king and had become a monk at Winchester. Vortigern persuaded him to accept the crown after all, while leaving him, Vortigern, to administer Britain on Constans's behalf. To this Constans agreed.

420–437. King Constans, the eldest son of King Constantine would have been wise to have kept to his resolution to avoid the perils of the crown and to have remained a monk. Shockingly, Vortigern used his position of power to organise the assassination of King Constans by a group of Picts; then to have the traitors whom *he himself* had appointed to the task put to death; and finally to seize the crown himself. He ruled for two separate periods.

437–455 and again in 460–480. King Vortigern. We are now at last in a period in which Geoffrey's *Historia* overlaps with what is recorded by other historians. This is not, however, to say that the *Historia* agrees with the other historians on every detail.

According to the *Historia*, the murder of King Constans for which King Vortigern had been responsible eventually started to become widely known, and in consequence various peoples revolted against Vortigern. In self-defence, the wicked king made a treaty with two invaders from Saxony, **Hengist** and **Horsa**, household names in history for ever afterwards. Again according to the *Historia*, it was to them that we owe some of the names of the days of the week which we use to this very day, in honour of the gods and goddesses of their country: the god Woden for the fourth day of the week; Freia, the most powerful goddess of all, to whom the sixth day was dedicated; and Saturn for the seventh day.

King Vortigern and his new allies defeated the Britons. To their leader, Hengist, he gave much land. Hengist then introduced his daughter Renwein (a name which survives as the modern name Rowena) to the king, and, disastrously, Vortigern became impassioned by her even though she was pagan and he Christian. After consultation with Horsa, Hengist handed his daughter over to Vortigern in exchange for the province of Kent, without even consulting the then ruler of Kent, and in consequence King Vortigern incurred the enmity of his previous allies and even of his own sons, **Vortimer**, Katigern and Paschent. Eventually the Britons deserted Vortigern and appointed his eldest son, Vortimer, king in his place.

455–460. King Vortimer succeeded in expelling the Saxons from Britain after four notable battles, during one of which both Horsa and Vortimer's brother Katigern were killed. After his final victory, King Vortimer set about restoring to the Britons all the possessions that his father and others had removed from them, and also, at the request of a newly arrived Christian missionary, St. Germanus, restoring their churches.

Becoming jealous, King Vortimer's stepmother Renwein, King Vortigern's pagan wife and Hengist's daughter, gave Vortimer poison to drink, with the result that King Vortigern was for a *second* time restored to the throne.

460–480. King Vortigern once more. At the instigation of his wife, King Vortigern sent messengers to Germany, to ask her father, Hengist, to return to Britain. Hengist did so, bringing a huge Saxon army. The result was treachery, betrayal and mass murder, and the virtual takeover of Britain by the Saxons. Towards the end of his life, Vortigern started consulting magicians, and thus the *Historia* introduces into English history a young man called Merlin. Merlin's mother was the daughter of a king, but no one knew who his father was, and indeed his mother claimed that his father did not exist other than in some ghostly form.

Asked by King Vortigern to prophesy the future, the young Merlin said that Hengist would be killed; that **Aurelius Ambrosius** would be crowned king, would restore peace and would bring the Church back to its former influential status, but would die of poison; and that King Vortigern's brother Uther Pendragon would succeed him but also die of poison.

The very next day after Merlin had made this prophecy, Aurelius Ambrosius came ashore, and almost at once was anointed king by the Christian clergy. Disgusted, first by King Vortigern's betrayal of his father King Constantine, secondly by King Vortigern's betrayal of his brother King Constans, and thirdly by the almost entire obliteration of Christianity in Britain that King Vortigern had been responsible for, King Aurelius Ambrosius had King Vortigern burnt alive.

480–501. King Aurelius Ambrosius had been too young to take up the crown when King Constans died in AD 437 and had therefore been smuggled abroad, to be raised in the household of King Budicius of Brittany. Not long after having been eventually declared King of Britain, Ambrosius, a man of great courage and military skill, first, as we have seen, had King Vortigern put to death, *at last* bringing that king's remarkable succession of reigns to an end; then forced the Saxons to retreat to Albany (Scotland); and finally launched an attack on Hengist – Christians versus pagans. After some desperate but indecisive battles, the Christians were victorious and Hengist was beheaded and, as the *Historia* puts it, 'packed off to Hell'.

Thereupon, Hengist's son Octa begged Aurelius for mercy on behalf of himself and his fellow Saxons. Aurelius took pity on them, granted them by treaty a region near Scotland where they could live in perpetuity, and then retired to London, where he ruled wisely and justly.

Wickedness had not completely been stamped out, however. One of Vortigern's sons, Paschent, the youngest, survived. He employed a Saxon called Eoppa to poison King Aurelius, and thus was one of Merlin's prophecies fulfilled.

King Aurelius was succeeded by his brother **Uther**.

CHAPTER SEVEN

55 BC–AD 633 Interrupted: the Era of King Arthur

AD **501–521. King Uther Pendragon**, more commonly called **King Uther**, succeeded his brother King Aurelius. Like his brother Aurelius, Uther had been smuggled abroad after the murder of Constans.

As soon as Uther became king, the Saxons who, under Hengist's son Octa, had been given land by King Aurelius Ambrosius, broke their treaty and started invading the rest of the country. After a series of battles, the Britons, led by King Uther, succeeded in routing the Saxons.

Then, travelling to London to be crowned with appropriate ceremony, King Uther found himself captivated by the most beautiful woman in Britain, Ygerna, who, however, was the wife of Gorlois, the Duke of Cornwall.

With his passion for the Duchess of Cornwall becoming more than he could bear, King Uther turned for advice to Merlin, who had developed a reputation as a prophet. As the story goes, Merlin's monstrous solution was to offer him drugs that would make him resemble her husband in every respect. Uther ignobly lent himself to the imposture and succeeded in deceiving the Duchess into committing adultery without realising it.

'That night,' says the *Historia*, 'she conceived Arthur, the most famous of men and whose great and wonderful actions have justly rendered his name famous to posterity.'

King Arthur

Further battles between King Uther and Gorlois followed. In the last of them Gorlois was killed, and King Uther married the widowed Ygerna. She bore him their son, Arthur, and a daughter, Anna.

Betrayed by spies, King Uther was poisoned and died, which brought the war between the Britons and the Saxons to an end. The leaders of the Britons then assembled and suggested to the Archbishop Dubricius that Arthur, even though only fifteen years old, should be crowned king. The archbishop agreed, as did some of the other bishops, and bestowed the crown on Arthur.

521–542. King Arthur. Even at that tender age, Arthur was 'of such outstanding courage and generosity together with sweetness of temper and inborn goodness that he was loved by everyone'. Recognising that the kingship of the whole island was his by right of inheritance, he at once marched to York, to do battle with the Saxons, Scots and Picts, whom he quickly overcame. Victory after victory followed, during the course of which huge numbers of the Saxons, Scots and Picts all over the country were killed, and also Irish, who had recently invaded Britain.

After these victories, King Arthur started rebuilding churches and establishing and restoring religious communities. When he had brought back the whole country to its former dignity, he married Guinevere – descended from a noble Roman family and 'the most beautiful woman in the entire island'.

Next, he completed the conquest of Ireland, took a fleet to Iceland and conquered it, and then at last returned to England and for the next twelve years governed his kingdom in peace.

It was during that period that one of the most famous events in all history, the institution of the Knights of the Round Table, took place. He invited distinguished men from far-distant kingdoms to join him, and developed a code of courtliness in his household that people all over the known world were inspired to imitate. Even men of the noblest birth thought nothing of themselves unless they wore the arms of Arthur and dressed as his knights did. An order of chivalry was formed, symbolised by the Round Table that he had built for the purpose and which, as the name suggests, had no head, implying that everyone sitting at it was of equal status.

By then, such was his reputation that kings of far-off countries trembled at the thought that they might be attacked by him. When this came to his ears, it led him to conceive the idea of conquering all Europe; and, after necessary preparations, he set out on that mission.

Successively, Norway, Denmark then Gaul accepted his rule. Returning to Britain, he established a great city, unnamed by the *Historia* but to become known as Camelot.

Finally, provoked by Roman delegates who came to complain that he had been insulting the Senate by not paying the yearly tribute that was traditionally due, he resolved to attack Rome, with the help of the conquered leaders who now owed him homage. Entrusting his kingdom jointly to his nephew Mordred and Queen Guinevere, he set off with his army from Southampton. During the course of many adventures and battles, he ended up defeating all the Roman legions that he came up against, by which time Britain, as the *Historia* notes, was 'mistress of thirty kingdoms'.

Triumphing over further Roman legions in hard-fought battles, he had almost reached Rome when word was brought to him that his nephew Mordred had become a treacherous tyrant, and was living in adultery with Guinevere.

The king immediately cancelled the planned attack on Rome and returned to Britain, where several battles culminated in one final great battle in which Mordred was killed and King Arthur fatally wounded. After handing the crown to his cousin Constantine, the son of the Duke of Cornwall, Arthur was carried off to the Isle of Avalon and, in Geoffrey's words, died there 'in the year 542 after Our Lord's Incarnation'.

~

Virtually all historians today would say that none of this, or almost none of it, happened, but I beg my readers to hesitate to be as sure as the experts are before doing their *own* careful investigation into the matter.

I am by no means without support in urging such a course. Two leading historians of that period, Leslie Alcock, Reader in Archaeology at University College, Cardiff, in his *Arthur's Britain,* published in 1971, and John Morris, former Senior Lecturer in History at University College, London, and author of the painstakingly researched *The Age of Arthur: A History of the British Isles 350 to 650*, published in 1973, prove conclusively that Arthur was as real, in his existence and in at least most of the achievements attributed to him, as anyone else who has ever lived. Let it be remembered, furthermore, that this was believed for very many centuries and by very many highly intelligent people at a time when, before huge quantities of records had been destroyed all over Europe, there was much more evidence in existence than is now available to us.

CHAPTER EIGHT

55 BC–AD 633 Resumed and Concluded

AD **555–563. King Keredic**'s origin is unrecorded. Early in his reign, the Saxons sent to Ireland for **King Gormund**, 'King of the Africans', who had invaded Ireland with an enormous fleet and conquered the entire country. King Gormund therefore invaded England with 160,000 Africans and devastated Britain, ravaging the fields, setting fire to cities and burning almost the entire country. The natives of Britain, including the priests of the Church, were largely destroyed, and King Keredic ended up retiring to Wales. During this period, 563–616, there was a succession of three unnamed kings.

Once he and his Africans had completed his destruction of most of Britain, the inhuman tyrant Gormund handed a large part of it over to the Saxons, whose treason had been the cause of his landing. Such Britons as survived sought refuge in Cornwall and Wales, and many of the priests went to Brittany in Armorica.

For a long time the Britons made no effort to recover the former greatness that had been theirs since the original arrival of Brutus more than 1,500 years earlier.

597. Augustine, later to be St. Augustine, a monk of the Order of St. Benedict who until then had been the prior, the superior of a monastery in Rome, was sent by **Pope (St.) Gregory (the Great)** to England, to preach Christianity there. Among the Britons, Christianity had been accepted from the time of Pope Eleutherius in the second century and, far from ever losing its influence, had continued to flourish, though deprived of contact with Rome. During the same period, however, the Anglo-Saxons, separately from the Britons, had completely eliminated Christianity from their culture and England had fallen back almost completely into barbarism, and the last survivors of the Britons' Church hierarchy, the Archbishops of London and of York, had fled into the mountains of Cambria, as Wales was then called.

Arriving in Kent, Augustine was quickly successful in converting King Ethelbert of Kent and soon afterwards the rest of the Anglo-Saxon population, and then founded seven bishoprics, himself becoming the Archbishop of the principal one, that of Canterbury.

He also founded a bishopric in the territory west of England that was still inhabited by the Britons, but this eighth one gave rise to a bitter dispute. Saying that they already had their own archbishop, the Britons refused to submit to the Saxons, who had deprived them of their own fatherland. They had no interest whatsoever in the Saxons or their religion (even though of course it was fundamentally the same religion as theirs); and, in their words, they had as much wish to communicate with the Angles as they had to communicate with dogs!

607. In response, the kings of Kent, Northumbria and elsewhere assembled a large army and set out for the city of Bangor in Wales, intending to destroy the churchmen who had scorned Augustine. Eventually they reached Chester, where monks and hermits from everywhere in Britain had gone for refuge. After a battle King Ethelfrid of Northumbria obtained occupation of Chester and, on discovering why the monks had gone there, at once loosed his soldiers onto them, and 1,200 monks were martyred – not a method of resolving ecclesiastical disputes that St. Augustine, who had died three years earlier, would have supported.

The Saxon tyrant King Ethelfrid then marched his army to Bangor itself. There, however, confronted by the Britons' leaders, he was wounded and at last forced to retreat. Some 10,000 of his soldiers were killed.

Of utmost importance: the change that Christianity brought about in the way of life of the inhabitants of England during the next few generations was dramatic. Before the arrival of St. Augustine in 597, there had been virtually no written literature, no industrial arts, no peace for more than the briefest stretches of time, and no social intercourse between one district and another. The Christian Church arrived in England as, amongst much else, a civiliser; and within a few years the English warriors, who until then could have been justly described as barbarous heathens, became hard-working farmers, eager scholars, peaceful law-givers and earnest priests. It was not merely a change of *religion* that had taken place, but also a peaceful revolution from mindless barbarism to the beginnings of culture and, progressively, civilisation.

616–625. Under a treaty entered into by all the princes of the Britons, **King Cadvan** was chosen as king of the entire realm on the understanding that, under his command, the Britons would immediately cross the River Humber in pursuit of King Ethelfrid. At the last moment, however, peace was made between the two kings, and it was agreed that Ethelfrid should be king of the part of Britain on the far side of the Humber, the north side, and Cadvan king on the south side. Remarkably, it was not long before they became firm friends.

There followed, in consequence, a domestic event which was to have constitutional importance. King Ethelfrid put aside his wife and, on taking another woman in her place, then went on to conceive such a hatred for his wife that he banished her from Northumbria. She, pregnant at the time of her dismissal, went to King Cadvan and begged him to try to persuade her husband to allow her to return. This Cadvan did, but unsuccessfully, and she therefore remained in his household until the birth of her child, a son. Very soon after that, Cadvan's own queen, who had become pregnant at about the same time as Ethelfrid's wife, gave birth to a son; and the two boys were brought up together in a manner suited to their royal blood. Cadvan's son was named **Cadwallo** and Ethelfrid's son was named **Edwin**.

When the two boys reached near-adulthood, their parents sent them to King Salomon, King of the Britons of Armorica, in order to learn there the lessons of knighthood and courtly behaviour. All three became close friends, and, when they joined the king in battles against his enemies, Cadwallo and Edwin were well known for their bravery and gallantry.

Many years later, their parents both having died, Cadwallo and Edwin returned to Britain to take up their inheritance of the government of the country, with Cadwallo as king in the south and Edwin, though not technically as king, in the north.

625–633. King Cadwallo, who was the Saxon Edwin's overlord, was asked by Edwin for a crown of his own, so that he could celebrate the traditional ceremonials in Northumbria as Cadwallo did south of the River Humber. King Cadwallo, however, was persuaded by his nephew Brian to reject Edwin's request, and responded with a message to the Saxon Edwin to say that his own countrymen, the Britons, had refused him permission to grant that request. Thereupon Edwin lost his temper and said that in that case he would have himself crowned without Cadwallo's permission.

War ensued. King Cadwallo was put to flight and crossed to Ireland. Edwin then led his army across most of Britain, burning cities and inflicting misery on both the townsfolk and the farmers of the country. Because Edwin, by now thoroughly paganised, had taken to consulting a magician from Spain, who was always able to warn Edwin where Cadwallo was about to land with his invading fleet, Cadwallo failed repeatedly in his attempts to return to Britain to give battle again, and eventually decided to visit his old friend King Salomon of the Armorican Britons, to ask for this king's help.

After many adventures during his journey, King Cadwallo finally reached Armorica. King Salomon, although he received him kindly, was reluctant to spare more than a few thousand soldiers to help him, but he did work out a solution with him: that Brian, who, it will be remembered, had persuaded Cadwallo not to give Edwin a crown, should cross over to Britain and find a way of killing Edwin's magician. Edwin would then no longer be warned when Cadwallo was about to arrive there.

Brian accomplished his mission, and soon afterwards King Cadwallo landed in Britain with 10,000 soldiers whom King Salomon had put under his command. After a great victory, in which Edwin was killed, Cadwallo marched through all the Angle provinces. According to Bede, he then embarked on a campaign to wipe out the entire race, including even the women and small children. It is thought by some that Bede was relying on a tainted source, however. Undoubtedly Cadwallo was respected after his death since a future king unrelated to him, King Caedwalla of Wessex, was named after him. Undoubtedly, too, Cadwallo died a Christian.

633–643 and 654–664. King Cadwallader, King Cadwallo's son, at first governed Britain honourably, and England enjoyed a period of peace and prosperity. In the twelfth year of his reign, however, he fell ill and civil war broke out among the Britons. There followed a severe famine which was followed by a pestilence which destroyed so many people that those who survived were unable to bury the dead. Indeed they had to leave their country, among them King Cadwallader, who set sail to take refuge in Armorica, where, with all his company, he was made welcome by King Alan II, the nephew and successor of King Salomon.

For the next eleven years, the population of Britain was very much smaller than it had been at any time since the original arrival of Brutus nearly 2,000 years earlier, with only a few Britons remaining, in remote forests in Wales and the north of Britain. At last, however, the deadly plague subsided, whereupon, regrettably, the few Saxons who still remained there at once returned to their old habits, and sent a message to Germany to tell them that the country, now abandoned by its native population, would fall easily into their hands if they would come over to occupy it.

'The odious race', the *Historia*'s title for them, came over in hordes, and occupied the almost-empty land from Albany in the north down to Cornwall in the south, sharing it with only a few pockets of Britons who lived precariously in remote parts of the woods in Wales. Any further influence of the Britons, the people who had founded Britain, on their country's future was on the point of becoming non-existent.

Not without one last gasp, however. A few decades later, the Britons who had gone overseas gathered their strength for a final effort. Encouraged by King Alan, who offered his help, King Cadwallader determined to return to his former kingdom and started to prepare his fleet.

It was not to be; at least not then. Suddenly, the *Historia* tells us, he heard an angel, declaring, in a voice of thunder, that God did not wish the Britons to rule in Britain any more, until the time arrived as prophesied earlier by Merlin to King Arthur. 'Go to Rome,' said the voice. 'Visit Pope Sergius there and do penance, and you will be numbered among the blessed. And the British people, as a reward for their faithfulness, will occupy the island again at some appointed time in the future.'

King Cadwallader went into careful consultation with King Alan. Together they reached the conclusion that the voice that King Cadwallader believed he had heard was authentic, and, with the agreement of King Alan, King Cadwallader sent his son Yvor and his nephew Yni to rule in his place over the few Britons who remained there. He himself renounced all worldly concerns and journeyed to Rome, where he was sacramentally confirmed by Pope Sergius and remained until, attacked by a sudden illness, he died in 689, twenty-five years after he had been driven out of his kingdom.

For nearly eighty years Yvor and Yni struggled to regain the kingdom for the Britons, but their efforts were in vain. Plague, famine and civil discord had caused the Britons to degenerate too far.

At this point:

- *British* power on the island was at an end and *English* rule began.
- Britain was no longer the united country it had been until the fifth century, because, following the Saxon conquest, Britain was divided into seven separate Saxon kingdoms.
- The original British people had, as we have just learnt, even ceased to be *called* British.

~

Astonishingly, the Saxons now radically changed their character and ceased completely to be an 'odious race'. They lived peaceably among themselves, cultivated the land, and rebuilt the cities and castles that had been destroyed. Under their leader King Adelstan, the first of their kings, they ruled over the whole of Loegria, most of present-day England other than Cornwall. Yvor and Yni did continue to harass the Saxons for many years to come, but, says the *Historia*, 'little good it did the Britons', who were able to make no further serious attempt to recover their land and simply lived on in a state of misery.

~

This is the point at which the *Historia* comes to an end.

It is surely worth stressing the *Historia*'s importance in any study of England's history. What Geoffrey claimed to have produced, let us remind ourselves, was a translation by him of a detailed account of the political founding of the whole of Britain, an account which included that of the country's original Royal Family, itself of royal blood in its very origin. If, therefore, we accept what the *Historia* says as authentic, we are able to trace our present-day Royal Family back to the Royal Family of Troy without missing a single link.

Also important: although King Arthur had briefly featured in the *Historia Brittonum* of a Welsh monk named Nennius, written some three centuries earlier, for the basic outline of what we know or think we know about Arthur we are indebted solely to Geoffrey of Monmouth. It is primarily because of Geoffrey that the name of Arthur became known first of all throughout Europe and then throughout the Western world, and that schoolchildren, generation after generation until recently, were brought up on King Arthur and learnt how to conduct themselves in gentlemanly and ladylike fashion under the inspiration of King Arthur and his court.

Does the *Historia*, however, deserve to be trusted as an important source of information? I suggest that we should hesitate to accept as certain today's virtually universal verdict that it does not.

In the first place, doing so would involve supposing our ancestors over many centuries, and not only in England but in Europe as well, to have been possessed of a near-universal naivety, and this must be open to doubt. It is not as though the *Historia* was never questioned, after all. Less than fifty years after its appearance, the twelfth-century historian, William of Newburgh, in the preface of his *Historia rerum Anglicarum* ('History of English Affairs'), denounced it with the words 'only a person ignorant of ancient history would have any doubt about how shamelessly and impudently he lies in almost everything'. It was despite being thus put on the alert that the scholars of the generations that succeeded him gave it universal approval; and, as its first translator, Aaron Thompson, pointed out, they had better opportunities for assessing it because there were more monuments still in existence and traditions were more fresh and uncorrupted than at any time later.

Secondly, there are features of the book that a forger would be unlikely to invent since they would not be helpful to its credibility: features that include occasional unnamed kings and nearly 250 years of no historical records at all.

Thirdly, in an early passage dealing with the renaming of New Troy as Lud City, the future London, there is a sentence, 'Since Gildas has given a full account of this quarrel I prefer to omit it, for fear of debasing what so great a writer has so eloquently related', which is clear evidence that the *rest* of the narrative was *not* taken from Gildas, unless Geoffrey was being extraordinarily cunning.

Finally, there are questions that are seldom asked and I have never seen answered.

What motive could Geoffrey and Walter, the Archdeacon of Oxford who had invited him to translate the book, have had for perpetrating such a shocking fraud? And how could the two have expected to get away with it? What if someone had demanded to see the original that Geoffrey had supposedly translated?

I now leave it to my gracious readers to make their own judgements, based on further research if they think fit, begging them to ensure that they are guided by *evidence* rather than purely by the number and impressiveness of those supporting the generally accepted position.

PART IV

THE FOUNDING OF ENGLAND

CHAPTER NINE

The First English People: Introduction

As to the time of King Cadwallader's son and nephew, Yvor and Yni, onwards, historians are in general agreement on the outlines of England's history.

The Saxons, who had replaced the Britons in most of the country, consisted of three separate tribes: the Jutes, from what is now part of Denmark and of northern Germany; the Angles, from the south of Denmark; and the Saxons, from present-day Hanover in Germany.

By the end of the sixth century, the country had become divided into seven separate kingdoms, now commonly called the Heptarchy, a word derived from the Greek words for 'seven' and 'sovereignty'. These kingdoms were:

- Founded by the Jutes: Kent, dating from 449.
- Founded by the Saxons: Sussex, Wessex and Essex, dating from 477, 495 and 527 respectively.
- Founded by the Angles: Northumbria, East Anglia and Mercia, dating from 547, 575 and 586 respectively.

~

In 664, the same year that King Cadwallader died, a synod, a Church council, to be known as the Synod of Whitby, was summoned to be held at Whitby in present-day North Yorkshire. Notwithstanding the efforts of St. Augustine at the end of the sixth century, there remained some small liturgical differences between St. Augustine's

Church in England and the Celtic Church in Wales, possibly the most obviously important of which was the date for celebrating Easter. It was agreed at the synod that all would follow the Roman Church in this and other disciplinary matters.

For approximately the next 300 years, first one of the seven kingdoms became the most powerful, and then another. It was during this period that the English monk and great scholar, St. Bede of Jarrow (a town in present-day Tyne and wear), wrote, amongst much else, his *Ecclesiastical History of the English Nation*, which earned for him the title 'Father of English history'.

In 757, nearly 150 years after the beginning of the reign of King Ethelfrid, the supremacy in England passed from Northumbria to **Mercia**, with **King Offa** becoming King of Mercia.

Now at last, we have reached the stage where the history of the part of the world to be known as England is no longer mere background of which we should have some awareness, but includes, as its basics, material that, as already mentioned, should be learnt by heart and fully absorbed. For the remainder of this book, therefore, the Royal Houses of England will be set out in a formal manner suitable for this new purpose.

CHAPTER TEN

The First English People: the Houses of Mercia and Wessex

Introducing the House of Mercia

King Offa ('Offa the Mighty')

Reigned 757–796, the greatest king since the earliest days to have reigned in England up to that time. While he was king, the chiefs of East Anglia, Essex and Kent became his vassals. Most notably, he built an immense ditch, known today as Offa's Dyke, running 140 miles from the River Dee to the River Severn, to protect England from invasions by the Welsh.

During his reign the Danes, inhabitants of what are now called Norway and Sweden and also known as the Vikings, began invasions of the country which involved plundering and burning towns and monasteries and sailing back home with their booty.

The supremacy of the House of Mercia ended with King Offa's death and, after a period of eight years during which no monarchs reigned, passed to the House of Wessex, the supremacy of which lasted for two centuries.

Introducing the House of Wessex

King Egbert

Reigned 802–839. From the time that Egbert became King of the West Saxons, Wessex began to replace Mercia as the dominant kingdom of England.

King Ethelwulf

Reigned 839–858. King Egbert's son.

King Ethelbald

Reigned 858–860. The eldest son of King Ethelwulf and the grandson of King Egbert.

During the century before the reign of King Alfred the Great, many invasions had taken place, with overseas warriors robbing everyone and everything – including kings, churches and even churches' altars – of their most valuable possessions. Their victims called them 'Wicingas', the word which still survives in our dictionaries as Vikings, and meant 'robbers'. When there was nothing more to steal, the 'Wicingas' turned to mass killing, and the ancient and respected kingdoms of Northumbria and Mercia effectively ceased to exist.

Wessex did not suffer the same fate, thanks, as we are about to see, to the military genius and courage of King Alfred.

King Ethelbert

Reigned 860–866. The second son of King Ethelwulf.

King Ethelred

Reigned 866–871. The third son of King Ethelwulf.

CHAPTER ELEVEN

King Alfred the Great

871–899: the fourth and youngest son of King Ethelwulf

Even among the monarchs of all nations in all history, King Alfred the Great is surely unique in the number and extent of his many wonderful qualities. Sadly, the treatment of him during the last 200 years seems to have been less than adequate. In this chapter I will outline what I maintain ought to be included, and used to be included, in any serious treatment of him. The most important source is a Welsh bishop and scholar, Asser, one of a group of learned men whom Alfred invited to become part of his court.

The soldier. During the reigns of each of his three elder brothers, Alfred often led his country's armies, *even though he was no more than twenty-two years old* when the last of those brothers died and he became king. By then, the Danes controlled the East Angles, the Northumbrians and the Mercians. Only King Alfred's West Saxons had not been conquered by them, and they were exhausted and dispirited, having fought some ten battles during the previous year. Alfred, with only a small army, defeated the Danes nevertheless, and extracted from them a promise, on oath, never to return.

Seven years later, in shameless violation of their solemn oath, the Danes launched another invasion, with a huge army, and laid waste the entire country. At this point, in 878, Wessex might easily have become extinct, for nothing was left of King Alfred's 'kingdom' save a few square miles of marshes, and even those seemed destined to be lost. The country called England, which was to have such great

King Alfred the Great

influence in the future, and indeed with the help of Scotland was to control a full quarter of the world and *all* the oceans of the world, was within a hair's breadth of never coming into existence.

This time the numbers of the Danes were so overwhelming that King Alfred was forced first to retreat and then to hide himself in the woods and marshes of Ethelney in Somerset. Here it was that the famous event, until recently known to every schoolchild, of King Alfred burning the cakes took place.

After hiding for a year during which he reorganised his army, King Alfred launched a series of attacks on the triumphant Danes whenever opportunities presented themselves. In 883, he regained control first of Northumbria and then of Mercia, mainly present-day Derbyshire; and, although the Danes returned to the attack not infrequently in the following years, he almost always routed them. Almost incredibly, during the period 871–878 he is believed to have fought no fewer than fifty-six battles, most of them land battles but some of them on sea; and everywhere he restored the spirits of the English as well as striking fear into their enemies.

The war came to an unusual end. King Alfred made a peace with the Danes that was guaranteed to be both lasting and to the contentment of all those involved. First, he agreed that the Danes should rule eastern and northern England, which by then were sadly under-populated. Secondly, he was influential in the conversion and reception into the Church of the Danish warrior-leader Guthrum, who then changed his name to Ethelstan and indeed invited Alfred, his former enemy, to be his sponsor and godfather. Thirdly, he captured and garrisoned London, and was recognised as king of all of England other than that part still controlled by the Danes.

In 886, treaties entered into between Kings Alfred and Ethelstan, defining the boundaries between the two kingdoms and other details of what had been agreed. These treaties and their contents became formally known as the Danelaw.

The seaman. King Alfred showed himself to be aware, more than any previous English monarch had ever been, that the safety and natural strength of the island of Britain must depend ultimately on its navy. Accordingly, he went to the labour of making himself highly skilled in seafaring matters and devoted three years to building and fitting out a fleet that was capable of giving chase to any Danish pirates that came near to Britain, and was of course eventually to achieve complete dominion of the British seas.

Further, with a marvellous technical skill that he had acquired by the most intensive study, he devised a new kind of construction for ships. The result was warships that were twice as long and twice as tall as any others, the longest, tallest, and swiftest that there had ever been until then, and with the ability, in addition, to go very close to shore and even into creeks, all of which made these ships – thanks to the king's own design, let it be remembered – virtually invincible.

Surely the most remarkable of all, under the heading of military matters, is that, by contrast with the other three military 'Greats', Alexander, who sighed when there was nothing left for him to conquer, Charlemagne, who used warfare to create the great Western Empire, and Otto, who used the same means to create the Holy Roman Empire, King Alfred's more-than-fifty battles were in every case *purely* for the purpose of *defence*. He had not the smallest interest in going overseas in search of foreign lands to conquer in ruling great empires.

Not only that, but, by incorporating the defeated Danes into his own people rather than continuing the war against them until he had driven them completely out of England, he actually strengthened his country greatly, by increasing the number of his loyal subjects.

The legislator. As soon as conditions permitted, King Alfred set to work constructing a body of laws that were just and salutary. Starting by identifying and promoting such good laws as had been enacted by his predecessors Kings Ina, Offa and Ethelbert, he added several of his own, all of them designed to create a body of legislation for keeping public peace and safety and preserving the respect due to the Christian Church and its representatives. He also took the greatest care to make sure that the execution of the laws was perfect and that justice was administered with exact fairness throughout the entire kingdom.

There is more. King Alfred introduced what was for England the entirely new principle of trial by jury in which verdicts were decided by twelve men of undoubted respectability, who were obliged to pass judgement on oath as to the evidence relating to any crime or other relevant fact. Thus he was the initiator of what is, right up to our present day, one of the most valuable privileges both of British subjects and of people in overseas countries to which the English common law has spread.

In total, what King Alfred produced in his law code, basically an adaptation of the laws of Moses in the Old Testament to suit Anglo-Saxon conditions, was the largest and best-preserved English legal documentation before the Norman Conquest of 1066 that survives.

The administrator of his kingdom. Before his reign, some parts of England had been divided into areas of land known as shires, a term still honoured by appearing at the end of the names of many of our present-day counties. King Alfred made additions to these shires, to the extent that they covered the whole kingdom, and subdivided them into what were called hundreds and subdivided those hundreds into districts called tenths, with every district being responsible for dealing with robberies committed within its boundaries.

Gentle and mild as King Alfred was in the governing and administration of his subjects, nothing could be more rigorous than the demands made by him on judges and magistrates. Up until his reign, bribes and 'presents' had been seen as a routine means of circumventing justice. In his time and for some time afterwards, the conduct of judges and magistrates was continually examined with scrupulous care, and any faults, however small, were punished with great severity.

The civiliser. When King Alfred came to the throne, the whole country was close to being a desert, and even feeding themselves adequately was difficult for the populace. He gave every possible encouragement to agriculture, and within a few years the English everywhere were not merely surviving well but prosperous. Further, he rebuilt monasteries which had been destroyed during the wars and even was responsible for the foundation of new ones, both because he wanted to spread piety throughout his kingdom and because they could provide education for his subjects.

He valued education above everything else, holding uncompromisingly the belief that the arts and sciences created a much more solid base for an agreeable and happy life than riches ever could; and he devoted every necessary effort to making it possible for *everyone* to receive a sound education.

In the arts. It has been generally recognised that, in every country, the state of architecture is a sure indication of to what degree the arts flourished at any particular time, something very much evidenced in the civilisations of the classical Greeks and Romans. King Alfred adorned his kingdom with several magnificent churches and other buildings, and he himself, having *taught himself* – in addition to everything else that he taught himself – the science of architecture, directed the builders. Up until the time of his reign, most houses were made of wood and mortar. He taught his subjects how to build houses with stone and brick, and this was not only valuable in itself but led to a massive flourishing of the practical visual arts, such as architecture, metal-working, and working in gold, silver and jewellery, in many of which notably beautiful specimens survive.

The scholar. Having suffered greatly from lack of education in his upbringing, because of being continually at war, and having not even learnt to read until he was twelve, he made up for the time lost as surely no one else has ever done. Even though he only turned to learning Latin at the age of thirty-eight, he *became the greatest scholar in his kingdom*, outstripping all his subjects in almost every branch of human knowledge.

His literary output would have been remarkable even if he had had no other calls on his time. He translated from Latin the Preface of Pope St. Gregory's book of *Pastoral Care* of 590; Orosius's *History against the Pagans* of about 420; the enduringly famous and influential *On the Consolations of Philosophy* by Boethius, of 524; possibly Bede's massive *Ecclesiastical History of the English Nation* of 731, though modern scholars believe it was done by contemporaries of his under his influence; and, according to one credible source, Florence of Worcester, the entirety of the New Testament of the Bible. And he had made considerable progress on translating the Psalms – he had completed the first fifty – when death overtook him.

Arguably as great an influence for England's future as anything was his decision that the Roman alphabet should be adopted in place of the original Saxon alphabet, which up until then had always been used in Saxon books. It is to King Alfred the Great, primarily, that we owe the letters from these very words that you are now reading.

Simply the person. To an incomparable extent, in him were united the soldier, the statesman, the scholar and, not least remarkably, indeed for what he was admired for most of all in his lifetime by those who knew him best, his saintliness.

Perhaps of interest is what the Christian term 'saintliness' involved in his case. This is some of what Asser records.

Of his yearly income, half was used for the purpose of administering the country and his household, while the other half was divided into four parts. One part was to be given to the poor, not only those of England but also those who came to him from any country anywhere. The second part was given to the two monasteries that he had built, and to those inside the monasteries who had dedicated themselves to the service of God. The third part was for all the other monasteries in the country, and some of those in Ireland as well. The fourth part was given to a school that he had founded.

Also prominent in his general conduct was the special reverence that he always showed towards the bishops in his realm and the other officials of the Church. Whenever he reasonably could he went to listen to sermons. He also asked servants of his to read the Bible to him during the day.

~

For a worthy summary of what we have learnt about King Alfred so far, here is the eminent seventeenth-century soldier, scholar, writer and politician Sir Henry Spelman:

> O, Alfred, the wonder and astonishment of all ages! If we reflect on his piety and religion, it would seem that he had always lived in a cloister; if on his warlike exploits, that he had never been out of camps; if on his learning and writings, that he had spent his whole life in a college; if on his wholesome laws and wise administration, that these had been his whole study and employment.[2]

All these, moreover, were the accomplishments of a man who almost throughout his life was very sickly. Early in his youth he was afflicted with a disease so painful that the time came when he thought himself unlikely to survive. Survive he did, but at the age of twenty, on the *very day* of his wedding in 868, he was struck with another disease – unknown to all physicians, Asser says – which tormented him day and night until his death, with scarcely a day passing without his feeling some great pain or aching.

~

Thus the man to whom England owes so much of what it can be proud of, right up to our present day.

CHAPTER TWELVE

King Edward I ('the Elder') and King Ethelstan

King Edward I ('the Elder')

Reigned 899–924. The 'the Elder' title was given him by later historians to distinguish him from King Edward II, known as King Edward the Martyr.

King Edward I was the son of King Alfred the Great. Arguably the most important feature of his reign was that he brought near to completion the process that King Alfred had started, whereby England – not yet *called* England – became a single kingdom under the control of the Royal House of Wessex.

King Ethelstan

Reigned 925–939. The son of King Edward I, the grandson of King Alfred the Great, and the second king after King Arthur, many centuries previously, to lay a formal claim to the whole of Britain, including Scotland and Wales.

When he came to the throne, the main part of his realm was in the south of England, in Wessex, which by then was an ancient kingdom and, thanks mainly to his grandfather, had come to stretch from Cornwall to Kent. In 927 he rode up north of the River Humber and entered York. The princes who until then had reigned north of York were intimidated by the unprecedented scope of his power and at once acknowledged his authority, giving him control of Mercia and Northumbria as well as Wessex.

The inhabitants of the various kingdoms of the Welsh and the Scots, led by King Constantin, then submitted too, and he was justly hailed by poets and chroniclers as *Rex Totius Britannia* – King of the *Whole* of Britain.

Step by step, he consolidated and then increased his power throughout the land, and this even though a massive confederation of Britons was in constant opposition to him. In 937, he completely defeated his opponents at the Battle of Brunanburh, following which a completely new concept, kingship of the English, emerged from nowhere. Since all those who acknowledged him as their lord also spoke the same language as he did, he thought it appropriate to adopt a magnificent new title, *Rex Anglorum* – King of the English.

England had at last been founded. By a single battle there had been brought into existence a new nation stretching from the Firth of Forth in Scotland to the English Channel in the southernmost part of England – a nation that was in due course to be the most powerful nation on earth.

Among his extraordinary achievements, he even had a decisive voice in what this new country was to be called. Out of several contenders, 'Anglia' triumphed, and the name Angleland, that is to say Englalonde in the language of its inhabitants, was adopted. Thus, at last, came into being the country the kings and queens of which are the subject-matter of this book.

PART V

BEFORE THE REFORMATION: KINGS OF ENGLAND ONLY

CHAPTER THIRTEEN

The House of Wessex

B Y THE BEGINNING of the tenth century AD, the Royal House of Wessex had gained control of the area that was to become known as England. By the end of that century, most of today's prominent English towns were *already* prominent towns, the currency was regulated, foreign trade was an important feature of the economy and the essential institutions of local government were established – none of which had taken place by the start of the century in the year 900.

King Edmund I

Born c. 922 and reigned 940–946. Variously known as King Edmund the Elder, the Deed-Doer, the Just and the Magnificent, he was the eldest son of King Edward the Elder (899–924), by that king's third marriage, and the grandson of King Alfred the Great.

King Edred *or* Eadred

Born c. 923 and reigned 946–955, having come to the throne on the death of his elder brother King Edmund I.

King Edwy the All-Fair

Born c. 941 and reigned 955–959. The elder son of King Edmund I, he became king at the age of fifteen on the death of his uncle

King Edred. His short reign was tarnished by disputes with both nobles and churchmen.

King Edgar the Peaceful

Born c. 942 and reigned 959–975. He was the younger son of King Edmund I and came to the throne at the age of sixteen. During his reign the unity of England achieved by his predecessors was consolidated. In addition, the system of measurements throughout England was standardised.

King Edward the Martyr

Born c. 962 and reigned 975–978, and recognised today as a saint. The eldest son of King Edgar the Peaceful's three children, he succeeded to the throne at the age of only thirteen. He was murdered in Corfe Castle in Dorset, possibly, it is thought, on the instigation of his stepmother the Dowager Queen Aelfthryth, the mother of the king who immediately succeeded him.

King Ethelred II 'the Unready'

Born c. 966 and reigned 978–1013 and 1014–1016. 'Unready' means, not 'unprepared', but 'ill-advised'. Since the time of King Ethelstan the whole of Britain had been unmolested, but during the reign of King Ethelred, the Danes ravaged it repeatedly and horribly.

The main events of the reign in summary

985. He married Egilva, daughter of the Earl of Northumbria, by whom he begot the future King Edmund Ironside, his immediate successor.

991. In order to buy off the marauding Danes, the king undertook to pay them a yearly tax of £40,000, a vast sum at that time, called the Danegeld. It was raised by taxing each hide – as much land as could be tilled with one plough in one year – at the rate of twelve pence.

994. King Swein of Denmark invaded England and besieged London, but was bought off for £16,000.

1002. King Ethelred's first wife, Queen Egilva, died. Shortly afterwards he married Emma, daughter of Richard I, Duke of Normandy. They were the parents of the future King St. Edward the Confessor.

1013. King Swein invaded England again. This time King Ethelred was forced to flee to Normandy, and King Swein replaced him as King of England.

1014. On the death of King Swein, King Ethelred was restored to the English throne.

1016. King Ethelred died.

King Edmund II, Edmund Ironside

Born c. 993 and reigned in 1016 only. There were two claimants to the throne: King Ethelred's son Edmund Ironside, and Canute, the son of King Swein of the Danes.

King Edmund Ironside was King Ethelred's eldest son by Egilva, his first wife.

CHAPTER FOURTEEN

The House of Denmark

King Swein ('Forkbeard'), King of the Danes

Born c. 960 and reigned 1013–1014. After two previous invasions of England, King Swein of Denmark and his Danes were finally victorious, with King Ethelred of the House of Wessex fleeing to Normandy. King Swein then conquered the whole of England, but died a year later, to be succeeded by his son Canute. Canute, however, was unable to reign immediately; and instead, King Ethelred was restored to the throne and reigned until his death two years later.

King Canute (Cnut) the Great

Born c. 995 and reigned 1016–1035.

(i) The main events of the reign in summary

1016. Canute gained the English throne two years after the death of his father King Swein Forkbeard in 1014. In 1018 he succeeded to the Danish throne as well, bringing the crowns of England and Denmark together. Military victories in 1026 were to add Norway and part of Sweden to his kingdoms.

1017. Wishing to make himself more acceptable to the English, he married Queen Emma, the late King Ethelred's widow. She bore him a son, **Hardicanute**.

1018. He made **Godwin** – a very ambitious noble of, remarkably, unknown Christian name – Earl of Wessex.

1027. With England settled in a state of peacefulness and prosperity, King Canute considered it safe to undertake a pilgrimage to Rome. He left the government of the country in the hands of the new Earl of Wessex, by then the most powerful of the earls.

1031. Occasional invasions by the Scots led King Canute to travel to Scotland, where, without needing to resort to violence, he compelled King Malcolm to do homage to him as overlord.

1035. On his death his kingdoms were divided between his three sons: **Swein**, who became King of Norway; **Harold Harefoot**, who became King of England north of the Thames; and **Hardicanute**, who became King of Denmark and of England south of the River Thames. In practice, King Harold Harefoot ruled all England until his death in 1040, whereupon his brother Hardicanute became the ruler of all England.

(ii) Of special interest

A wise and successful king, Canute re-established the laws of the great King Edgar the Peaceful; divided the whole country of England into four great earldoms, those of Northumbria in the north, East Anglia in the east, Mercia in what is now the Midlands, and Wessex in the south; supported existing laws and addressed common grievances; strengthened the currency; and set about improving relations between the monarchy and the Church, repairing all the churches and monasteries that had suffered from Viking plundering, building new churches and undertaking the patronage of monastic communities.

He is best known for an anecdote first related by the twelfth-century historian, Henry, Archdeacon of Huntingdon, in his *Historia Anglorum*. Wishing to rebuke his courtiers for their flattery of him, King Canute placed his throne by the seashore and commanded the incoming tide to halt rather than wet his feet and robes. The tide of course continued to rise as usual, and, as Archdeacon Henry put it, 'dashed over his feet and legs without respect to his royal person'. Said the King: 'Let all men know how empty and worthless is the power of kings, for there is none worthy of the name, but He whom heaven, earth, and sea obey by eternal laws.' He then hung his gold crown on a crucifix, and, 'to the honour of God the almighty King', never wore it again.

King Harold I ('Harefoot')

Born c. 1016, the second son of King Canute, and reigned 1035–1040.

1036. Princes Alfred and Edward, sons of King Ethelred the Unready, returned to England from Normandy, whither they had gone after King Ethelred's death. On their arrival, King Harold had the elder, Prince Alfred, seized, brutally blinded, and killed. Prince Edward hastily returned to Normandy.

1040. On the death of King Harold, his half-brother, Hardicanute, son of Canute and of Emma, was invited to become king in his place.

King Hardicanute (Harthacanut)

Born c. 1019, the third son of King Canute and younger half-brother of King Harold I on his father's side and of Edward the Confessor on his mother's side. Reigned 1040–1042.

1040. On the death of Harold, his half-brother, Hardicanute, came from Denmark with a large army. Swiftly securing possession of the whole of England, he then had the body of his half-brother removed from its place of honour in Westminster, publicly beheaded, disposed of in a sewer, and retrieved and thrown in the Thames – from where, however, London shipmen rescued it and had it buried in a churchyard.

During his reign King Hardicanute doubled the size of the English fleet and, in order to pay for this, severely increased the rate of taxation.

1041. He invited his other half-brother, Prince Edward, back from exile in Normandy, and is thought to have made him his heir to the English throne.

1042. Attending a wedding, he suddenly collapsed and died.

CHAPTER FIFTEEN

The House of Wessex Again

King St. Edward the Confessor

Born probably in 1003 and reigned 1042–1066. King Edward was the son of King Ethelred II by Emma, Ethelred's second wife, and King Hardicanute's brother.

(i) The main events of the reign in summary

1044. Reluctantly agreeing to the wishes of the nobles and the people to take a consort, he was the first king in English history to choose someone non-royal for his wife and consort: Edith, the daughter of the powerful noble Earl Godwin and famous for both her beauty and her accomplishments.

1051. Because Godwin was constantly rebellious, the King and his council, which was known variously as the Witenagemot and the Witan, declared him an outlaw and banished him and his family from England. This council just mentioned was an assembly of the most important noblemen acting as the king's official advisers and is thought to have existed in Anglo-Saxon England since as early as the seventh century. Its functions included that of choosing the member of the Royal Family deemed most suitable to be the next king.

William Duke of Normandy visited England, and apparently received from King Edward the promise, which he may not have had the authority to make, of the crown on his death.

King St. Edward the Confessor

1052. Godwin and his family were permitted to return to England. Godwin was restored to his earldom and all his former positions of power.

1053. Godwin died, to be succeeded by his son Harold as Earl of Wessex.

1066. King Edward the Confessor died.

(ii) Of special interest

King Edward is now little respected by most historians. He tends to be represented as well-intentioned and pious but weak in character and unworldly, and his reign as largely unfortunate in its results. He was, however, in fact one of England's most important and long-lastingly effective kings. Please consider the following:

- He was responsible for the very existence of the buildings of England's Houses of Parliament today and of what surrounds them, although most of the buildings themselves are no longer the same. Early in his reign, he turned the cathedral called St. Peter's Cathedral, situated in the part of London called Thorny Island, into a great building, and then, in 1059, built a monastery there, endowed it with a magnificent abbey, and at the same time built for himself a palace next door to it.

  Thus came into existence both Westminster Abbey and, at its side, what is still officially called the Palace of Westminster, occupying eight acres of land and now, rebuilt after having been largely destroyed in a fire in 1834, including the House of Lords, the House of Commons and Big Ben. Moreover, Westminster Abbey was the very first church in England to be built in the Romanesque style, which was the ancestor of the Gothic style in which all the great church buildings were built from the twelfth century onwards. King Edward was responsible for the introduction into England of the greatest architecture that the world has ever known.

- He was responsible for a very large number of religious foundations, started up and existing *at no cost* to his people. In those days, kings inherited estates which provided sufficient money for their ordinary expenses and expenses of running the country, and taxes were not levied other than in time of war or other emergencies.

- King Edward even *abolished* a tax, the Danegeld that in his father King Ethelread's time had first been paid to the Danish fleet, and then, when no longer needed for that purpose, had been paid ever since into the royal exchequer. As was perhaps without precedent and was certainly never to happen again, King Edward even went so far as to command that what had been received from this tax until then should be returned to those who had paid it.

- In 602, King Ethelbert and in 693 King Wihtred had published laws, known as dooms, for the kingdom of Kent, and other monarchs had published similar laws for Wessex and Mercia. King Edward united all these laws into a single code and made various amendments and additions, and this code of laws became 'common' to the whole of England, and indeed they were known as Edward the Confessor's Laws, to distinguish them from the later laws passed by the Norman kings after 1066.

  To a remarkable extent King Edward's laws are *still in force today*, under the title of the common law of England. By any yardstick, they are one of the wonders of the world; and are honoured as such not only in England but also by countries – such as the United States of America, Canada, Australia, New Zealand and, if it could be called a country, Hong Kong – that have come under the influence of those laws as a result of having been ruled from Britain at any time and have kept them as a precious inheritance when eventually ceasing to be ruled by Britain.

- In the administration of his justice, he walked in the steps of King Alfred the Great, whom he proposed to himself as a model, in his insistence on the integrity of his judges.

- Although he never had any wish to go to war, when he thought it necessary to do so he did not shirk that responsibility.

- Notwithstanding his constant attention to all his duties as a monarch, his primary aim was to lead a life of piety, his obvious success in which was to earn him after his death the title of 'Confessor', given in recognition of a saintly life.

~

Here is an assessment of his reign by the seventeenth-century Member of Parliament and author John Gurdon in his *History of the Parliament*:

> Edward the Confessor, that great and good legislator, reigned in the heart of his people. The love, harmony and good agreement between him and the great Council of the nation, produced such a happiness is to be a measure of the people's desires in all succeeding reigns.[3]

Can any praise of a king be more exalted than that?

He died in 1066, aged sixty-three, and, famously, posterity for succeeding ages longed for the revival of the happiness of the good Confessor's reign.

To this day, kings of England at the coronation both receive the crown that bears King Edward's name and is an imitation of the original, and put on his ecclesiastical garments known as the dalmatic and maniple.

King Harold II

Born in 1022. Reigned from January to October 1066. Did not marry.

(i) The main events of the reign in summary

1066. In January he was chosen by the Witan to succeed King Edward and crowned at Westminster Abbey. In September a rival claimant for the throne, King Harald Hardrada of Norway, invaded England in Yorkshire with the support of Harold's brother Tostig. King Harold at once led his army north on a forced march from London and defeated both at the Battle of Stamford Bridge. Immediately afterwards, William Duke of Normandy landed with an army in Sussex. Harold marched his army back to intercept William, and was defeated and killed at the Battle of Hastings.

(ii) Of special interest

Although Harold had been the brother-in-law of the late king, there was only a minimal amount of royal blood running through his veins (his mother was a cousin of King Canute) and there was no precedent or rational justification for the choice of someone with no royal blood. How it came about that the Witan, the group of people responsible for choosing the next king after the death of King Edward, made the choice of him, the son of the Earl Godwin, rather than making the obvious choice of a grandson of King Edmund Ironside, is a mystery, as also it is a mystery that historians never seem to advert to this mystery.

PART VI

BEFORE THE REFORMATION: KINGS OF ENGLAND AND DUKES OF NORMANDY

CHAPTER SIXTEEN

The House of Normandy

King William I (usually 'William the Conqueror', sometimes 'William the Bastard')

Born c. 1028 and reigned 1066–1087. He was the illegitimate son of Robert I, Duke of Normandy, which gave rise to difficulties in Normandy when he succeeded to the dukedom. Although he was acknowledged as Duke William II of Normandy from 1035 onwards, his hold on Normandy was not secure until 1060. In 1051 or 1052 he married Matilda of Flanders, the niece of one king of France, the granddaughter of another, and also descended from the Royal House of Wessex. They had nine, possibly ten, children, two of whom, William and Henry, were to become king of England in succession to him.

(i) The main events of the reign in summary

1066. On King Edward's death, Duke William, his first cousin once removed, maintained that King Edward had promised the English throne to him, and that the leading English noble Harold Godwinson had solemnly sworn to support his claim. On Harold's taking the throne in defiance of these claims, he built and put together a large fleet of some 700 warships, invaded England, and, partly because Harold had just had to fight off Harald Hardrada's invasion in the north of England, decisively defeated Harold at the Battle of Hastings on 14 October. He was crowned King of England on Christmas Day. He was the great-nephew of Queen Emma, who

King William I ('William the Conqueror')

had been wife successively to King Ethelred and King Canute, but that was too remote a family connection to the throne to be relevant, and his entitlement to it was therefore technically 'by conquest'.

1067. The Saxons in the west of England rose up in a revolt which King William suppressed.

1069. The Saxons rose up again, this time in the north and assisted by the Danes. King William's response was a devastation of the country so complete that, in the Domesday Book – see below, 1086 – that part of England was marked 'waste'.

1071. In East Anglia, a final, long-drawn-out struggle of the Saxons for independence, led by Hereward the Wake, ended with King William victorious and his conquest of England complete.

1072. King William invaded Scotland, and forced King Malcolm III to pay homage to him.

1079. In Normandy, King William's eldest son Robert led a rebellion against his own father. King William defeated him and spared his life.

The New Forest in southern England was created, by the enclosure of several thousand acres as a royal hunting ground.

1086. The Domesday Book, arising from a general survey of landholdings made in 1085 and putting on record the extent and value of the land, the population and the land's owners, of which the Saxon landowners had by then been reduced to a small minority, was completed.

1087. A quarrel with King Philip I of France led to his invading France. While besieging the city of Mantes and trying to burn it down, he fell from his horse and died from the injuries that resulted.

(ii) Of special interest

The Battle of Hastings is arguably the most famous and important battle in the history of England and indeed of Britain; its consequences, under the merciless Normans, were far-reaching:

• The Norman-French language, originally introduced into England by King Edward the Confessor, whose early life had been spent in Normandy, was for the next 300 years the language spoken in England by the upper classes.

- Norman manners and architecture became part of the culture of the country.
- Almost all the land in England was confiscated from the Saxons and taken over by the Norman invaders.
- To protect themselves from counter-attacks by the remaining Saxons, the Normans built more than forty large castles, of which many still survive, including Windsor Castle and part of the Tower of London.
- The feudal system, to be described in chapter 19, became fully established.
- The Jews established a presence in England for the first time. According to Albert M. Hyamson OBE, in his *A History of the Jews in England* first published in 1908, 'it has been suggested that a large sum of money was paid by the Jews to William so that he should permit them to settle in England.'

King William II ('William Rufus')

Born c. 1056 and reigned 1087–1100. He was the second son of King William I. The reason for the nickname 'Rufus' was said by the earliest authority on the subject, William of Malmesbury writing in 1127, to have been that his complexion was unusually ruddy.

(i) The main events of the reign in summary

1087. Prince William was named heir by his father, King William the Conqueror, in place of his elder brother Robert, who was granted the dukedom of Normandy. William now succeeded his father to the throne.

1088. The new king's uncle, Odo of Bayeux, launched a rebellion of barons in Normandy in support of King William's brother Robert's claim to the English throne. King William crushed it impressively.

1089. King William started to levy heavier taxes on the Church than had ever been levied before.

1090. Robert of Normandy continued to be rebellious, and King William led an invasion of Normandy in order to try to subdue him.

1091. King Malcolm III of Scotland invaded England from the north. King William defeated him.

1092. The war with Scotland continued, and King William gained control of Carlisle and Cumberland.

1093. King Malcolm III and the Scots launched another invasion of England. King William defeated them at the Battle of Alnwick, at which King Malcolm was killed.

Falling ill and wishing to make amends for the wrongs he had done to the Church, King William appointed Anselm as Archbishop of Canterbury.

1095. Northumbria, in the very north of England, launched a rebellion, which King William defeated.

1097. Anselm had from the start opposed King William's policy, rapacious without precedent, towards the Church. Now unable to withstand King Williams's violence, he withdrew to Rome, not to return until the next reign.

1098. The Welsh rebelled. King William suppressed the rebellion.

1100. King William was killed by an arrow, shot by Sir Walter Tyrrell, while hunting in the New Forest.

(ii) Of special interest

As we have seen, King William I had thought his son William to be more suitable for the throne of England than his elder son Robert, to whom he gave the Duchy of Normandy. Many of the barons in England did not agree, and King William II's reign was unstable throughout. The apparent accident, a strange and unlikely one, of Sir Walter Tyrrell's arrow, has been thought by many to have been a deliberate murder organised by his younger brother, Henry, who in consequence became the next king; and there are grounds for suspicion, since it was also believed, though never conclusively confirmed, that Prince Henry was in the New Forest at the time of the accident.

King William II has been held by most historians to have been a bad king and to have practised every sort of vice. He has, however, had occasional defenders, who, for instance, have held that he was a wise ruler who maintained order and justice in England, and have pointed out that he was a victorious general. His role in his long-running clash with Archbishop Anselm and his unprecedented financial appropriations from the Church justify his bad reputation in part, but there is no evidence of his being perverse in the passing of laws and the administration of justice, and he was undoubtedly a magnificent warrior, constantly engaged in suppressing rebellions and always successfully.

King Henry I

Born 1068 and reigned 1100–1135. Manner of accession: the fourth son of William I, and King William II's brother, the next in line.

(i) The main events of the reign in summary

1100. King Henry issued a Charter of Liberties, pledging that he would govern well. He married King Malcolm III of Scotland's daughter Edith, uniting the Saxon and Norman lines. She adopted the additional name of Matilda with the intention of improving her relations with the English.

1101. King Henry's brother, Robert of Normandy, invaded England in an attempt to take the throne from his brother. The attempt failed and ended with both signing the Treaty of Alton, which confirmed Henry as King of England and Robert as Duke of Normandy.

1106. Another war between Henry and Robert broke out. It ended with Henry defeating Robert and taking control of Normandy as well as England.

1118. Queen Matilda died.

1120. King Henry I's only son, Prince William, was drowned on a ship, the *White Ship*, on a journey from Normandy to England, leaving his sister, who was also called Matilda, as King Henry's heir.

1121. King Henry married Adela of Louvain, which is in present-day Belgium.

1126. King Henry persuaded the barons to accept his daughter Princess Matilda as the lawful successor to the throne.

1128. Princess Matilda married Geoffrey Plantagenet, Count of Anjou in France, thus laying the foundation of the Plantagenet line which, with seven kings in succession, was to rule England from 1135 to 1399 and, more than any other dynasty, was to give England its long-enduring form and character. Geoffrey's name 'Plantagenet' was derived from a 'twig of broom-shrub', *planta genista* in Latin, that he was accustomed to wear in his cap.

(ii) Of special interest

King Henry expanded greatly the English empire. In the south he won Normandy from his elder brother Robert after Robert had claimed, unsuccessfully, the crown of England. In the north he subjugated to some extent the King of Scotland and in the west completely the various princes of Wales.

During King Henry's reign, the crusades were launched for the first time. His elder brother Robert, but not he, took part in the First Crusade.

The official reason for launching the crusades was to recover the Holy Land, approximately present-day Israel, from the Turks, who had captured Jerusalem and were making pilgrimages for Christians to the Holy Land no longer possible. There were nine crusades in total, over a period of 174 years, finally ending in 1270.

Matilda, Holy Roman Empress and Queen of England, and King Stephen

Born 1102, the daughter of King Henry I. She was arguably Queen from 1135 until her death in 1167. King Stephen reigned, by usurpation of the throne from her, from 1135 to 1154.

(i) The main events leading up to and including the disputed reigns in summary

1092. Stephen, son of King William I's daughter Adela, was born. Usually known as Stephen of Blois, he was brought up in France, where he married Matilda, daughter of the Count of Bologne. He was the son of King Henry I of England's sister Adela and was therefore King Henry's nephew and King William I's grandson. His claim to the English throne when King Henry died in 1135 was in consequence more remote than the claim of another Matilda, who was King Henry I's daughter and direct descendant.

1110. Princess Matilda, when aged eight, became engaged to be married to King Henry V of Germany, who in the following year was to become the Holy Roman Emperor.

1114. Princess Matilda, by then aged fourteen, and Emperor and King Henry V, were married. Right from the start Matilda entered fully into public life as Queen and Empress.

1120. Prince William, brother of Empress and Queen Matilda and King Henry I's only son, was, as already noted, drowned on a journey from Normandy to England. Although England had never before been ruled by a queen, King Henry declared his daughter to be his heir to the throne, and extracted from his barons an oath of loyalty to her and her successors.

1125. Queen and Empress Matilda's husband Henry, the Holy Roman Emperor, died, and Matilda returned to her original home in Normandy.

1127. Stephen of Blois, nephew of King Henry I, swore to support the claim of Queen and Empress Matilda to the throne of England.

1128. King Henry I persuaded his widowed daughter Matilda to take as her second husband Geoffrey of Anjou, which she did only reluctantly, because she was by then twenty-eight and Geoffrey was only fourteen.

1133. Queen Matilda gave birth to the future King Henry II.

1135. King Henry I died. At once Stephen of Blois usurped the throne from Matilda, receiving the backing of powerful people in England, and was crowned King of England. In return he allowed the barons to build castles on their estates, unwisely in that it was to lead to warfare between barons for long into the future.

1138. Robert of Gloucester, an illegitimate son of King Henry I and a half-brother of Queen Matilda, rebelled against King Stephen, starting a civil war that was to last for fifteen years and was notable for its cruelty and bloodshed.

King David I of Scotland invaded England in support of Matilda, who was his niece.

1139. Queen Matilda and Robert of Gloucester invaded England, and at once established a court in Gloucester in the south-west.

1141. King Stephen was defeated and taken prisoner. The English clergy then declared queen Matilda to be the 'Lady of England and Normandy', a title considered to be suitable as a preliminary to her coronation as queen. Partly because the nobles thought that this could lead to her husband Geoffrey of Anjou, a

Norman, playing a significant part in the government of England, however, her attempt to be crowned in Westminster received unexpected opposition from the Londoners and was unsuccessful. She was never formally declared queen and indeed was fortunate to be able to escape from Westminster to Oxford. There she was besieged and eventually was once again fortunate to be able to escape, and left Stephen with the usurped crown.

1148. Queen Matilda handed over her claim to the English throne to Henry, her fifteen-year-old son by her second husband, Geoffrey of Anjou, and left England to spend the rest of her life mainly administering Normandy, part of her son's future territory.

1153. A compromise at last brought the civil war to an end: Matilda's son Henry became both Stephen's adopted son and his official successor to the throne as King Henry II.

1154. King Stephen died and Queen Matilda's son King Henry II succeeded him, in effect in his mother's place. In addition to continuing to be directly involved in Normandy, Matilda played a considerable part in the administration of England as his adviser, and in 1160 even acted as mediator between Henry and his Chancellor Thomas à Becket when their close association and friendship came to an end.

(ii) Of special interest

It must be doubtful that King Stephen ever felt that he had profited from his usurpation of the throne. His life as king was one of constant warfare and anxiety, all of which eventually ended in his complete defeat and the loss of the throne and all traces of such dignity as he had once had.

Queen and Empress Matilda, on the other hand, surely falls into the category of having been one of history's greatest and most remarkable women. There is good reason, moreover, to suppose that she would have ruled exceptionally well. She showed unfailing competence in her administration of Normandy and in her advice to her son King Henry; she worked extensively and cooperatively with the Church; she founded a number of Cistercian monasteries; and she was renowned and admired for her piety.

CHAPTER SEVENTEEN

The First Two Kings of the House of Plantagenet

King Henry II

Born 1133 and reigned 1154–1189. The son of Henry I's daughter Matilda, and therefore Henry's grandson and William I's great-grandson. In 1151, he had married Eleanor of Aquitaine, the richest and most powerful woman in Europe and eleven years his senior.

(i) The main events of the reign in summary

1154. Henry succeeded King Stephen to the throne at the age of twenty-one. The extent of the possessions over which he ruled was extraordinary. From his mother Queen Matilda he inherited England, Normandy and the Maine; from his grandfather King Henry I, Anjou and Touraine; and, from his wife Queen Eleanor, Poitou and all the French provinces from immediately south of the River Loire down to the Pyrenees mountains forming the border between France and Spain.

1155. King Henry appointed Thomas à Becket as Chancellor of England, the senior political position in England after the King himself. Becket was not of noble birth, as Chancellors usually were, but was a commoner of exceptional ability.

Pope Adrian IV, the only Englishman ever to have been Pope, published a papal bull – a particular kind of public decree issued by a pope – titled *Laudabiliter*, which gave to King Henry the feudal overlordship of Ireland and the Church's permission to invade Ireland and solidify the relationship between the Irish Church and Rome. The genuineness of this bull has been disputed – unjustifiably in this writer's opinion, however, since, even though no contemporary copy exists, there are references to it in documents written in the 1200s. Indeed it is generally accepted as genuine.

1162. Archbishop Theobald died, and King Henry used his influence with the bishops and monks in England to get Becket appointed Archbishop of Canterbury, even though Becket was a worldly man and not even an ordained priest. On being ordained a priest and then consecrated Archbishop of Canterbury on two successive days, however, Becket at once resigned from the office of Chancellor and all his other civil offices.

1164. Up until this time, crimes committed by the clergy were exclusively dealt with by the Church in England, which had the strict right to self-government and did not come under the jurisdiction of kings. King Henry sought to change this, and summoned a council at Clarendon Palace in Wiltshire where he set down in writing a number of demands, known to posterity as the Constitutions of Clarendon. One of these demands was that clergymen charged with criminal offences should be tried by civil courts. Becket at first agreed to put his signature to the constitutions. He then decided that he could not, after all, accept them and appealed to the Pope to release him from what he had signed his agreement to, by means of the authority in such matters that only popes possessed. In the conflict that resulted, Becket, with his life under threat, fled to France, where for six years he lived in exile, still as Archbishop.

1170. Pope Alexander III threatened England with an interdict which would suspend all public church services throughout England. King Henry was persuaded to become reconciled with the Archbishop, who then returned to England to take up his position again. Soon, however, the quarrel was reopened, eventually leading to Becket transmitting an excommunication by the Pope of the English bishops who had opposed him. In a fit of rage, King Henry uttered some hasty words which led four knights to hasten to Canterbury and murder Becket in the cathedral. King Henry did public penance for his responsibility in this sacrilegious crime, and Becket's tomb became one of the most important destinations for sacred pilgrimages in Europe.

1171. At the Council of Cashel, King Henry was accepted by all the Irish kings as Lord of Ireland, their feudal suzerain (the title given to a sovereign who had some authority in a state of which he was not the direct ruler).

1173. Thomas à Becket was officially canonised as a saint – an unusually early canonisation since most do not take place until at least fifty years after a person's death.

1173–1174. Princes Henry, Richard and Geoffrey led an unsuccessful rebellion against their father.

1183. King Henry's three sons led a second rebellion, during the course of which Prince Henry died of a fever. Soon afterwards Geoffrey was killed in a tournament.

1189. Prince Richard succeeded in expelling his father from Touraine. Finding that Prince John, his favourite son, was also involved in the expulsion, King Henry died of a broken heart.

(ii) Of special interest

King Henry II, the first king to come to the throne unopposed since King Harold in 1066, started his reign as undoubtedly a well-motivated king. At once he had many castles that had been built by barons without permission in previous reigns torn down. He negotiated with King Malcolm IV of Scotland the return of Northumbria and Cumbria in the north to England, and, with a short military campaign, established himself as the superior of the provinces in Wales.

At least as important for the future as anything else he did, he consolidated the system for the administration of justice that is one of the foundations of the greatly revered English common law.

Under his energetic and wise rule in the early days of his reign, England became a land of prosperity and peace, to such an extent that the twelfth-century historian, William of Newburgh, was able to write in his *Historia rerum Anglicarum* ('History of English Affairs') that 'a virgin could walk from one end of the realm to the other with her bosom full of gold and suffer no harm, and that evil barons had vanished like phantoms' – an astonishing testimony to what the King had accomplished and to his power.

In almost all his activities, military and in the administration of justice, his chief agent and adviser, Thomas à Becket, was fully involved. Early in King Henry's reign, Theobald, the Archbishop of Canterbury, had brought to his attention this man of exceptional ability, the son of a prosperous London merchant. King Henry and Becket quickly became close friends and constant companions, and not long afterwards Becket became King Henry's chief minister, his Chancellor, and was even given the task of bringing up and training King Henry's son, Prince Henry.

In 1161 everything changed. Archbishop Theobald of Canterbury died, and, with motives by no means free from self-interest, the obvious next move for King Henry was to get Becket appointed as the new Archbishop of Canterbury.

King Henry was by then a mighty monarch, ruling over a greater part of Christendom than had ever been directly ruled before, and unhampered by any form of Parliament. His rule was by no means total, however. There was in those days an institution whose power was even greater than the king's: the Church, which was not only a religious organisation but was also a political unit that was independent of the monarchy and even superior to it, and, in addition, the owner of about a third of the land in England, all of which had been acquired by gifts and none of it by conquest.

This organisation had its own independent administration of its affairs, its own set of laws and its own system of justice. It even had its own collection of great and beautiful buildings, prominently placed and superior in grandeur to any of the palaces and manor houses of any others in the kingdom, even to those of the king; and its members were not subject to the king even in criminal matters.

Indeed, ultimately, the king was subject to the Church, which wielded authority as much over the king as over his humblest subject, and had the right to excommunicate him. Moreover, in extreme cases, the head of the Church, the Pope, even had the right to dismiss him from his office as king and to free his subjects from the duty to obey him, a right which was very occasionally exercised, as we shall be seeing in a later reign.

The ordinary people of England certainly did not find this objectionable. The monasteries and other Church landowners were the easiest of landlords; they provided schooling free of charge everywhere in the country for anyone who wanted it; they were hospitals, looking after, again free of charge, anyone who was ill; and they were always available to help those who got into financial difficulties – paupers, as such, simply did not exist. They even had the responsibility of keeping the roads in good repair, at no cost to the king or to anyone else in the country.

That is the background against which, as his reign proceeded, King Henry became, on the one hand, increasingly convinced that he 'knew best' as to the efficient and effective administration of England, and, on the other hand, increasingly frustrated by the independent-mindedness of some of the Church's senior members. Kings Alfred the Great and Edward the Confessor had had no such thoughts, but that did not deter King Henry. When Archbishop Theobald of Canterbury died in 1162, he was ready with a seemingly ideal solution in his quest for greater control of the administration of his kingdom: for his close friend and ally Thomas à Becket to be appointed in his place. Together they could administer the affairs of the Church as competently and profitably as they had together been administering the affairs of England.

At first Becket, not even a priest, let alone a bishop, and clearly dismayed, refused to take up the office. He eventually allowed himself to be persuaded, however, but then after being ordained and consecrated, found himself in conscience obliged to resign from being Chancellor, much to the annoyance of King Henry.

Morally, Becket had no alternative. Intrinsic to the fact of England and the Church being in every way two completely separate and different political organisations was their having two completely separate heads. If Becket had continued to be at Henry's command in addition to being the head of the Church in the country, it would have been only one small step for England and the Church to have become a single organisation with a single head, with Henry – ludicrously given that he was only a layman – chief executive of the Church as well as chief executive of England.

There were further and worse clashes, coming to a head when King Henry decided that clergymen who committed ordinary crimes, including robbery and murder, must be tried in the ordinary courts of justice rather than in the Church's courts. At first Becket compromised further than he ought to have done. Eventually, however, he found himself making it clear that he was not prepared to act otherwise than in accordance with the Church's traditional status of being superior to the monarchy in religious matters, where-upon King Henry started behaving in a manner which eventually caused Becket, fearing for his life, to flee in disguise to France. There he was well received by King Louis VII.

Eventually a compromise was reached and Becket returned to England. Almost at once, however, an occasion arose which caused Henry, himself in France at the time, to fly into a rage and give utter-ance to what could well be the most dramatic error of communication in all history, in its importance and in the extent of its unintended consequences:

'Will no one rid me of this turbulent priest?'

His courtiers were well accustomed to Henry's occasional uncontrollable rages and normally would have taken little notice. This time, however, four of the knights in attendance on him took him at his word and at once set off across the Channel for Canterbury. They arrived at the cathedral on 29 December 1170, when Becket was at the high altar and about to start saying vespers, and told him that he was to go to Winchester with them to submit to the King's will. When he refused, they went outside to pick up their weapons, and returned to fall on him with their swords and hack him to pieces.

The sacrilegious murder of an archbishop in his cathedral and while at its altar appalled the whole of Christendom, and not least King Henry, who humiliated himself to the extent of doing heroic penance fully under public gaze, first undertaking a fast and then walking barefoot, and wearing nothing but a woollen shirt, to the newly established shrine of Thomas à Becket at Canterbury. On the following day, England's king allowed himself to be publicly scourged in turn by every single bishop, abbot and monk there, each taking his turn to flog him. Finally, he lay all night and all of the following day on the cold stones in front of the new shrine.

They were very different days from today.

The horrifying crime blighted the last years of King Henry's reign. And no wonder: he was now a king who had been responsible for the brutal murder by four armed assassins of an unarmed man who had not only been his best friend and most treasured compan-ion but was also, in his intelligence, industriousness and all-round competence at the highest level, one the most impressive people ever to be involved in the running of England's affairs, and both admired and liked by everyone as well.

At least, though, King Henry had been responsible, materially speaking, for every single step of his late friend's greatness. On the one hand, he had been responsible both for Becket's appointment as Chancellor and for his appointment as Archbishop of Canterbury. On the other hand, he had been responsible for the martyrdom which led, first, to Becket's body being laid in a gold-plated shrine covered in jewels, secondly, to his being canonised and then venerated throughout Christendom, with the date of his death soon being established as an official feast day throughout England and some of France, and, finally, to his shrine becoming a destination for pilgrimages from all over Europe, and indeed to its being the focus for the entirety of Geoffrey Chaucer's *The Canterbury Tales* – until ... until 1536, as we shall be seeing.

~

It is during this reign that the Age of Chivalry is generally reckoned to have begun. Ultimately based on the laws and principles written down by King Alfred the Great, chivalry was a social and ethical system greatly influenced by the Church to make warfare as civilised as it was possible for warfare to be. It combined unfailingly honourable conduct in battle with knightly piety, which included fighting for the Church and giving war trophies to churches and monasteries, and courtly manners, which covered etiquette, decorum and sophisticated conversation.

King Richard I ('Coeur de Lion' or, in English, 'the Lionheart')

Born 1157 and reigned 1189–1199. He was the third son of King Henry II and Queen Eleanor. As well as King of England, he was at various times Duke of Normandy, Aquitaine and Gascony, Lord of Cyprus, Count of Poitiers, Anjou, Maine and Nantes, and Overlord of Brittany. His eldest brother had died before he was born. His second brother, Henry, had fallen ill and died shortly before the death of their father. Twice Richard, together with his brothers, had rebelled against his father, the second rebellion leading to their father's death.

(i) The main events of the reign in summary

1187. Saladin, Sultan of Egypt and Syria, captured Jerusalem and much of the country surrounding it on behalf of the Mohammedans, sometimes known as the Saracens. This part of the world had been an important centre of Christian pilgrimage until it was first conquered by the Mohammedans in the seventh century. In the eleventh century Pope Urban II had called for a crusade, a military campaign to restore the Holy Land to Christian control so that pilgrims could again have access to the holy sites that had been features of the life of Christ. There were to be nine crusades in all, the first one launched in 1096 and the last in 1271. Prince Richard's response to the conquest by Saladin was to announce that he would 'take up the cross' for what would be the Third Crusade for the restoration of the Holy Land to Christendom.

1189. The England that King Richard inherited was peaceful, well-administered and prosperous. He at once started raising money for the crusade, and, when the preparations were completed, he became the first ruler in northern Europe to join the Third Crusade. He left the government of his kingdom in the capable hands of William Longchamp, the Bishop of Ely, whom he appointed Regent, a regent being someone assigned official responsibility for ruling a kingdom when the reigning monarch is too young, absent or incapacitated.

1192. Three military victories ending with the complete defeat of Saladin and his Saracens were followed by peace with Saladin and a guarantee of free access of pilgrims to Jerusalem. King Richard was then captured and taken prisoner by the Archduke of Austria and handed over to the Holy Roman Emperor, Henry VI of Germany, who demanded a ransom of the vast sum of 100,000 marks, the equivalent of about £70,000 in the currency of the early Middle Ages, when, for instance, the annual pay of a schoolmaster was less than £1 per year.

1194. The ransom was raised in England by means of various taxes. King Richard was released from captivity, returned briefly to England, and then left to fight in France, never to see England again.

1199. While besieging the Castle of Châlus in the Limousin province of France, where he was putting down a rebellion, he was mortally wounded and died.

(ii) Of special interest

As did his contemporaries, posterity regards King Richard as the personification of gallantry, chivalry and Christian virtue, and as the greatest and most heroic of all England's Christian kings, and to a large extent, his reputation is justified – which is not, however, to suggest that he comes anywhere near to King Alfred the Great in his virtues, in his accomplishments, or in his benefits to future generations.

Although, in total, King Richard spent no more than six months of his eleven-year reign in England, the country was well governed in his absence, and he left the large empire that his father had inherited increased in extent and in an excellent state: everywhere respected, prosperous and peaceful.

CHAPTER EIGHTEEN

The House of Plantagenet's King John

King John

Born 1166 and reigned 1199–1216. He was the fifth son and eighth child of King Henry II and Queen Eleanor, and the youngest brother of King Richard I, the second of his elder brothers. He married, first, Isabelle of Gloucester; secondly, Isabella of Angoulême.

(i) The main events of the reign in summary

1199. With no fewer than four elder brothers, it was remarkable that King John was ever king – so unlikely, indeed, that his father called him John Lackland in jest soon after his birth, and the name stuck. As it turned out, only one of his brothers, Prince Geoffrey, had a surviving child, and only one other of them, Prince Richard, survived for long enough to come to the throne of what was then the greatest dominion in Europe, stretching from the border between England and Scotland to the Pyrenees, the mountains dividing France and Spain.

1204. The first five years of King John's reign ended with England having lost most of the parts of France that the Norman Conquest of 1066 had united with England.

1205. A dispute arose between the monks of Canterbury and King John, and involving Pope Innocent III, about who should be the new Archbishop of Canterbury after the death of the last Archbishop, Hubert Walter.

King John

1206. Stephen Langton was appointed Archbishop of Canterbury by Pope Innocent III but King John refused to accept him.

1208–1212. In response, Pope Innocent III issued an interdict against England, banning almost every kind of church service; then excommunicated King John; then took the final step and declared that King John was no longer the rightful king of England.

1213. After a conflict of ever-increasing intensity lasting for eight years, King John gave in and submitted to the demands of Pope Innocent III, and they became completely reconciled. He then went even further than what the Pope had demanded. He swore fealty to the Pope – fealty being, under the feudal system that ruled in many countries in the Middle Ages, the duty of faithfulness of a tenant or vassal to the lord to whom he owes this duty – and in doing so made England a fief of the Holy See, which England remained, at least in theory, until the reign of King Henry VIII.

In the same year started one of the best-known episodes of English history, a momentous conflict between King John and the barons, the biggest landholders, who were legally his vassals. The conflict also involved Archbishop Stephen Langton of Canterbury in alliance with the barons.

1214. King Philip II of France defeated the English at the Battle of Bouvines.

1215. With King John in a much-weakened situation after his defeat at the recent Battle of Bouvines, the conflict with the barons ended with a meeting between the barons and King John at Runnymede. At this occurred, if we are to trust the most widely held view of the significance of Magna Carta, the great event of King John's reign: his putting his seal on that document – finding it objectionable but deciding that the weakness of his position left him with no alternative. Magna Carta is still considered to be part of the constitution of England and of the constitutions of many countries that were part of the British Empire that was to come into existence. It even played a notable role in the creation of the American constitution after the so-called War of Independence of the late eighteenth century.

Pope Innocent III used his authority to annul Magna Carta, and excommunicated the barons. King John then defied the barons and attacked the north of England, their main stronghold.

1216. The barons turned to France for assistance in their war against King John, with the eventual result that Prince Louis of France, son of King Philip, invaded England and reached as far as the Tower of London. In response, the barons invited Louis of Normandy, the son of King John's rival, Philip of Normandy and King of France, to help them. At one point during the course of the war that resulted, King John, while crossing the Wash, the wide bay at the north of present-day Norfolk, lost all his baggage, including his financial possessions, and then died very shortly afterwards, aged forty-nine and in the seventeenth year of his reign.

~

Those are the bare facts about the king who, according to the Robin Hood stories in books and in films, was 'the wicked Prince John' before he became king, and, according to most historians, became very much wickeder when king.

(ii) Of special interest

For an authoritative assessment of King John, both as a person and as a king, here is a useful summary given by the nineteenth-century historian John Lingard in his eight-volume *History of England from the First Invasion by the Romans to the accession of William and Mary in 1688* at the end of his chapter on King John:

> History has recorded only his vices; his virtues, if such a monster could possess virtues, were unseen or forgotten. He stands before us polluted with meanness, cruelty, perjury, and murder; uniting with an ambition which rushed through every crime to the attainment of its object, a pusillanimity which often, at the sole appearance of opposition, sank into despondency.
>
> Arrogant in prosperity, abject in adversity, he neither conciliated affection in the one, nor excited esteem in the other. His dissimulation was so well known that it seldom deceived: his habit of suspicion served to multiply his enemies; and the knowledge of his vindictive temper contributed to keep

open the breach between him and those who had incurred his displeasure. Seldom perhaps was there a prince with a heart more callous to the suggestions of pity. Of his captives many never returned from their dungeons, if they survived their tortures, they were left to perish by famine ...

John was not less reprehensible as a husband than he was as a monarch. While Louis took from him his provinces on the continent, he had consoled himself for the loss in the company of his beautiful bride; but he soon abandoned her to revert to his former habits. The licentiousness of his amours is reckoned by every ancient writer among the principal causes of the alienation of his barons, many of whom had to lament and revenge the disgrace of a wife, or daughter, or sister ...

The picture of King John given above, which of course could hardly be a worse one, appears on the face of it to carry considerable conviction, presented as it is by an undoubtedly scholarly and thorough historian. Nevertheless, we have a duty to ask ourselves: are there any sound reasons to disagree with at least some of what he has just said, or even with much of it?

Astonishingly, that summary by Lingard is not really supported by him in the chapter of his book in which it features. It is as though he is mechanically reproducing the commonly accepted picture of King John, rather than giving a carefully weighed-up conclusion based on the evidence that he has just provided.

Also important is that, of the allegations made against King John that are so widely accepted, *all* of them are based on *posthumous* reports. What this means is that future generations would have to base their opinion of him on authors who were writing some time after his death, when what they said would have been much more difficult to disprove – it is notoriously difficult to prove a negative. Furthermore, because the earliest of these authors were monks and King John was frequently in conflict with members of the Church, we are far from being able to rule out the possibility that they had axes to grind.

One such monk was Roger of Wendover, of the Abbey of St. Albans, author of *Flowers of History*, a book full of horrifying anecdotes about King John, which has always been considered to be, and used as, an important source of information about him. Should we, let us ask ourselves, judge it to be as trustworthy as most historians of the period have assumed it to be?

In fact, more than one modern historian has found favourable things to say about King John, though no historian of whom I am aware goes anywhere near to the relatively favourable judgement of him that I believe ought to be made.

Here, for instance, is a modern author, Alan Lloyd, on page 123 of an important book published in 1972 of which I shall be making some use in this chapter, *The Maligned Monarch: A Life of King John of England*: 'That Wendover did not pen his account of John's reign until a decade after the king's death ... [and] that he laced it with the most improbable and demonstrably inaccurate detail did not deter his readers, who lapped it up.'

Writing still later than Roger of Wendover was another contemporary monk of the same religious order, Matthew Paris, who took it upon himself to develop further, and considerably worsen, Wendover's representation of King John, 'with picturesque distortion upon distortion to produce a libel of John so hypnotic that it was to bemuse biographers of the maligned king centuries afterwards', to quote Alan Lloyd once again.

So it has continued century after century, with, for instance, the author Kate Norgate, in her book *John Lackland*, published in 1902, going so far as to refer to what she called King John's 'super-human wickedness'.

Now very much on the alert, we must remind ourselves that King John deserves to be looked at as anyone deserves to be looked at: as innocent until *proved* guilty. Let us therefore examine some of the individual allegations against him, on which that summary by Lingard was based.

First and surely foremost, we shall be finding that monarchs subsequent to King John undoubtedly committed crimes such as these:

- Mass murder.
- Judicial murder, a much more pernicious form of murder than 'mere' murder, in that it involves people being put to death by tyrants who are making deliberately perverse use of the law in order to commit that horrifying, perhaps ultimate, injustice.

- Oppression of the ordinary people of England, let alone of the poor.
- Disruption of society.
- Breaking their coronation oaths.
- Instituting religious disarray.
- Stealing property from the monasteries and from any other institutions of the Church.
- Passing unjust laws.

That is a surprisingly large collection of crimes for a monarch described as Lingard described King John not even to be *accused* of, let alone *found guilty* of.

~

Now we can turn to another important fact, which would be unusual in someone quite as evil as King John is supposed to have been. This is that King John has had credible supporters. Much more impartial accounts than those of Wendover and Paris have been published from time to time until well into the last century.

Here are some undoubted facts relating to King John's reign that can be gleaned from what I believe to be the best treatment of him of all, *The Maligned Monarch*, and from similarly well-researched sources.

The reign was by any standards a remarkable one. As also already noted, King John early in his reign lost most of the vast territories in France that had been up till then subject to kings of England, which meant that he ceased to be Duke of Normandy, Count of Anjou, and Lord of Touraine and Maine; and for much of the rest of his life he was engaged in warfare to try to win them back. There is nothing unseemly or inappropriate in an ambition to recover what has been lost by defeat in war, as opposed to an ambition to conquer territory belonging to others. Indeed this is implicitly confirmed by historians in his case, since it is his loss of the English possessions in France and failure to recover them that have led historians to regard him as a poor ruler.

The reign included two memorably dramatic events. One, of course, was the meeting with the barons at Runnymede ending with the signing of Magna Carta. The other, starting early in his reign, was the long-drawn-out clash, running from 1205 to 1213, with, first of all, the monks in Canterbury, which was the headquarters of Christianity in England, and then Pope Innocent III, over who should be the new Archbishop of Canterbury after the death of the existing one.

As to which of the parties in this conflict had right on their side in this dispute, this is not as obvious as may at first appear, and as historians commonly lead us to assume. Two pieces of background must be borne in mind. One is that English kings, at their coronation, promised on oath to preserve the official freedoms of the Church, which included the right to choose its own bishops, priors and other top dignitaries. The other, however, is that this was a right which kings tended to try to minimise in its extent, and not wholly unreasonably. Attached to those offices of the Church were baronies, and these not only provided their possessors with income but also gave them certain legal powers with which they could exercise considerable influence in state matters. Understandably, kings would not want such offices to be given to their enemies, and therefore the election of the most senior prelate of all, the Archbishop of Canterbury, was of considerable interest to any king of England.

When Archbishop Hugo died in 1205, the monks most directly responsible for the election of his successor were far from straightforward in how they proceeded. Assembling secretly during the night, they elected Reginald, their own superior, without the agreement either of the King or of the other bishops in England, and quickly sent their nominee to Rome for confirmation.

Fortuitously, however, King John learnt of this while the nominee was on his journey. With the support of the bishops in the province of Canterbury itself, who considered it reasonable, given the tradition of kings' involvement in the selection of candidates and the reasons for it, that King John should object, the King at once ordered that another election should take place. The result of this election was that his preferred candidate, John de Gray, the Bishop of Norwich, became a second archbishop-elect; and a second group of messengers was then sent to Rome, asking for confirmation of this second election.

Pope Innocent took time to make a careful and thorough enquiry. At the end of it he rejected both elections, and on obviously valid grounds. He declared the first one void because of its irregular and surreptitious procedure, and the second one void because, at the time that it took place, the first one had not been annulled in the appropriate way prescribed by the laws of the Church.

Who was to be appointed in their place? There happened to be in Rome at that time an Englishman, Stephen Langton, who was rector of Paris University and whom Pope Innocent III had recently made a cardinal, the cardinalate being the highest dignity in the Catholic Church after the Pope. Believing that King John would accept him, the Pope arranged for him to be appointed to the office of Archbishop of Canterbury and then consecrated him.

King John's immediate response was flatly to refuse to accept Cardinal Langton as Archbishop, maintaining that the recognised prerogatives of the English kings entitling him to have a say in the matter had been overridden. Nor was his indignation without any justification. Certainly Pope Innocent, as head of the Church of all Christian countries, had the strict right to make an independent appointment of an archbishop; but to do so was far from usual in any Christian country at that time.

What King John did at once, wisely or unwisely, was to vow that Langton should never set foot in England as Archbishop; and from that point on, he and Pope Innocent were in outright conflict.

Pope Innocent III's manner of proceeding, by contrast with that of King John, was with deliberation and without haste, with determination but also with prudence.

First, in 1208 he declared an interdict on England. Most church services there were forbidden, the church bells remained silent, and the dead were buried in unconsecrated ground. That proved to be ineffective in bringing about King John's submission, and in 1209 Pope Innocent excommunicated him. Finally, in 1214 the Pope absolved all King John's subjects from the duty to obey the King and called upon all Christian princes and barons to dethrone him, whereupon the King's powerful rival Philip of France started preparations for enforcing the deposition.

At that point King John recognised that he had no realistic choice other than to capitulate. With a tactic that some historians have been horrified by and others have applauded, he submitted himself completely to the Pope, and even went so far as to take the very oath of fealty to the Pope that vassals used to take to their lords in those days, and to vow complete submission to Pope Innocent and his successors, from which he never withdrew.

This action of King John's has blackened his name ever since. A king laying his dominions at the feet of a foreign clergyman?

As Lingard points out in his chapter on King John, however, we should not measure the actions of our ancestors by what seems to us right and proper in our own time. In the thirteenth century, there was nothing at all degrading about vassalage, and in fact most of the princes in all Christian countries were vassals, some of them of foreign monarchs and others of the pope of the day. Like his predecessors John was already a vassal of the king of France for his surviving French territories. What is more, the barons in King John's realm, who would shortly be extorting Magna Carta from him, fully supported him in taking this step.

~

Of interest is that King John was respected by the ordinary people of England even when the kingdom was under interdict. It was not they who were his opponents, but some of the barons, his rivals for power. As Alan Lloyd, the author of *The Maligned Monarch*, puts it: 'The struggle was with a minute and highly privileged group of his subjects.'

Although King John's abilities as a soldier are usually denigrated, he was in fact a brave warrior, constantly having to be engaged in warfare, always the leader of any troops under his command, winning battle after battle, and clearly an impressive military leader and strategist. Alan Lloyd in chapter 19 of his book says: 'The inference that he was a feeble soldier is a false one. No mediaeval English warrior dealt so successfully with the Scots, Welsh and Irish.'

And while a good claim could be made that King Edward I was in fact his superior in this, that Lloyd could say what he said on John's behalf is an impressive testimonial. He was in fact recognised as a good soldier well before he came to the throne, and indeed by one of the greatest of all soldiers of that era, his elder brother Richard, who, when he became King Richard I on the death of their father, at once put John in charge of an English army assigned to obtain the submission of the Welsh princes. Even though he was only twenty-two, John handled the expedition faultlessly.

He could even be fairly described as *heroic* in the military field, as he campaigned over long periods during the most adverse of conditions, sometimes having to travel with his troops for long distances in bad weather, with scarcely any rest, and even though in a state of constantly wretched health towards the end of his life. Nothing even remotely approaching such virtues was to be seen in the reigns of monarchs much more highly respected by most historians, such as King Henry VII, King Henry VIII and, of course, Queen Elizabeth I.

While he was engaged in these seemingly endless conflicts of various kinds, he somehow found time to develop significantly the English navy, showing wisdom, imagination and administrative competence in the manner in which he carried this out. As may be remembered, this fundamental institution for England's future as a world power had been founded by King Alfred the Great. By the time of King Richard and King John it had become very much reduced, but King John restored it, bringing into existence a standing fleet and a permanent navy comprising about fifty royal galleys.

He was also undoubtedly an excellent administrator. The nineteenth-century mediaevalist Bishop Stubbs, a leading historian of his day, saw fit to make special note of this, and one obvious piece of evidence of it is that we know more about his activities than we know about those of any of his predecessors because he insisted on copies being made of all his letters, which indeed show him to have been a hard-working monarch.

Against the background of what we have seen so far, it is perhaps time to remind ourselves once again of the devastating words of Lingard:

'History has recorded only his vices; his virtues, if such a monster could possess virtues, were unseen or forgotten.'

No evident virtues? King John respected the laws of the country and the principles of equal justice. He did not suppress popular causes. He was unusually interested in the administration of justice, and important features of the English law such as the need for relevant witnesses and competent juries advanced during his reign under his supervision. In 1204, he even undertook a reform of the currency, issuing new coins of better design, and he made it a punishable offence to use clipped coins. (In those days, and indeed until well into the twentieth century, coins were made of a precious metal such as gold or silver, and the metal could be shaved from their circumference by the unscrupulous.)

At this point, some of us may be rubbing our eyes in disbelief, wondering if we have read correctly what has just been written. *He respected the laws and the principles of equal justice? He even made notable improvements to the laws and the legal and currency systems?* What can Magna Carta have been about? Is this *really* the king described by Lingard?

You may feel like rubbing your eyes again, good readers, as you read what now follows.

1. He was responsible for the foundation of Oxford University as an institution consisting of colleges. Up until the time of King Richard I, the institution was no more than an informal guild of scholars based at Oxford. It was under King John's rule that the boarding of students in various buildings under principals was developed, and also that, in 1214, a Chancellor of the University was first mentioned.

2. London Bridge, an elaborate construction that at this point was to be built in brick for the first time and with a drawbridge in the middle for tall ships, had been originally commissioned by his father King Henry II, but owes much of its construction to him. When the project, which had no precedent in England, was proving difficult, he took a close interest and in due course produced a solution by recommending the services of a French expert on bridge building, a Master Isambert, who had gained a high reputation as the designer of important bridges in France. Thus, although the bridge that he was responsible for completing was replaced in 1831, we owe to King John the origin of one of the more notable features of the London of today, which indeed even features in a nursery rhyme.

3. He even founded *a new city*. After losing Normandy in 1206, he visited an area of land with a negligible population called Liverpool. Recognising its importance, including its potential importance as a port, because of where it was situated, he gave it a Royal Charter and thus brought into existence the first piece of conscious urban planning in England that had taken place since

the days of the Romans. As is officially acknowledged today, he was even responsible for the original street plan on which the city is still based.

4. Although he is almost universally accused of having been in high degree irreligious, some historians have noticed such things as King John's personal interest in the life of St. Wulfstan of Worcester and his friendships with several senior clerics, most especially with Hugh of Lincoln, who was later declared a saint. And at least one twentieth-century historian of the Middle Ages, Lewis Warren, has pointed out that the chronicler accounts – the accounts recorded in chronicles, records of events in date order – were subject to considerable bias. The King was 'at least conventionally devout', maintains Warren, citing as evidence John's pilgrimages and his interest in religious scripture and commentaries.

Even his lengthy quarrel with the Pope needs to be put into perspective when judging his religious inclinations, for he never came close to questioning the status of the Pope as head of the Christian Church. The reality is that there can be no doubt that King John was a genuinely God-fearing man. In addition to what has just been noted, which included his friendship with a future saint, he enjoyed good relations with other clerics even when England was under interdict and, as is seldom mentioned by historians, he was the actual founder of the magnificent Beaulieu Abbey in Hampshire, which he then endowed with extraordinary generosity, giving it many income-producing manors in various parts of the country, large amounts of money and building materials.

Finally, when he evidently realised that he was close to death during the night of 18 October 1216, he asked for the last sacraments and received them from the Abbot of Coxton, just a few hours before he died.

5. He is said to have been treacherous, and all historians seem to be agreed that he betrayed his brother while King Richard I was overseas engaged in the crusades.

I see no reason to believe that last allegation. In the first place, there is an important principle relating to the weighing-up of evidence, a principle that indeed is part of the common law of

England: '*Falsus in uno, falsus in omnibus*', which means 'False in one thing, false in everything'. What this amounts to is that, once a witness has been caught out giving just *one* piece of false testimony, *nothing* that he says is to be trusted thereafter, so that everything he says needs to be independently checked before it is believed. The sources of information for King John's treachery, principally the two monks Wendover and Paris, are the same sources as those that we have seen to be unreliable on other matters concerning King John. In the second place, on his death-bed King Richard nominated Prince John as his successor to the kingdom, which is far from indicating that he regarded him as untrustworthy.

'His virtues, if such a monster could possess virtues, were unseen or forgotten.'

I suggest that such forgetfulness is to be regretted.

~

Finally, what of Magna Carta, the signing of which is much the best-known of the events that took place during the reign of King John, and which is part of the very *constitutions* of several countries today?

Here is Lord Sumption, a Justice of the Supreme Court, and one of Britain's most senior present-day judges and also a distinguished mediaeval historian, in a speech at a conference of the Franco-British Council in London in June 2015:

I have no problem about the values which the charter is commonly supposed to express. But I have the utmost difficulty in finding them anywhere in the charter. The document is long. It is technical. And it is turgid ... It is not even a document for all Englishmen but only for the small minority who were free, male and relatively rich.

To those who revere Magna Carta because of what they have heard and read about it, I say that, if you read it, which can be done in a modern translation, you will find that, for the most part by far, in clause after clause, it is about the relationship between the king and the earls, barons and other landowners. It does state a number of important principles relating to all classes of people. There is nothing in those of any significance that was new, however, since England had been a Christian country for many centuries by then, and in recent centuries had been living under the laws of King St. Edward the Confessor.

What, moreover, is sometimes left unmentioned is that two further versions of it were enacted soon afterwards, one in 1217 and one in 1255, each one significantly modifying the original in favour of the king and even deleting several of the original's clauses, and also that, although, as we shall be seeing, King Henry III submitted to it in 1266, soon after that it became virtually forgotten – for several centuries scarcely noticed, as far as English law was concerned.

I do not exaggerate. In the Middle Ages' greatest treatises on law of all, Sir John Fortescue's greatly admired fifteenth-century works *On the Laws and Governance of England* and *The Governance of England*, Magna Carta makes no appearance. Monarchs had resumed their traditional role of being genuine kings of the country, which meant, amongst other things, their being ultimately the sole fount of law.

What started bringing Magna Carta into the prominence that it enjoys today was the treatment of it by a leading lawyer and author on law writing later in the seventeenth century, Sir Edward Coke, an important legal figure towards the end of the reign of Queen Elizabeth I and in the reign of King James I. In various books of his, including his massive four-volume work *Institutes of the Lawes of England*, he repeatedly wrote about Magna Carta, very much trying to raise its status and, in consequence, trying to reduce the status and authority of monarchs, so that they would cease to have the authoritative status that kings of England had always enjoyed up until then.

We are not obliged to be influenced by Sir Edward Coke in this respect. Even at the time that he was writing, what he said was challenged, principally by another leading lawyer of the same period, Lord Ellesmere; and modern authors have gone so far as to accuse Coke of misconstruing the charter and of less than complete honesty in his analysis of it.

Furthermore, when the time came that King John decided that he should appeal to the reigning Pope about the document that he had signed, Pope Innocent III, in a lengthy document, showed himself to be appalled by the charter and could have used no stronger terms to condemn it than he did. The barons, he declared, had ignored their solemnly taken oaths of fealty; and he went on to say:

> [We] utterly reject and condemn this settlement. Under threat of excommunication we order that the king should not dare to observe it and that the barons and their associates should not insist on it being observed. The charter with all its undertakings and guarantees we declare to be null and void of all validity for ever.

He went further. He then excommunicated the barons, and, when Archbishop Stephen Langton refused to publish the excommunication, the papal commissioners in England suspended him from all Church functions in England, which Pope Innocent then confirmed; and Langton was only released from his suspension on condition that he left England and did not return until peace was restored, which meant that he remained abroad until 1218, after the death of King John.

By far the most contentious part of the charter was its Clause 61, as it is now called by modern historians (the original was unnumbered), very near the end of the document. Under this clause a council of twenty-five barons would be created to monitor and ensure King John's future adherence to the charter. If John did not conform to the charter within forty days of being notified of a transgression by the council, the twenty-five barons had the right to seize John's castles and lands until, *in their judgement*, amends had been made. That is to say, they had acquired the legal right to make war on the king if they, in their own judgement, without any question of due process of law in arriving at their judgement, formed the opinion that he had violated any of the liberties – which in practice were *their* liberties – that he had guaranteed with his signature.

King John was horrified. So was Pope Innocent III. So too, perhaps, will be those of my readers who understand and appreciate the principles of monarchy outlined in chapter 1. What this amounted to, he said, *was his being subject to twenty-five over-kings.* 'Why not ask for my kingdom?' was how he summarised that clause.

I maintain that, as was accepted in practice by everyone up until the time of Sir Edward Coke, Magna Carta is philosophically and intrinsically wrong, with scarcely anything to be said in its favour. In order to see why, it is perhaps sufficient to look at the principles of monarchy outlined in chapter 1, against the background of which it simply does not make sense in any constitution that includes a traditional monarchy.

As explained in chapter 1, a monarch in England is a fount of law, a *source* of law, an element of the law known as the prerogative or royal prerogative, which is defined in dictionaries in such terms as 'the right of the sovereign, theoretically subject to no restriction'. This can only mean that, subject only to divine law and to hallowed custom relating to monarchs, a monarch is *above* the law, which is the opposite of being subject to it and *not compatible* with being subject to it. A fount or source cannot be part of what it gives rise to, and certainly cannot be part of what it controls.

In all Christian countries including England up until the sixteenth century, this is how authority was structured. Barons ruled their local areas and had legal authority over those who lived there. Kings ruled the barons, and they normally ruled their other subjects through the barons. And the reigning pope had authority over the king, including even the right to dismiss him. There is of course nothing of any significance left of that system today, but there were virtually no protests against it during most of the history of the period. Even King Henry VIII had accepted the system in its totality before, as we shall be seeing, he rebelled and set up the new church with him as its head because there was no other way in which he could marry a woman with whom he was – to put it delicately – much taken.

This system of authority also meant that the whole of the western section of Christendom, as it was called in those days, which was the equivalent of the Western Europe of today, was virtually a single country, headed by a single ruler. Indeed, the only really significant difference between one country and another was its language, and even that difference was relatively minimal because of every educated person being fluent in Latin.

One of the biggest changes that King Henry VIII and his successors brought about in setting up a new church, one that belonged only to their country, was that, effectively, it spelt the end of Christendom, and the replacement of it by the concept of the Europe that we know today, with Europe being a geographical area rather than a culturally united area, and with the countries in it having very little in common with each other compared to what they had had before. It is by no means obvious that this was a change for the better. And it certainly did not make sense to King John's successors and their subjects. With the single exception of King Henry III, who, as we shall be seeing, was forced to submit to it towards the end of his reign, they ignored Magna Carta in practice, and continued to do so until the reign of King James I early in the seventeenth century.

Should we be shocked at the notion that a constitution in which Magna Carta or anything equivalent played no part should have lasted for so long, and with no significant protest? I suggest not. Although no institution can be perfect and, in the case of the institution with monarchy at its head, bad kings are possible, the system had on the whole worked well during the recorded history of up to the point that we have just reached, and continued to work well for some centuries afterwards; and it is to be doubted that any other system would work better.

The reality is that, once a king becomes to a greater or lesser extent controlled by his inferiors, special interests come into the picture. The politicians, without a long-term interest in what they are doing because of the relative shortness of their careers, are going to find it tempting to advance their own interests.

None of the foregoing is to suggest that the authority of a king is so extensive that he has 'the right to govern wrong'. We shall be looking at this in more detail when we come to the reign of King James I.

~

This is what we have now seen:

King John was a fine warrior and an exceptionally good administrator; responsible for advances in the all-important matters of both the system of justice and the administration of justice in the kingdom; the founder of the city of Liverpool and of the wonderfully beautiful Beaulieu Abbey; one of the founders of Oxford University; and responsible for the completion of London Bridge.

Against this background, surely a claim that he was even a great king could be justified. This is not to suggest that he has even the remotest claim to King Alfred's title 'the Great', or that he was anything approaching a saint. One can have degrees of greatness, however; and I am certainly suggesting that none of his successors has an objectively better claim to be considered a great king than he has.

I shall be making use of him as a yardstick against which to measure later monarchs who have enjoyed vastly better reputations than his.

CHAPTER NINETEEN

Interlude: the Feudal System

WE HAVE REACHED the point where the story of England's kings and queens will become difficult to understand without at least an outline of the principal social relationships outside family relationships in England, Wales and Scotland.

The feudal system prevailed throughout almost all civilisation in very similar forms to those in England at that time. In order to understand it as it was in England then, the starting point must be a brief look at the technical terms *vassalage*, *homage* and *fealty*, which are of the highest importance for an understanding of the Middle Ages and of some of the politics in the next few chapters.

Under the feudal system …

- All the land in England belonged to the Sovereign, as 'Lord Paramount'.
- The Sovereign divided the land into 'fiefs', which he gave to his nobles, technically his 'vassals', to be *held* by them – not *owned* – as his tenants-in-chief under these three mutually agreed conditions:

    (i) The Lord Paramount undertook to protect his vassals.
    (ii) The vassal undertook to serve the Lord Paramount without payment for forty days in the year and to supply the lord's castle with certain provisions.
    (iii) Included in the undertaking was an agreement by the vassal to serve his lord in times of war and to do other specified duties in times of peace.

- The lords, the Lord Paramount's vassals, sublet their land under similar conditions to their own vassals, who were called mesne tenants, as were their sub-tenants.
- Thus, whenever the king wanted to go to war and needed an army, he summoned his vassals, who in turn summoned *their* vassals. With this system, the king was able to gather for himself an army of up to 60,000 men.
- *Homage* was the ceremony in which a vassal, in effect a feudal tenant, pledged reverence and submission to his liege lord, and received in exchange his *investiture*, the symbolic title to his new position, so called because originally the new holder of an office was *clothed* ('invested') in special garments which symbolised his new power. What the homage symbolised was the acknowledgement by a vassal to his liege lord that he, the vassal, was, literally, his man (*homme*) – that is under his ownership, though with important limitations that prevented this from being anything resembling slavery.
- The oath of *fealty* implied lesser obligations than did the oath of homage, not least in that one could swear 'fealty' to many different overlords with respect to different land holdings, whereas homage could only be given to a single liege lord – necessarily since, obviously, if one were to pledge one's service as a soldier to more than one liege lord, one might find oneself bound on oath to fight on two opposing sides at the same time.

CHAPTER TWENTY

The Last Five Kings of the House of Plantagenet

King Henry III

Born 1207 and reigned 1216–1272.

(i) The main events of the reign in summary

1216. King Henry III came to the throne in the middle of the war known as the First Barons' War and was crowned king at the age of nine. Because of his minority, William Marshall, who had loyally served no fewer than four previous kings and had received the title the Earl of Pembroke, was appointed Protector – administrator of the kingdom in a sovereign's place – of King Henry and Regent of the kingdom. Marshall ruled ably and was popular.

1217. Most of the barons who had been fighting against King John abandoned their rebellion, rallied round the new King of England and deserted King Louis VIII, who had been assisting them. A large French fleet attempting to bring support to King Louis was destroyed by a leading noble who had played an important part in the administration of King John's kingdom, Hubert de Burgh. King Louis then entered into a peace treaty with the English representatives of King Henry and returned to France.

1219. The Earl of Pembroke died and Hubert de Burgh became King Henry's Chief Counsellor. England continued to be governed well.

1230. King Henry, now aged twenty-two, and ruling personally rather than through senior ministers, invaded France in an attempt, unsuccessful, to reconquer the provinces that had originally been ruled by his father.

1232. Hubert de Burgh was replaced as King Henry's Chief Counsellor by Peter des Roches, Bishop of Winchester. The new appointment, not a success, was one of the main causes of bad government in England during the next twenty-six years.

1236. King Henry married Eleanor, the second daughter of the Count of Provence. They had five children. One result of the marriage was that many foreigners from the French provinces flocked to England and acquired important offices in the state and in the Church, with one of Queen Eleanor's uncles, Count Boniface of Savoy, even becoming Archbishop of Canterbury. Increasingly, the government of England was by people completely ignorant of the principles of English government and English law.

1238. Simon de Montfort, the Earl of Leicester, a French nobleman directly descended from King Henry I, married King Henry III's sister, Princess Eleanor, and started to play a role in English politics.

1242. King Henry started an expensive war in a quest to regain the lost French possessions. Once again, he was unsuccessful.

1258. The barons rebelled against the King, with Simon de Montfort, the King's brother-in-law, taking up the leadership of the rebellious barons and succeeding in seizing power in England. There followed a meeting of a hundred barons in Oxford, known to history as the Mad Parliament, at which the barons presented a list of grievances and drew up what became known as the Provisions of Oxford. In accordance with these, both King Henry and his son Prince Edward, the future King Edward I, swore to accept the following:

1. That twenty-four barons should be appointed to reform the government.
2. That there should be three Parliaments every year.
3. That the king should have a permanent body of fifteen people to advise him.
4. That accounts of public money should be rendered each year.

The King submitted to these provisions, which considerably limited a monarch's power. Not least notably, the publication of his assent was the first official document ever to be issued in the English language.

1261. Pope Urban IV absolved King Henry from his oath to keep the Provisions of Oxford. In those days, it was accepted by everyone, although later disputed, that popes had the right and power to relieve people from oaths, under the authority that had been given by Jesus Christ to St. Peter and his successors as recorded in Matthew 16:18–19.

1264. With King Henry continuing to refuse to accept the Provisions, civil war broke out in England. At the Battle of Lewes King Henry and his brother Richard were taken prisoner. Under a treaty called the Mise of Lewes, Prince Edward, King Henry's son, gave himself up as a ransom for his father; but King Henry did not regain his former power and Simon de Montfort became the sole master of his entire kingdom.

1265. Simon de Montfort, in the King's name, summoned what was called a 'parliament': two knights from each county and, for the first time in England's history, two representatives from each city and each, as a town was then called, borough. Although far from truly representative of the people, this has been regarded by many as the first House of Commons. The event was followed by a reaction in favour of the King. The nobles who had been opposing the King deserted de Montfort under the leadership of the Earl of Gloucester. Having escaped from confinement, Prince Edward swiftly raised an army and, at the Battle of Evesham, accomplished the defeat of de Montfort, who was slain in the battle.

1266. Regrettably to those who believe in traditional monarchy, the Dictum of Kenilworth was signed, a dictum being a formal announcement from an authoritative source, to be accepted by everyone. In it, although King Henry III was restored to his full authority and the Provisions of Oxford were annulled, the King agreed to be submissive to Magna Carta.

1267. The Dictum of Kenilworth was replaced by a set of laws that became called and known to history as the Statute of Marlborough, Marlborough being where Parliament met in order to enact it. This, the newly agreed basis for royal government, is the oldest piece of statute law in the United Kingdom that to this day has never been repealed and parts of which are still valid.

(ii) Of special interest

What the new system of government established by the Dictum of Kenilworth amounted to was that a king was no longer *truly* king in reality, even though everyone at the time accepted both that monarchy as such was a divinely instituted system of government and also that the monarch was officially responsible for the passing of laws and the administration of justice.

What the dictum further amounted to was:

1. The king's role had effectively been taken over by a group of people of which he was merely one member, with no decisive voice.

2. The person born for the job of governing people in the realm, and conscious throughout his life of the duties he had been born to carry out, was replaced by a group of very different people. This was a significant revolution. On the one hand a traditional monarch, by the nature of things, was subject to relatively few conflicts of interests in the exercise of his role, the main ones being temptations to put pleasure before duty and to over-indulge himself on the trappings which come with the role. On the other hand, those now in a position to exercise political control were people who in the great majority of cases would inevitably be motivated at least partly by self-interest and were all too likely to use their power to increase their domination over their social inferiors. Furthermore, they would have no training at all in the principles of good government.

But is not democracy, the reader may wonder, the ideal form of government for a country?

The running of a country is an operation of the utmost complexity, requiring extensive knowledge and experience, in such areas as: politics and political history; social organisation and social history; law and justice; and much else. The thought that, for instance, a large public corporation could be successfully run for the benefit of its shareholders and employees by people who (a) have no business training, and, moreover, (b) are replaced in their entirety every few years by the votes of shareholders who have no understanding of the business and little knowledge of the top executives in it, can at once be seen to be an absurdity. That, however, is the form of government that modern democracy is; and even that is before taking into account the fact that talent, education and moral integrity are by no means as likely to secure the election of a democratic country's leaders as are such qualities as salesmanship, 'the gift of the gab', 'spin' and even deceitfulness.

~

During this reign both the concept and the term 'Parliament' came into existence, as part of the legal system. Although monarchs were still responsible for the laws, they needed to have broad acceptance of their policies in order to be sure of the cooperation of their subjects, which in practice meant consulting the nobility and the senior clergy on important decisions. The events at which the consultations took place were originally called Great Councils, and during this reign such councils evolved into the Parliament of England.

King Henry III is little respected by historians. It is said that, although he wanted to rebuild the great empire of his grandfather King Henry II, and to be a crusader such as his uncle King Richard I had been, he achieved neither, being weak, extravagant, reckless and an incompetent general.

That picture, however, is mainly based on the *Chronica Majora* of Matthew Paris, who gave us cause to be shocked in his account of the reign of King John. There are also these two facts to take into account:

1. The civil war ended in 1267 with the monarchy and its full authority completely restored.
2. King Henry was well-known and respected as a person of unusual piety. His alleged extravagance took the form, not of indulging in anything resembling licentious activities, but rather of holding lavish religious ceremonies; feeding every day 500 of the poor and helping orphans; giving support to his favourite religious orders;

helping to develop the universities of Oxford and Cambridge which had begun to grow in importance; erecting in Chancery Lane a home for Jewish converts to Christianity, who, by the time he died, amounted to about 10 per cent of the Jewish population in England.

His greatest extravagance – or, arguably, by no means extravagance – of all? He had a particular devotion to his holy predecessor King St. Edward the Confessor, and, starting in 1245, and employing hundreds of craftsmen, he spent twenty-five years completely rebuilding King St. Edward the Confessor's Westminster Abbey, the building in which almost every monarch since William the Conqueror has been crowned, and creating the most magnificent piece of architecture that Christian Europe had yet seen – the Westminster Abbey that can still be viewed today even though, in its interior, it is only a shadow of what it was because of the ruthless destruction inflicted on it by the Puritans in the 1640s.

We should perhaps hesitate to be disparaging of someone responsible for such an extraordinary and long-lasting achievement.

Edward I (nicknamed 'Longshanks' because of his height)

Born 1239 and reigned 1272–1307. Son of King Henry III. Married, first, in 1254, Eleanor of Castile in Spain, by whom he had sixteen children; secondly, Margaret of France, by whom he had three children.

(i) The main events of the reign in summary

1272. Edward succeeded King Henry III to the throne, as King Edward I, on his way back from a crusade and was proclaimed King during his absence. From the beginning of his reign he considered an important part of his role as monarch to be (a) that of law-giver, and (b) to consolidate his kingdom by adding Wales and Scotland to it.

1274. He was crowned in Westminster Abbey and received the homage of King Alexander III of Scotland.

1277. Prince Llewellyn of the Welsh, who had assisted Simon de Montfort during the reign of King Henry III, refused to swear allegiance to King Edward.

1279. King Edward enacted the Statute of Jewry, which obliged Jews to wear a distinctive yellow badge and required them to respect the prohibition of lending money at interest already in force for Christians.

1282. King Edward invaded north Wales and defeated Prince Llewellyn, who was allowed to retain only the small amount of territory consisting of Anglesey and the district surrounding Mount Snowdon.

1284. After defeating a second rising in Wales, he annexed Wales to England and made it subject to England's laws, as it has remained ever since.

1286. King Alexander III of Scotland died, leaving his granddaughter Margaret as the only direct heir to the Scottish throne.

1290. On 18 July King Edward announced that all Jews in the kingdom were to leave it on 1 November of the same year. According to Albert M. Hyamson, in his *History of the Jews in England*: 'About 16,000 Jews, who had gradually been restricted to seventeen towns, left England. The King, possessed by no vindictive passion for persecution, took steps so that they should be allowed to depart in peace, without molestation, and they were allowed to take all movable property with them.'

On 26 September, Princess Margaret, the heir to the Scottish throne, died, leaving three claimants to that throne: John Balliol, Robert Bruce and John Hastings, all of them descended from King David I of the Scots, who had reigned from 1124 to 1153.

1291. Since the reign of King Edward the Elder in 899–924, the kings of England had been recognised as feudal overlords of Scotland. The Scottish Council now appealed to King Edward in this status to decide which of the three should be King of Scotland. He decided in favour of John Balliol, who accepted the kingdom as vassal of King Edward and did homage to him.

1295. King Edward summoned what became known as the Model Parliament, generally considered to be the origin of Parliament as it now exists and representing the Lords, the Commons and the Clergy.

John Balliol, now King of Scotland, refused to join King Edward on his campaign in France and entered into a pact with France to form the 'Auld Alliance'.

1296. King Edward became involved in a war with France. Despite the official and traditional status of King Edward as Overlord in Scotland, the Scottish nobles not only refused to fight for him in that war, but entered into a secret treaty with France. In consequence, King Edward invaded Scotland and deposed King John Balliol and sent him as a prisoner to England, took over the throne of Scotland, and removed the Crown Jewels and the Stone of Scone to Westminster. The Stone was to remain there until 1996, when it was returned to Scotland. Scotland ceased to be a kingdom and became a dependency of England.

1297. Led by William Wallace, a Scottish knight, the Scots rose up against English rule and defeated King Edward at the Battle of Stirling Bridge. Wallace was appointed Guardian of Scotland.

1298. England invaded Scotland again and this time defeated William Wallace, at the Battle of Falkirk.

1299. John Comyn, nephew of the imprisoned King of Scotland, John Balliol, became Regent in his uncle's place.

1300. Up until then, the law courts had been united under a single head, the Justiciar. They were now divided into three: the King's Bench; the Court of Common Pleas; and the Court of the Exchequer.

1301. King Edward made his son and heir, the future King Edward II, Prince of Wales. In doing so, he founded the tradition, existing to the present day, whereby the monarch's eldest son is given the title of Prince of Wales at some point in his life that is considered to be appropriate for the bestowing of this honour.

1303. John Comyn defeated the English at the Battle of Roslin, whereupon King Edward invaded Scotland and inflicted defeat on it for the third time.

1305. William Wallace was executed in London.

1306. Robert Bruce, until then faithful to King Edward, murdered John Comyn in a church in Dumfries, rebelled against England, and was crowned King of Scotland at Scone.

1307. King Edward responded by launching his fourth invasion of Scotland, but died while on the journey.

(ii) Of special interest

King Edward I was a valiant crusader; subjugated Wales; defended the Crown's territories in France; expanded and improved both the administration of England and the judicial system; was the founder of Parliamentary practice; and launched a determined and long-lasting campaign, which enjoyed successes without proving ultimately successful, to bring Scotland under his dominion. He truly earned the loyalty of his subjects. He also built many castles in England and Wales that were intended to function as both fortresses and royal palaces.

King Edward II

Born 1284 and reigned 1307–1327. Son of King Edward I. Married Princess Isabella of France.

(i) The main events of the reign in summary

1307. King Edward travelled to France to negotiate a marriage with Princess Isabella, daughter of Philip IV of France. While in France, he left in complete charge of his kingdom Piers Gaveston, a knight from Gascony in France who had previously been expelled by King Edward I but whom he, King Edward II, had just made Earl of Cornwall.

1308. The marriage took place. The barons, with Thomas Earl of Lancaster at their head, demanded the dismissal of Piers Gaveston on the grounds of misgovernment. King Edward submitted to the demand but made Gaveston Lord Deputy of Ireland.

1310. Parliament set up a committee, the Lords Ordainers, to control the King by regulating his household and reforming – which meant revolutionising – the government of the kingdom. The King's cousin, Thomas Earl of Lancaster, took charge of the committee.

1312. King Edward recalled Piers Gaveston from Ireland, but Gaveston was kidnapped by the King's opponents, led by the Earl of Warwick, who put him to death.

1314. In Scotland, a new leader, Robert Bruce, had been winning fortress after fortress from the English, with Stirling

Castle alone still holding out but its governor saying that he would capitulate unless relieved before St. John's Day, 24 June. King Edward invaded Scotland with a huge army, but was routed by Bruce at the Battle of Bannockburn and only just escaped from being captured. The independence of Scotland was established.

1320. A father and son both named Hugh Despenser became King Edward's new favourites – a favourite in those days being an intimate companion of a ruler or other important person.

The Scots, with the Declaration of Arbroath, declared their independence from England.

1322. The Earl of Lancaster, the King's cousin, led a rebellion of the barons in England. It was crushed by King Edward and his forces at the Battle of Boroughbridge in Yorkshire. Lancaster was beheaded.

1326. Queen Isabella started an adulterous affair with Roger Mortimer, the first Earl of March. With her encouragement, Mortimer invaded England from France. He landed in Suffolk, accompanied by the Queen and the Prince of Wales, the future King Edward III, and the Queen and Mortimer successfully assumed royal authority, and, as a first step, took the two Despensers captive and had them hanged.

1327. Now under the control of Queen Isabella and Mortimer, the Parliament met and, surely extraordinarily, pronounced King Edward II guilty of such crimes as being too indolent to be able to distinguish between right and wrong, obstinately refusing the advice of the wise and listening to 'evil counsel'. It then deposed him and declared his son Prince Edward to be king. Even more extraordinarily, King Edward II is said to have confessed that the articles containing the allegations were indeed true, and that he was unworthy to reign. He was imprisoned in Berkeley Castle, and in the same year he died, and is believed by many to have been murdered.

(ii) Of special interest

What is often said about King Edward II is that he was a failure in government, in warfare and as a husband, and had favourites whom he allowed to wield excessive influence in the country. It is further sometimes alleged, especially by historians writing long after his reign, that his relationships with his favourites included homosexuality.

While he was still alive with his son reigning in his place, however, there were people with strong motives to blacken his name, and if necessary to invent crimes and character defects. Never allowing ourselves to forget that history is written by the victors, therefore, and remembering too that he was betrayed politically by a wife who was at the time publicly committing adultery, it is worth enquiring into the possibility that he was in reality a man and king of worth.

Relevant in this context is how he died. From the time of his death, accounts circulated that he was murdered in Berkeley Castle by being impaled on a red-hot poker rammed right up into his bowels, an allegation that is suggestively appropriate to the allegations of homosexuality. The story was not widely accepted at the time, and has never been widely accepted since by historians. Nor was homosexuality on his part, involving first Piers Gaveston and then the two Despensers, widely supposed in his lifetime or for some time after his death.

Whatever may be the truth, the entire case against King Edward is insufficiently supported.

King Edward III

Born 1312 and reigned 1327–1377. Son of King Edward II. Married Philippa of Hainault.

(i) The main events of the reign in summary

1327. At the start of King Edward III's reign when he was aged fifteen, after his father King Edward II had been deposed, the government of the kingdom was in the hands of his mother Queen Isabella and Roger Mortimer.

1328. King Edward married Philippa of Hainault, great-granddaughter of King Philip III of France. They had fourteen children and she was a popular queen.

1330. King Edward took over the government of the kingdom. He had Roger Mortimer executed, and confined his mother to luxurious imprisonment for the rest of her life.

1332. Parliament was for the first time divided into two houses: the House of Lords and the House of Commons.

1333. David Bruce, son of Robert Bruce, was crowned King of Scotland as King David II. King Edward invaded Scotland, defeated the Scots at the battle of Halidon Hill, and placed on the throne Edward Balliol, the son of King John Balliol whom King Edward I had deposed.

1337. Although the traditional Salic Law, then prevailing in France, excluded the female sex from being monarchs, King Edward III claimed the French throne by a right coming through his mother the late Queen Isabella, the daughter of the French king Philip IV. Nor is it impossible that his claim was valid, because it does not necessarily follow from the absence of a right for the throne to pass *to* a woman that such a right cannot pass *through* a woman. King Edward's claim had the momentous effect of launching the Hundred Years War that was to last from 1337 to 1453.

1339. King Edward launched the first campaign in the war. Although he won the great naval Battle of Sluys, the campaign was unsuccessful.

1346. King David II of Scotland invaded England, and was defeated and taken prisoner at the Battle of Neville's Cross.

King Edward launched the second campaign against France. Mainly due to the superior skill of the English archers, he routed the French at the Battle of Crécy, in northern France. In that battle his eldest son, Edward, to be known as the Black Prince, started to play an important part in English history, distinguishing himself greatly in that battle and going on to conquer other parts of France, which he then ruled from Bordeaux until, after returning to England, he died in 1376, one year before his father.

1347. King Edward laid siege to Calais, the town in France closest to Dover at the other side of the English Channel, and captured it after eleven months. It was to remain British until some 200 years later, in the reign of Queen Mary I.

1348. King Edward founded the Order of the Garter, still the highest order of chivalry in England.

1348–1350. In the terrible event known as the Black Death, about a third of the population of England and Wales died.

1352. Under the very first Statute of Treason, it became high treason to bring about death of the king or his eldest son; to give assistance to the king's enemies; or to counterfeit coins.

1356. The third campaign against France. At the Battle of Poitiers, the Black Prince routed the King of France and took him prisoner.

1357. King David was released from captivity, and returned home to Scotland.

The Black Prince made an expedition to Spain, to support King Pedro ('the Cruel') of Castile, who had been deposed by his brother. There he won the Battle of Navarrete and helped King Pedro to regain his throne.

1369–1370. King Edward launched his fourth, and last, French campaign. According to a contemporary French historian, Jean Froissart, 3,000 unarmed inhabitants of Limoges, who had deserted the English cause, were killed in what therefore became known as the Massacre at Limoges, and this took place in breach of the rules of chivalry, because King Edward was 'inflamed with passion and revenge'. It is fair to mention, however, that Froissart has frequently been challenged.

1371–1374. His health by then shattered, the Black Prince returned to England, leaving military affairs in France in the hands of his much less able brother, John of Gaunt, with the result that the English lost all their dominions in France other than Bordeaux, Bayonne and Calais.

1377. King Edward died.

(ii) Of special interest

King Edward III was responsible for two notable features of today's Britain.

In 1337, he established by royal charter the Duchy of Cornwall for his son, 'the Black Prince'. According to the charter, the eldest son of a reigning monarch automatically becomes Duke of Cornwall and in possession of landholdings to give him financial support.

The invention of this title and what goes with it was a remarkably imaginative and beneficial idea on the part of King Edward. Built into it is the fact that, the monarchy being hereditary, the heir to the throne could spend much of his lifetime 'waiting in the wings' and, because of the dignity of his position, being very limited in how he could occupy himself. What this constitutional innovation did was to make the heir financially independent, and what this has meant is that the heir has access to whatever financial resources he needs in order do what he sees as beneficial to the nation.

The other innovation of King Edward's that remains as vivid today as ever was his institution of the Order of the Garter. As every British child used to learn, while Catherine Grandison, the Countess of Salisbury of that time, was dancing at a court ball at Calais, her garter suddenly slipped from her leg. When the courtiers nearby sniggered, the King, a man of superior character, picked up the garter and graciously and gallantly put it on his own leg, saying as he did so, in the language spoken at the time and in the hearing of all: '*Honi soit qui mal y pense*' – 'Shame on him who thinks evil of it.' 'Soon,' King Edward added, 'you shall see this garter set so high that you will think it an honour to wear it'; and those words '*Honi soit qui mal y pense*' became, as they still remain, the motto of the Order, which he formally inaugurated with a great feast and joust.

In addition to its being the first of the orders of chivalry, it is also the most prestigious, and we can indeed bow our heads in admiration at the kingly inventiveness and far-reaching constructiveness of the third of the House of Plantagenet's King Edwards.

King Richard II

Born 1367 and reigned 1377–99. Grandson of King Edward III and son of King Edward's eldest son, the Black Prince, who died before he would have come to the throne.

(i) The main events of the reign in summary

1377. King Richard II succeeded to the throne at the age of ten, having lost his father, the Black Prince, at the age of nine. Until 1389, the kingdom was ruled in his name by his uncles John of Gaunt and Thomas of Gloucester.

1381. John of Gaunt, who was the third of the surviving sons of King Edward III, and Thomas Duke of Gloucester, the last of King Edward's sons, instituted a poll tax, a tax levied on all irrespective of the level of their wealth. Undoubtedly extortionate, it quickly resulted in the event known as the Peasants' Revolt. Approximately 100,000 rebels from Essex and Kent marched on London, demanding (a) the abolition of the system of villeinage that put a category of peasants legally under the control of the landowners, and (b) a general pardon – and doing considerable damage as they proceeded. King Richard, although not yet England's ruler, first met the men of Essex and granted their demands, whereupon they dispersed, and then met the men of Kent and bought them off with promises of freedom from the serfdom that was part of the system of villeinage. A notable result was that, although villeinage was not officially abolished at that time, the landowners ceased to enforce it as rigidly, and it gradually died out.

1386. A group of five nobles who became known as the Lords Appellant (makers of an 'appeal') sought to impeach King Richard's favourites, because of what they considered to be tyrannical rule. Immediately successful, they established for themselves the right to govern England for one year.

1387. The Lords Appellant launched a successful armed rebellion against King Richard. By the end of it they were in control of the country with King Richard as a figurehead.

1388. In what became known as the Merciless Parliament, some of the King's favourites were impeached. Several of them were executed.

1389. King Richard, now aged twenty-two, dismissed his guardians, took over the government of the country, and appointed William of Wykeham as Lord Chancellor, the senior executive position in the government. For eight years the King's rule was successful and respected.

1397. King Richard made himself an absolute monarch and took vengeance on three of the Lords Appellant. One of them spent the rest of his life in prison; one of them died in prison; the third was beheaded.

John of Gaunt's son, Henry of Bolingbroke, accused the Duke of Norfolk of having uttered 'treasonable words'. It was agreed by all that the matter should be settled by single combat, as was the custom in those days; but, just as the combat was about to start, King Richard took the matter into his hands and banished both of the combatants from the kingdom, Bolingbroke for ten years and Norfolk for life.

1399. John of Gaunt, the father of Henry of Bolingbroke, and King Richard cancelled the legal documents that would have allowed Bolingbroke to inherit his father's estate automatically. This meant that Bolingbroke would need to ask King Richard for his father's estates when the latter died. King Richard then went on a military campaign in Ireland. While he was there, Bolingbroke invaded England in order to claim back his unjustly seized estates, quickly gained enough power to have himself declared King Henry IV, and then had King Richard II confined to prison, where, at the age of thirty-three, the King died in mysterious circumstances. Bypassing the true heir to the throne, King Richard's seven-year-old son Edmund de Mortimer, the new king, Henry IV, had himself crowned prior to Richard's death.

(ii) Of special interest

How King Richard died in prison has always been a subject of speculation. Some have suspected that the new king, Henry IV, had his predecessor murdered, but there is no evidence to support that claim, and indeed King Richard's body was put on public display in St. Paul's Cathedral not long after his death and showed no signs of violence.

There were two momentous events outside the arena of politics during the reign.

One was that King Richard's Lord Chancellor, William of Wykeham, Bishop of Winchester, founded New College in Oxford in 1379 and then, in 1382, Winchester College, the first of the great public schools still in existence today. The other was that John Wycliffe (a) made the first complete translation of the Bible into English since King Alfred the Great had made a start on it about 500 years earlier, and (b) founded a heretical movement called the Lollards, which preached contradictions to various teachings of the Church, with the consequence, after his death, of his works being officially burnt, his body being removed from its grave and burnt as well, and the ashes cast into the River Swift.

Also noteworthy: in 1398 Geoffrey Chaucer completed his lengthy poem *The Canterbury Tales*, which in due course earned him renown as the Father of English Literature and the privilege of being the first poet to be buried in Poets' Corner in Westminster Abbey.

As to the poll tax which had to be abandoned, there was never to be another one until 1989, when the then Prime Minister Margaret Thatcher introduced one, officially called the community charge, which lasted little longer than the first one.

CHAPTER TWENTY-ONE

The House of Lancaster

King Henry IV

Born 1367 and reigned 1399–1413. He was the eldest son of John of Gaunt, who was the fourth son of King Edward III, and prior to his reign was the Duke of Lancaster. His first marriage, when he was aged twelve, was to the non-royal Mary de Bohun, daughter of the Earl of Hereford. Their son Henry became Prince of Wales when his father seized the throne from King Richard, and was later to become King Henry V. Mary died in 1394, and therefore never became queen. In 1483 he married his second wife, Joanna of Navarre, daughter of King Charles of Navarre.

(i) The main events of the reign in summary

1400. A year after King Henry IV seized the throne, the Earls of Kent, Rutland, Huntingdon and Salisbury launched a rebellion to restore King Richard. The Earl of Rutland betrayed the rebellion, however, and it was quickly suppressed. Kent, Huntingdon, Salisbury and others were executed.

1401. Henry and Parliament had passed the act *De heretico comburendo* (translatable as either 'Concerning the burning of the heretic' or 'That the heretic is to be burnt'), making the public teaching of heresy punishable by being burnt at the stake. Later in the year an official persecution of the Lollards was launched, and one of the promoters of the Lollard heresy, William Sawtrey, originally a Catholic priest, was condemned for heresy after due investigation, degraded from priest to not-even-doorkeeper in seven successive stages, and then sentenced and publicly burnt at the stake.

1402. The Duke of Albany led Scotland in invasion of England, but was defeated at the Battle of Homildon Hill.

1403. The Percy family in Northumberland, headed by the Earl of Northumberland and Henry, known as Hotspur, the Earl's son, launched the first of three rebellions. Hotspur was defeated and slain at the Battle of Shrewsbury.

1405. The Earl of Northumberland launched his second rebellion, this time in favour of Edmund Mortimer, a prisoner of King Henry's who by descent was the rightful heir to the English crown. Again the rebellion was suppressed, and Northumberland fled to Scotland.

1406. King Henry, never strong in his health, fell victim to what was possibly a form of leprosy which included disfigured skin, though he was to live for a further seven years.

1407. King Henry conceded to the House of Commons the sole right to originate grants of money, in doing so severely hampering his ability to act as king, and submitted to a demand to name sixteen counsellors and to be guided by their advice.

1408. Once again the Earl of Northumberland took up arms against King Henry, this time to be defeated at the Battle of Bramham Moor and killed.

1413. Worn out by illness, revolts and constant shortage of money, King Henry died at Westminster at the age of forty-five.

(ii) Of special interest

It is important for any sort of realistic understanding of the Middle Ages to recognise that capital punishment for heretics was not as illogical and barbaric as at first sight it may appear to have been. Nowadays the right to practise the religion of one's choice within reason is almost a dogma, depending for its base on the supposition that religious belief can be no more than a matter of opinion. That was not the position of those who lived in the Middle Ages. They held firmly (a) that there was one true religion, a *demonstrably* true one; (b) that this religion was the one founded by Christ and presided over by the legitimate successors of St. Peter, the first Bishop of Rome; (c) that these legitimate successors of St. Peter had complete authority, given to St. Peter in Matthew 16:16–19, to teach and to legislate throughout Christendom; and (d) that this authority even included the right and the power to dismiss kings from office, a power that was very occasionally used.

They further held that certain crimes were serious enough to merit the punishment of being put to death. Murder was one such crime and remained so in Great Britain until the death penalty for murder was abolished in 1965. Heresy they considered to be a more serious crime than murder. Murder, it was argued, brought about death only in the *present* world. Serious though that was, it was only temporary in the context of eternity, whereas persuading people to believe in a heretical doctrine was to make them ineligible for Heaven, and consigned to Hell, for *eternity*, because one of the conditions for salvation was wholehearted acceptance of the dogmatic teachings of the Catholic Church.

Thus the logic of heresy being one of the capital offences of the time and the most serious of them all. To hold a heretical belief in private was not a crime, but to promote one in public and to infect others with it very much was, and was all the more serious a crime in the case of someone officially representing the Catholic Church and betraying his office, as in the case of John Wycliffe, who earlier had even been Master of the Catholic college of Balliol in Oxford.

Finally, the Lollard heresy was not only religious in character but had *political* effects as well, because it alleged that no ruler, either spiritual or temporal, had any authority while in a state of mortal sin, which Lollardy judged to apply generally to non-Lollards.

~

To some extent King Henry's reign amounted to a continuation of the long-running war between the king and nobles, with the latter constantly trying to reduce the power of the king. Let it not be thought that the motives of the nobles were those of benefiting the ordinary people in the country. Their aim, in reducing the king's power, was the *increase* of *their* power; and they were successful to some extent, especially during 1407.

~

Otherwise, the main characteristic of King Henry's reign is that, from its very beginning, it marked the start of what was to be almost constant warfare throughout the rule of the House of Lancaster, even more so than the reigns of the King Edwards had been.

King Henry V

Born c. 1387 and reigning 1413–1422, King Henry V is 'Shakespeare's' Prince Hal, who, after merry dealings with Falstaff, grows up and, by then as King Henry, wins the battle of Agincourt.

(i) The main events of the reign in summary

1413. Henry succeeded the throne at the age of twenty-five or twenty-six on the death of his father.

1415. A group of nobles mounted a conspiracy to remove King Henry from the throne and replace him with Edward Mortimer, Earl of March, the son of the Edmund Mortimer who had been the legitimate heir during the reign of King Henry IV. The conspiracy was discovered and various parties involved in it were executed.

King Henry V attempted to win back the territories in France lost by his ancestors, which caused the resumption of the Hundred Years War that had started in 1337. At the same time he revived the claim to the French throne first made by King Edward III and invaded France with 30,000 men. After a five-week siege of the port of Harfleur in Normandy, the surrender of Harfleur was achieved; but the victors, ill from lack of food, had to retreat to the port of Calais.

King Henry achieved a great victory at the battle made famous throughout the entire world by 'Shakespeare', the three-hour Battle of Agincourt, a small village in the north-east of France. Thanks to the skill of the English archers with the longbow, some 20,000 French soldiers were defeated by 6,000 English soldiers.

1417. In a second campaign, King Henry invaded France again, and conquered several towns in Normandy.

1419. King Henry laid a siege lasting six months to the prosperous capital of Normandy, Rouen, at length starving it into surrender.

1420. King Henry entered into a treaty, the Treaty of Troyes, with King Charles VI of France. Under its terms, King Henry was: to marry King Charles's daughter Princess Catherine; to be Regent during the lifetime of King Charles; and to be King of France as well as of England after King Charles's death.

1421. King Henry returned to England with his new wife Queen Catherine.

1422. King Henry died just before he could succeed King Charles VI as King of France. King Charles died two months later. Henry's ten-month-old son succeeded them as king of both England and France.

(ii) Of special interest

King Henry V is England's most glorified king since the Norman Conquest, and second only to King Alfred the Great in the popular estimate of his worth. Indeed, some historians might even put him first. In the words of a modern historian, Desmond Seward, in the introduction in his book *Henry V as Warlord*, published in 1987:

> Henry V is one of England's heroes. The victor of Agincourt was idolised during his lifetime; his memory inspired one of Shakespeare's most stirring plays; and the Victorians considered him a perfect Christian gentleman: 'He was religious, pure in life, temperate, liberal, careful and yet splendid,' says Bishop Stubbs, 'merciful, truthful, and honourable, discreet in word, provident in counsel, prudent in judgement, modest in look, magnanimous in act, a true Englishman.'
>
> That brilliant historian of the mediaeval English, the late K. B. McFarlane, thought Henry 'the greatest man that ever ruled England.'

In these pages I have recorded numerous instances of where the popular image of a monarch, even among learned historians, is misleading. No popular image, however, I maintain, is more misleading than the one represented by that summary. Here is how its author, who took the trouble to consult French sources as well as English ones and is the only English historian I have come across who arrives at the reality of King Henry V, immediately continues in the same introduction:

> Nevertheless, his conquest of France was as much about loot as dynastic succession, accompanied by mass slaughter, arson and rape – French plunder was on sale all over England … The misery inflicted on the French by Henry's campaigns is indisputable. Any local historian in north-western France can point to a town, a château, an abbey or a church sacked by his men. When the English raided enemy territory, they killed anything that moved, destroyed crops and food supplies and drove off livestock … Occupied areas fared little better because of the *pâtis,* or protection racket, operated by English garrisons; villages had to pay extortionate dues in food and wine as well as money, failure to deliver sometimes incurred executions and burnings.

Mass slaughter, arson and rape. To any who may suppose that to be typical of how warfare was conducted in the Middle Ages, I say emphatically: no, that is not so. It was not, for instance, how Kings Edward I and III fought in France during their endless campaigns. Nor has any such conduct been even suggested of supposedly 'Bad' King John.

Indeed, I strongly doubt that there is a single precedent in Christian warfare for Henry's methods. Certainly the horrors of the Norman Conquest of England did not begin to approach it, with, for instance, rape not so much as being alleged. Nor was anything resembling what Desmond Seward has just outlined to be repeated until centuries later.

The reality is that arguably the most astonishing of all the achievements of the Church after the conversion of England by St. Augustine of Canterbury was its success in *civilising* warfare. Considering war to be a great evil, but realistically recognising also that it was inevitable in a world that would always contain sinners as well as saints, the Church did what it could to mitigate its disastrous effects and to reduce to the minimum its evils, and it succeeded in this throughout Europe to an extent that is unimaginable today.

Here are a few examples of the effects of the Church's influence:

- As already noted, the introduction and constant encouragement of the notion of chivalry.
- What was called the Peace of God, which protected from military hostilities clerics, monks, nuns, and eventually even the poor and pilgrims and merchants on a journey, and also created the right of asylum in sanctuaries – all this under pain of excommunication.
- What was called the Truce of God, which forbade any acts of private warfare from Saturday night to Monday morning, and eventually from Wednesday night to Monday morning and in the whole of Advent and Lent – again all under pain of excommunication.

Thus it was that the Middle Ages in which King Henry V lived was the era which created the tradition of comradeship, courtesy, and various civilised conventions between soldiers of opposing sides of which traces were still to be found as late as the beginning of the First World War; the era, indeed, of which it could be said, without romantic exaggeration, that a peasant could be ploughing tranquilly in one field while soldiers were killing each other in an important battle in the next field.

Nor can that last assertion be dismissed as mediaeval fiction. Professor Thorold Rogers, Professor of Political Economy at Oxford University in the mid nineteenth century and an important enough scholar to rate an entry in *Encyclopaedia Britannica*, was hardly able to believe his eyes as he pored over the huge array of original documents from which he composed his *History of Agriculture and Prices in England from 1259 to 1793*. In the preface to volume 4 he says wonderingly about the Wars of the Roses that were to start forty years after Agincourt:

Then came the civil war, the strangest civil war ever seen. No one suffered except the combatants. The people took no part in the strife. It was a long battle between two factions and their retainers ... A singular feature in this great war of succession is that it is a war of pitched battles, not of sieges. The partisans on either side seem to have made their way to some open heath and there to have fought out their quarrel.

And that is a system of the conduct of war that might as well never have been heard of by King Henry V, nor, as we shall be seeing, by any of the heroes, real or supposed, of the new era opened up by the Reformation and 'Glorious Revolution', such as Queen Elizabeth, 'Protector' Cromwell, Kings William III and George II, and, if he can be called a hero, the 'Butcher' Duke of Cumberland, let alone by any of the wartime leaders of the last hundred years or so of world history.

Mass slaughter, arson and rape. The reality is that the 'perfect Christian gentleman' who was 'the greatest man that ever ruled England' appears to have been a man who was thoroughly and unspeakably evil.

King Henry VI

Born 1421 and reigned 1422–1461 and then briefly restored to reign 1470–1471.

(i) The main events of the reign in summary

1422. As an infant aged ten months, Henry became King Henry VI of England on the death of his father, King Henry V. Two months later, under the terms of the Treaty of Troyes which had been signed by his father in 1420, he also became King of France on the death of his grandfather, Charles VI, who had disinherited his own son, Charles, in favour of King Henry V. This was however to be contested by the future King Charles VII, as will emerge.

Humphrey, Duke of Gloucester, became Regent of England, and John, Duke of Bedford, became Regent of France. Henry was knighted in 1426, aged four, and crowned King of England in 1429, at the age of seven, and King of France in 1431.

1429. Joan of Arc, a peasant-girl aged seventeen who had not learnt to read or write, and who lived in Domrémy in north-eastern France, persuaded a local garrison commander to take her on a journey to the court of King Charles VII in Chinon, in west-central France. There she managed to obtain a private audience with the king and made him two promises, conditional on his equipping her with armour and a horse and placing her at the head of his army.

King Henry VI

First promise: that she would bring to an end the siege of Orléans, a city near Paris, in the north of France. This, if true, was of the highest importance. By then that siege had been in process for about six months, and, as contemporaries are on record as having recognised, if the crushing defeat that the French had recently suffered at Agincourt were to be followed by a victory by the English at Orléans, which was now appearing to be probable, that could be expected to lead on inevitably to the conquest of the whole of France by the English.

Second promise: that she would arrange for Charles to be crowned at Rheims, where, by tradition, French kings were always crowned – an even more non-credible promise than the first one, because Rheims was in the depths of the part of France that was at that time completely controlled by the English.

To the understandable disgust of some of his military officers, King Charles dressed this illiterate girl in a suit of white armour at her request and put her in charge of his army, whereupon she launched her campaign to expel the English from France. First, she put new heart into the French defenders of Orléans, who by then had become badly dispirited, and, forcing the English to retreat, raised the siege. Then the force under her command overthrew and took prisoner the greatest soldier of his day, John Talbot, Earl of Shrewsbury, at the Battle of Patay. Finally, winning battle after battle on the way, she conducted King Charles successfully through the very heart of the enemy's country to Rheims, where he was crowned and formally enthroned as King Charles VII.

1430. Joan of Arc was captured by the Burgundians, who then sold her to their English allies. Monstrously, King Charles, for whom she had done so much and to whom, indeed, he owed his very kingship, made no attempt to rescue her.

1431. Joan of Arc was tried by a pro-English ecclesiastical court as both a heretic and a witch and, in accordance with the legal penalty for such crimes at the time, was burnt at the stake in Rouen, the capital of Normandy, on 30 May.

1437. At the age of sixteen, King Henry personally took over the rule of England from his advisers. During the remainder of his reign, the whole of France was gradually lost to the English, with the single exception of the port of Calais, which, as already mentioned, was not to be lost until the reign of Queen Mary.

1445. The marriage between King Henry and Margaret of Anjou took place. She was to be one of the most significant figures in the Wars of the Roses, and sometimes even the military leader of the Lancasters.

1453. The English were driven out of France, bringing to an end the Hundred Years' War. That war was shortly to be replaced by the Wars of the Roses, a long-running series of battles, this time on English soil, between the House of Lancaster and the House of York, which was to last until 1485, thirty-two years later, with the end of the reign of King Richard III.

Queen Margaret gave birth to their only son, Edward of Westminster, also sometimes known as Edward of Lancaster.

Possibly because of understandable despondency arising from the endless defeats and loss of territory that England had been suffering for most of his life, King Henry fell ill, with what amounted to a complete mental collapse – to the extent of being unable to speak or to be aware of what was going on around him. Richard, Duke of York, who had become the heir presumptive to the throne after the death of the Duke of Gloucester, was made Protector for the period, lasting more than a year, during which King Henry was incapable of governing.

1455. The arrival of this new member of the House of Lancaster meant that the Duke of York was no longer the definite heir presumptive to the throne and could no longer expect an unopposed and peaceful accession when King Henry died. Shortly afterwards, King Henry recovered his health and the Duke of York was dismissed from the office of Protector, to be replaced by a favourite of Queen Margaret's, the Duke of Somerset. The Duke of York then took up arms, starting the Wars of the Roses, a series of wars fought between these two rival branches of the House of Plantagenet:

- The House of York, which was descended from the second son of King Edward III; and
- The House of Lancaster, descended from John of Gaunt, the third son of King Edward III.

The leader of the Yorkists was Richard, Duke of York, who had just been dismissed from the Protectorship. The leader of the

Lancastrians was the favourite of Queen Margaret's, John Beaufort, Duke of Somerset.

1455–1471. Some of the battles of the Wars of the Roses:

- The Battle of St. Albans in 1455, with the Yorkists under the Duke of York victorious; the Duke of Somerset killed; and King Henry taken prisoner.
- The Battle of Blore Heath in 1459, with the Yorkists again victorious.
- The Battle of Northampton in 1460. The Yorkists, under 'Warwick the Kingmaker', as the Earl of Warwick, the richest and most powerful noble of that time, has always been called, were victorious for the third time, and took King Henry prisoner. Queen Margaret fled with their son Edward to Scotland.
- The Battle of Wakefield also in 1460, with the Lancastrians victorious.

    Still in 1460, Richard, Duke of York, publicly claimed the throne for himself. After complicated negotiations, the House of Lords settled for the compromise:

    (a) that King Henry VI of the House of Lancaster should hold the crown for the rest of his life, after which

    (b) the crown should pass to Richard, Duke of York.

    This compromise was greeted with indignation by Queen Margaret, since it eliminated her son Prince Edward from succession to the throne. In fact the Duke of York clearly had a better claim to the throne by right of birth than King Henry VI, because, as noted above, he was descended from the *second* son of King Edward III, whereas King Henry was descended from the *third* son, John of Gaunt.

    Within a few weeks of this agreement being finalised, Richard, Duke of York, was killed in battle. The agreement that he should succeed to the throne was eventually of some effect, however, in that his two sons became successively King Edward IV and King Richard III. Further battles:

- The Battle of Mortimer's Cross in 1461, in which the Yorkists were victorious once more.

- The Second Battle of St Albans, again in 1461, with Queen Margaret defeating the Earl of Warwick, and rescuing her husband, King Henry.

The drama of the constant changes in the fortunes of both Houses continued. Unfortunately for the House of Lancaster, although Queen Margaret was in many respects a remarkable military leader, her conduct in warfare was not always prudent, and her unpopularity became such that she was refused admission to London by the people of London. Not for nothing was she known as the 'She-wolf of France'. Earlier, the throne had been claimed by a new contender, Prince Edward, Earl of March, son of Richard, Duke of York, who, it may be remembered, was descended from the *second* son of King Edward III and, taking over the Yorkist cause, had asserted his right to the throne back in 1460. Now, taking advantage of Queen Margaret's unpopularity, he was able to enter London in triumph to be proclaimed King as King Edward IV, the first of the three kings of the House of York.

1470. By now King Edward was consistently acting as he chose rather than doing the bidding of Warwick the Kingmaker. In consequence Warwick took it upon himself to replace this king with one who would be more submissive to him. After failing in an attempt to install King Edward's brother, the Duke of Clarence, on the throne, he turned back to King Henry VI, who was still imprisoned in the Tower of London. Taking King Edward by surprise and forcing him to flee to France, he installed Henry VI as king once more, in a manoeuvre known as 'the Readeption' (from the Latin prefix *re-*, meaning 'again', and the Latin noun *adeptio*, meaning 'obtaining').

1471. In March of that year, Edward returned, landing in Yorkshire. Marching south and gathering adherents as he went, he first defeated and killed Warwick, at the Battle of Barnet, and then defeated Queen Margaret in the Battle of Tewkesbury, at which King Henry's son Edward was also killed. On the night that King Edward returned to London, King Henry VI was murdered in the Tower. Who committed the murder it is not known, but it is of course suspected that it was on the orders of King Edward. As to the fact of the murder, there is no room for doubt. In 1484, King Richard moved his body from Chertsey Abbey, where it had originally been buried, to St. George's Chapel at Windsor Castle, where it was found, several centuries later, with its skull damaged and signs of blood.

(ii) Of special interest

King Henry VI is little respected by historians. That was not the attitude of his contemporaries and the successors of his contemporaries during the next few decades; nor is it mine. He cannot be blamed for the complete change in the course of the Hundred Years War and the period of military calamity for England during the first ten years of his life for which Joan of Arc was responsible. As to the loss of all of France apart from Calais, since he was not a soldier, let alone a competent military leader, and some people have talents which others do not have, it may not be fair to put that to his discredit, although it must be said that defence of the realm was one of the duties of kings and that military competence was therefore an important kingly virtue. At all events, the century of warfare had been consistently disastrous for England, and it was better for the English that the war be brought to an end even by losing it than that it should continue.

During his lifetime he was regarded as genuinely heroic and, although never officially canonised, as a genuine saint, and miracles were attributed to him. Until well into the sixteenth century his shrine enjoyed great popularity as a destination for pilgrims. In the seventeenth century, however, he was disparaged in the plays attributed to William Shakespeare, in no fewer than three plays devoted to him, represented as hopelessly weak-willed; and this has influenced historians in that direction ever since.

What mattered to King Henry VI was not military achievement, other than strictly in a country's self-defence, but that his subjects and future generations could be educated in the highest degree both in religion and in the important secular subjects. He not only promoted this in his lifetime, but left behind him three great monuments whose influence has stretched, century after century, right up to the present day. These were:

- Eton College – 'The King's College of Our Lady of Eton besides Wyndsor', to give it its full title – which he situated next door to the royal property of Windsor. It is of course the best-known school, worldwide, that there has ever been, and for the best reasons. I have known of people, though far from the majority, who were unhappy there, but I have never known of any Old Etonian who would rather have been at a different school.

- King's College in Cambridge – 'The King's College of Our Lady and St. Nicholas in Cambridge'– founded in 1446 and completed a century later, and the possessor, in its chapel, of the greatest example of English late-Gothic architecture in existence.

- All Souls College in Oxford – 'The College of the Souls of All Faithful People Deceased in the University of Oxford' – the purpose of which was to enable graduates to engage in courses of advanced studies of arts, philosophy, theology, and civil and Church law that end with an exam that has been justly described as 'the hardest examination in the world'.

Monarchs are surely entitled to have included, as part of the judgement made of them, such monuments as they leave behind; and, according to this criterion, King Henry VI ranks along with the greatest of all. Many of his contemporaries held this view of him, and especially those who knew him best.

CHAPTER TWENTY-TWO

The House of York

King Edward IV

Born 1442; reigned 1461–1470; briefly deposed 1470–1471; resumed throne to reign again 1471–1483. He was great-great-grandson of Edward III.

The main events of the reign in summary

1461. As noted earlier, the Yorkists under Edward's leadership defeated the Lancastrian army at Mortimer's Cross. Edward then united his forces with those of his cousin, Richard Neville, the Earl of Warwick, proclaimed himself King, marched against the Lancastrians, and defeated them at the Battle of Towton, effectively bringing to an end the possibility of any valid Lancastrian claims to the throne in the future. He then continued to London where, with the full support of Warwick, he was crowned.

1464. King Edward married Elizabeth Woodville, a commoner and the widow of a commoner. Warwick was gravely displeased, and with reason, given that he had been negotiating with King Louis XI of France on King Edward's behalf for King Edward to marry either the daughter of King Louis or his sister-in-law. He was indeed enraged at being humiliated when it became evident that, while he was negotiating, Edward had secretly married this commoner.

1465. The deposed King Henry VI, after spending a year in flight, was captured and imprisoned in the Tower of London.

1469. Warwick broke completely with Edward, to the extent of joining King Henry's wife Margaret, the 'She-wolf of France'. He ended up entering into an agreement with both King Louis XI and Queen Margaret to restore King Henry VI if they would support him in a military invasion of England.

1470. Warwick's invasion took place and was successful, with King Edward forced to flee to Flanders, in the north of present-day Belgium. After first trying to put King Edward's youngest surviving brother, the Duke of Clarence, on the throne, Warwick engineered the restoration of King Henry VI to the throne: this being the already-mentioned Readeption. King Edward returned, however, and although starting with only a small force, increasingly gained support and finally was able to enter London unopposed and take prisoner King Henry, who, as we have seen, was to suffer a violent death in the Tower of London during the following year. King Edward and his brothers then defeated Warwick at the Battle of Barnet, where Warwick was killed.

1471. King Edward won the Battle of Tewkesbury and in doing so brought all remaining Lancastrian resistance to an end.

1475. Reviving the long-standing claim to the French throne, King Edward started a war with France, which continued until his death in 1483.

1476. William Caxton set up in Westminster England's first printing press. The first book produced by it was Geoffrey Chaucer's *Canterbury Tales*.

1478. King Edward's youngest-but-one brother, George, Duke of Clarence, who at one stage had joined Warwick the Kingmaker on the Lancastrian side against his brother, was convicted of treason against King Edward and executed, allegedly, though improbably, by being drowned in a butt of Malmsey wine.

King Edward V

Born 1470, the elder son of King Edward IV, and reigned for eighty-six days at the age of twelve during 1483.

The main events of the reign in summary

1483. In May, King Edward took up residence in the Tower of London, to be joined there in June by his younger brother, Richard, Duke of York. In June an English preacher, referred to by historians sometimes as Dr. John Shaw and sometimes as Dr. Ralph Shaa, preached a sermon in which he declared that, to his certain knowledge, King Edward IV, who had already been shown to be irresponsible by the standards expected of royalty, had in fact been contracted to be married to Lady Eleanor Butler at the time that he married Elizabeth Woodville and made her queen. That, according to the laws of the Church of the time, meant that his marriage to Elizabeth Woodville had been invalid, which in turn meant that King Edward and his brother Richard were illegitimate and therefore had never been eligible for the throne.

In addition, the children of Richard's elder brother, the Duke of Clarence, had been barred from the throne by King Edward IV, and an assembly of the Lords and Commons declared King Edward's uncle Richard, Duke of Gloucester, to be the legitimate king, which was later confirmed by an Act of Parliament titled *Titulus Regius*.

What happened to the two children after that is unknown. Majority opinion has it that they were murdered on the orders of their uncle, King Richard, as, for instance, in the play *Richard III* attributed to Shakespeare, in which Sir James Tyrrell, ordered by Richard III to murder them, smothers them with a pillow. We shall be looking at this further; for the time being it is only necessary for us to note that the accusation is unsupported by any genuine proof and that it was undoubtedly useful propaganda for the House of Tudor.

CHAPTER TWENTY-THREE

A Hunchback of Self-confessed 'Naked Villainy'?

King Richard III

Born 1452 and reigned 1483–1485. Son of Richard, Duke of York and brother of King Edward IV.

Duke of Gloucester before he became king, his mother was Cecily Neville. His wife and queen was his cousin Anne Neville. He was the fourth of four brothers. The eldest of them was King Edward IV, the father of King Edward V and Prince Richard; the second was Edmund, Earl of Rutland, who died in one of the Wars of the Roses battles at the age of seventeen; the third was George, Duke of Clarence, who, as we have seen, was convicted of treason and executed in 1478.

(i) The main events of the reign in summary

Prior to his accession in 1483, Richard had been sent by his brother King Edward IV to govern the north of England, which he did efficiently and with unfailing loyalty.

1483. King Edward fell ill. In danger of dying, he entrusted his son Edward to his brother Richard, Duke of Gloucester, as Edward's Protector. He then did die and his young son became King as Edward V but three months later was replaced as king by his uncle, who took the throne as King Richard III and at once appointed one

King Richard III

of his supporters, the Duke of Buckingham, as Constable and Great Chamberlain of England.

The Duke of Buckingham started a rebellion against King Richard, in order to put on the throne Henry Tudor, whose claim to the throne was of negligible validity. King Richard crushed the rebellion, and Buckingham was captured, tried and executed.

1484. King Richard helped King James III of Scotland to suppress a revolt by the Duke of Albany.

King Richard's only legitimate son, Prince Edward, died at the age of ten.

1485. King Richard's wife Queen Anne died.

Henry Tudor landed at Milford Haven with 2,000 French soldiers. At the Battle of Bosworth that followed, King Richard was killed, bringing his short reign to an end.

(ii) Of special interest

'Shakespeare's' play *Richard III*, written about a century after Richard's death, is representative of what most historians have said about King Richard ever since. In it King Richard III is, without exaggeration, the ultimate incarnation of evil. Indeed, right at the beginning he gives this indication of what is to be expected of him: 'I am determined to prove a villain.'

And prove a villain he does, murdering both King Henry VI and Edward of Lancaster; contriving the death of his own brother the Duke of Clarence; killing Lord Hastings; arranging the murder of his two child nephews in the Tower of London; poisoning his own wife in order to marry his niece; and so on throughout the play.

Given the circumstances both of his birth and of his appearance, we might hesitate to blame him: the play tells us that he suffered the terrible start of being born after two years in his mother's womb, and with a complete set of teeth, hair down to his shoulders, a withered arm, a humpback and one shoulder higher than the other.

~

Now *audi alteram partem* – let us look at the other side.

Although the 'Shakespeare' play, at least in outline, has tended to receive the approval of historians, there is overwhelming evidence that there is scarcely a word of truth in it.

As to Richard's appearance:

There is no definite evidence that King Richard was in any way deformed or otherwise strange in his looks. In 2012, a skeleton was found in Leicester which scientists have identified as probably being that of King Richard, and indicating a severe lateral curvature of the spine. There are, however, no *contemporary* references to any physical deformities, and no indications of such deformities in the earliest-known portraits of him. Indeed, a highly respected nineteenth-century author and Member of Parliament, the Right Hon. T. P. Courtney, relates that a contemporary of King Richard's, the Countess of Desmond, who as a young girl danced at the court of his brother Edward IV, maintained, when she was an elderly lady, that Richard was 'the handsomest man in the room except his brother Edward, *and was very well made.*' (Italics added.)

Further, among those who would have seen Richard III as an adult would have been the contemporary author of the Croyland Chronicle, a historical record that the Benedictine Abbey of Croyland, in Lincolnshire, started in the early Middle Ages and kept constantly up to date. The chronicler, although having no qualms about making *other* accusations about Richard, makes no reference to any physical peculiarities. Nor do any other contemporary writers.

As to Richard's character and the most important things that he is specifically accused of:

He was trusted by his brother King Edward, and respected and popular in the part of Britain that Edward delegated to him to administer.

There is neither any evidence nor any likelihood that Richard murdered King Henry VI.

He did not come to the throne in place of his nephew, the young King Edward V, on his own initiative. On the contrary, all the indications are that he was as much a trustworthy man of his word as anyone who ever lived, which was why his brother Edward IV was happy to appoint him as Lord Protector of his son, young Edward, if Edward should become king before he was of an age when he could rule.

What in fact happened was that, after Richard had taken the traditional oath of allegiance to King Edward V, as his young nephew had now become, Bishop Stillington, who had been a witness of what he now reported, testified that Edward IV had entered into a contract to marry Lady Eleanor Talbot before his marriage to Elizabeth Woodville. This meant that the marriage to Elizabeth Woodville was invalid and, in turn, that the young Edward V was illegitimate. As was its duty once there was serious doubt about Edward's legitimacy, Parliament gave its full agreement to the implications of what Bishop Stillington had revealed, and there followed one of the most magnificent coronations on record, with virtually the entire peerage being present and confirming the legitimacy of the coronation.

As to the two princes in the Tower of London, which in those days was not a prison but one of the royal residences, they were much more of a threat to the position of King Richard's successor, King Henry VII, than they had ever been to King Richard, and King Henry certainly did not lack the sort of ruthlessness that the murder would have needed. This is how Josephine Tey, in her novel *The Daughter of Time*, published in 1951 and written by her for the express purpose of restoring the reputation of Richard III, wraps this matter up.

First, she quotes a typical historian dealing with the period:

'It was the settled and considered policy of the Tudors to rid themselves of all rivals to the throne, more especially those heirs of York who remained alive on the accession of Henry VII. In this they were successful, although it was left to Henry VIII to get rid of the last of them.'

Then she gives the reaction to those words of the police detective who is her fictional hero in the novel:

He stared at this bald announcement. This placid acceptance of wholesale murder … He gave up. History was something that he would never understand. The values of historians differed so radically from any values with which he was acquainted that he could never hope to meet them on common ground. He would go back to Scotland Yard, where murderers were murderers.

As to Richard's conduct when King, here is just one important and undoubted fact – the verdict of the nineteenth-century Lord Chancellor, Lord Campbell, one of the most distinguished of all England's Lord Chancellors and Lord Chief Justices, as recorded in Chapter XXIV in Volume I of his *Lives of the Lord Chancellors of England*: 'We have no difficulty in pronouncing Richard's Parliament the most meritorious national assembly for protecting the liberty of the subject, and putting down abuses in the administration of justice that had sat in England since the reign of Henry III.'

All that in two short years. I believe that I can now safely rest my case on King Richard III's behalf.

CHAPTER TWENTY-FOUR

The House of Tudor Takes Control

King Henry VII. Deserving even of such modest praise as is sometimes accorded to him?

Born 1457 and reigned 1485–1509. He was the son of Edmund Tudor and Margaret Beaufort, neither of whom was royal. Margaret Beaufort did in fact have royal blood, but it was royal blood that was tainted. King Henry VI's great-grandfather, John of Gaunt, had had an illegitimate offspring by his mistress Katherine Swynford, before they were married. When they subsequently did marry, her family, the Beauforts, were legally declared legitimate, but even so they were barred from the throne. It was the son of the not genuinely royal Margaret Beaufort, Henry Tudor, who defeated King Richard III at the Battle of Bosworth and became king.

Henry Tudor had been born in Wales in 1457, but forced to flee to Brittany in France when fourteen years old. In 1486 he married Princess Elizabeth of York, daughter of King Edward IV and niece of King Richard III, and also King Henry's third cousin in that both were great-great-grandchildren of John of Gaunt. They had eight children. Perhaps uniquely in all history of all countries, Queen Elizabeth, as she then became, and in due course also became the mother of King Henry VIII, was the daughter, the sister, the niece, the wife, the mother and the grandmother of successive kings and queens of England.

(i) The main events of the reign in summary

1485. On 22 August, Henry Tudor came to the throne as King Henry VII after defeating King Richard III at the Battle of Bosworth.

1486. King Henry married Elizabeth of York, uniting the Royal Houses of York and Lancaster, which had been constantly at war until then.

1487. King Henry restored the Star Chamber, an institution of the past that had fallen into abeyance, and increased the number of its functions.

Lambert Simnel, of humble origin and an undoubted impostor, claimed to be the Earl of Warwick, nephew to King Edward IV, and thus the true king. He was supported in his claim by the Earl of Lincoln, and was actually crowned, as King Edward VI, in Dublin. The rebellion was eventually defeated.

1491. King Henry invaded France, but, shortly afterwards, entered into the Treaty of Étaples, in accordance with which he withdrew his forces from France in exchange for the promise of payment of £149,000, a large sum of money.

1492 and 1499. Another claimant to the throne, Perkin Warbeck, asserting that he was Richard, Duke of York, was expelled from France in 1492 under the terms of the Treaty of Étaples. In his attempt to overthrow King Henry, Warbeck reached as far as Taunton in Somerset with a large force before being defeated and becoming King Henry's prisoner, kept in the Tower of London. At first he was treated well by King Henry, and indeed, after admitting that he was an impostor, he was released from the Tower of London but kept under guard at court. After twice trying to escape from there, however, he was hanged, drawn and quartered in 1499.

1502. King Henry's eldest son, Prince Arthur, died. Consequently Prince Henry, the future King Henry VIII, became heir to the throne.

1503. King Henry's daughter Princess Margaret married King James IV of Scotland. This had important future consequences for both England and Scotland. The birth of their son, who would become King James V of Scotland, brought the House of Stuart into the line of descent from the House of Tudor; and this made King James V's grandson eligible, not only for the throne of

Scotland as the future King James VI, but also for the throne of England as the future King James I.

1509. Aged fifty-two, King Henry died at Richmond Palace.

(ii) Of special interest

King Henry VII tends to receive the respect of historians. The following is not untypical of what one can expect to read in any brief summary of his life: he brought the seemingly endless Wars of the Roses to an end and peace to the country; he pursued successful policies in the area of trade; and he left to his successors a united country after having established a new and powerful dynasty. It is, however, also accepted that he was strongly disliked by most of his subjects.

Generally representative is what is to be found in children's books.

From *A Nursery History of England*, published in the 1920s: 'King Henry VII was rather a wise king. He had some trouble in keeping the crown he had won, but he did keep it.'

From the most recent edition of the best-selling Ladybird *Kings & Queens*, published in 2014: 'Henry was a strong, learned and thoughtful king, who was fair in law-giving and very good at making and keeping money. His long reign brought peace and prosperity but he was never much loved by his subjects, as he lacked warmth and charm.'

Lest it be thought possible that books written for children are not sufficiently representative of historians in general, here are the closing words of probably the most thorough treatment of his reign, *Henry VII*, by Professor S. B. Chrimes, published in 1972:

'In the ultimate analysis, the quality of Henry VII was not that of a creator, but rather of a stabiliser, for lack of whom ships of State are apt to founder. For that quality, he stands out pre-eminent among British monarchs.'

~

The three quotations and that summary, even though they do not exclude the possibility of some serious imperfections in him and of his being unpopular with many of his subjects, must be close to being as opposite to what is factual as anything could be. What seldom, if ever, seems to receive even the smallest mention, even by historians writing for the adult market, is that there were few species of crime that King Henry's reign did not include, whether committed by him directly or indirectly. Indeed in that sense, which of course is far from a good sense, it is one of the most remarkable reigns in all English history.

For a start, his accession to the throne was fraudulent. Not only did he have no genuine claim of any kind, but he never succeeded in finding even a plausible *un*-genuine one. To take each of the only three possibilities of legitimacy in turn:

1. His royal descent through his mother, Margaret, of the House of Lancaster, whose royal descent was from John of Gaunt, the third son of Edward III.

    In the first place, this line had in the past been excluded from the throne by Act of Parliament. In the second place, there were members from the direct line of John of Gaunt senior to him and he therefore could not claim senior membership for himself until that direct line became extinct.

    In the third place, his mother was still alive, and indeed outlived him. If, therefore, either of them had the right to the throne, which in fact neither did, as we have seen, it was *she*, not he, who had this right.

2. Through his marriage to Princess Elizabeth, of the House of York, as has been suggested.

    In the first place, marriage to a member of a royal family had never before rendered a person eligible to be genuinely king; and he could only be king by what is called courtesy, a courtesy title being a title without any legal validity. In the second place, he was not even yet married to Princess Elizabeth, but only *pledged* to be married to her; and in any case he would hardly have welcomed, not only owing his crown exclusively to his wife, but owing it to a wife who was the representative of the rival and hated York family.

3. King by right of conquest.

    The majority of Henry Tudor's troops were English, and one cannot legally be a conqueror of a country of which one is already an inhabitant and citizen. A soldier in arms in his country can legally fight to *defend* it or to *preserve order*, but otherwise he is committing treason, and treason has always been held to be an even worse crime – and worthy of a more serious punishment – than murder.

Discussions with his advisers were lengthy and anxious. Their solution: to settle the crown on the head of himself and his heirs without any discussion at all, of either his right to the crown or the right of his future wife to the crown. In short, his assuming the title of King was a naked fraud.

Fully aware of this, Henry swiftly took steps to solidify his position as best he could.

His first step he had in fact taken well before the Battle of Bosworth. On Christmas Day 1483, two years before that battle, he had made a solemn oath in Rennes Cathedral in Brittany that he intended to marry Princess Elizabeth of York. She was the sister of one of the two Princes in the Tower, as they have been known to history, the elder of whom became King Edward V on the death of his father. After his victory at Bosworth, the new King Henry did what was necessary to fulfil his vow and he and Princess Elizabeth were married on 18 January 1486 at Westminster Abbey.

This new Queen was to feature uniquely in future history, incidentally. It is traditionally held that the image of the Queen on the 'court' cards of a standard pack of fifty-two playing cards is of her, which, if true, means that her portrait appears four times in every standard pack of cards sold anywhere in the world.

By the time he married Princess Elizabeth, Henry VII had taken his second step, which was to get himself crowned. His coronation took place at Westminster Abbey on 30 October 1485.

The union was of great significance for the future of the Tudor monarchy, as also for the future of England in general. The stained glass in the great rose window in the south transept of York Minster, commemorating their marriage, shows the combined red and white roses; and the joining of the Houses of Lancaster and York meant that the Wars of the Roses had finally come to an end.

The new King Henry's third step was to make sure that there was no opposition to his claim. In order to achieve this, he did what could hardly be more horrifying in its abuse of the legal system or more sinisterly immoral. He now declared himself King 'by right of conquest', and did so retroactively from 21 August 1485, the day *before* the Battle of Bosworth. Anyone who had fought for Richard against him could therefore be pronounced guilty of treason; which, in the first place, carried the death penalty, and, in the second place, gave Henry the right legally to confiscate the lands and property of King Richard III and transfer them to himself.

Henry's fourth step was to try to secure dynastic marriages for his children in order to strengthen his own position. Thus he arranged for the marriage of his elder son, Arthur, to Catherine of Aragon, the youngest daughter of, arguably, the greatest-ever Spanish monarchs, King Ferdinand and Queen Isabella, in doing so sealing an alliance with the then mighty Spain and giving the Spanish monarchy a strong motive to support him in his usurped position.

Fifthly and finally, he reintroduced an institution of the past known as the Court of Star Chamber (so called because of the stars on its ceiling), situated in the Palace of Westminster. The senior court in England, and supposedly for dealing with any wrongdoings by the lords and making them punishable for any abuse of power, it was in its new form purely an instrument of tyranny, and used to punish men who had offended him or his ministers. It had the express right to punish people who had not broken any law but had merely done actions which the judges deemed to be 'morally reprehensible': the Star Chamber could be completely subjective and arbitrary in its decisions, and, especially in future reigns, came to be used much more as an instrument of oppression than one of justice until it was abolished in 1641.

Also worth noting is the possibility that, as part of a programme to exterminate all those who had genuinely valid claims to the throne, King Henry was responsible for the deaths of the 'Princes in the Tower' that are commonly attributed to King Richard III. Certainly he had a motive for committing those murders, if they took place, which King Richard III had not had.

Tellingly, as well as interesting in its future consequences, Henry needed what no king had ever needed before, a personal bodyguard. He instituted for this purpose the Yeomen of the Guard, who are now England's oldest military corps, and indeed still wear a distinctive Tudor-style uniform.

~

There have been historians who have accepted that he was hated by most of his subjects during his reign. Two more events in his reign are even by themselves sufficient to make this no surprise.

One was the use by his officials of what has become part of the English language, Morton's Fork, a phrase which carries the meaning: a specious piece of reasoning in which contradictory observations lead to the same conclusion. Such reasoning is immoral even in an argument, of course, but what if it is used as an instrument to raise taxes?

The thought is shocking. A king is the person in a realm primarily responsible for the administration of justice, and in accordance with strict fairness. It is indeed arguably a monarch's most important duty. Yet, this is how his Lord Chancellor, Cardinal John Morton, Archbishop of Canterbury, and with King Henry's full approval, imposed taxes in order to fill the King's coffers. He decreed that no one was to be exempted from taxes. In his words to his tax collectors, as he required them never to take no for an answer and to tax all the King's subjects no matter what their circumstances:

> If the subject is seen to live frugally, tell him because he is clearly a money-saver of great ability, he can afford to give generously to the King. If, however, the subject lives a life of great extravagance, tell him he, too, can afford to give largely, the proof of his opulence being evident in his expenditure.

That such a crime against justice should have been committed by England's most senior representative of the Church, the Archbishop of Canterbury, and on the instruction of the man whose paramount duty it was to protect his subjects from injustice, is dismaying to an extent that is only rivalled by the failure of countless historians to give it due notice.

The result of 'Morton's Fork' was that, by the end of his reign, King Henry VII had accumulated the colossal personal fortune of £1.5 million, upwards of £1 billion of present-day money, and an amount unheard of and even scarcely to be imagined before his day.

For the second of the two events that I maintain are by themselves sufficient to have made King Henry hated, I simply invite my readers to return to the end of the last chapter and remind themselves of how Josephine Tey closed her book on King Richard III, using the hero of her book, Chief Inspector Grant, in the passage that begins: 'It was the settled and considered policy of the Tudors to rid themselves of all rivals to the throne ...'

Note the word 'policy'. Wholesale murder *as a policy*?

PART VII

THE REFORMATION: KINGS AND QUEENS OF ENGLAND, WALES AND IRELAND

CHAPTER TWENTY-FIVE

Still the House of Tudor

Introduction

What needs to be said to give an adequate picture of the next four reigns is different from what is to be found in almost any other historical work dealing with them to an extent that it would be difficult to exaggerate. It is therefore as well to introduce it with a mention of the main sources on which I have relied. Principally, there are two.

The most important of the two is *A History of the Protestant Reformation in England and Ireland* by William Cobbett. This first appeared in the 1820s, published in instalments. There are at least three remarkable things about this book. One is that even though Cobbett had nothing resembling academic qualifications, it is a solid and even brilliant work of scholarship. This is because of the second remarkable feature of it, which is that no fewer than four authors, all of them eminent in their fields, were involved in the best edition of it. The third is that, although it has stayed in print and sold well throughout the English-speaking world ever since its first appearance, no historian dealing with the period sees fit to mention it. Certainly I have never seen it mentioned in the bibliographies of books dealing with England's history.

The principal author, of the four eminent authors, is of course William Cobbett himself. He was a well-known politician, author and journalist of his time and, as he emphasises in the book, a staunch Protestant who cannot be suspected of Catholic bias. His evident motive for writing the book was out of fairness: to support the cause of Catholic emancipation at a time when Catholics in England were forbidden to enter certain professions or to become Members of Parliament, and when it was officially and legally a *crime* nationwide to attend Mass or to build a Catholic church.

A second contributor to the book was the author on whom Cobbett mainly based his history, John Lingard, whom we met in earlier chapters, and who was a Catholic whose groundbreaking scholarship is widely hailed. His *History of England, From the First Invasion by the Romans to the Accession of Henry VIII*, in eight large volumes, had appeared a few years earlier, in 1819; and, although Cobbett took full responsibility for the contents of his own book, it is clear from much of what is in it that Lingard's book was an important source.

A third contributor was another Catholic scholar, Cardinal Francis Aidan Gasquet, who lived in the second half of the nineteenth century and the early part of the twentieth century. He happened to come across Cobbett's book several decades after it had been originally published, and, at once recognising that it was potentially useful as a defence against anti-Catholic propaganda, he put together a new and improved edition of it. Realising that it was of the utmost importance for such a book that it should be *completely* error-free, he went through it critically, sentence by sentence, adding footnotes wherever either there were any doubts as to fact or he thought that a footnote would be helpful for any other reason, and also improving the construction of the book.

The fourth contributing author, Professor Thorold Rogers, like Gasquet, played no part in Cobbett's original version of the book, but an appendix consisting of material written by him was added by Gasquet in his revised edition. Rogers was a researcher and writer on economic history in England who was significant enough in that field to feature even today in current reference books such as the single-volume *Chambers Biographical Dictionary*.

Here, in Gasquet's words, is why Gasquet considered this appendix by Rogers, a Protestant, to be important enough to be included:

> It may pass through the mind of some readers that the picture drawn by Cobbett with such vigour, or even passion, must be an exaggeration, nay, a caricature. Yet the genius of the man

had divined and grasped the truth; and he only anticipated the results arrived at by the exact investigations of the present day. The late Professor Thorold Rogers, who devoted the whole of a laborious life to an enquiry into the economic history of England, comes, so far as this period is concerned, to the same conclusion as Cobbett himself. Indeed, the words in which he delivers what may be termed a scientific conclusion form almost a heavier indictment than that framed by Cobbett's imagination.

Let no one suppose that, because 'economics' is a technical and rather abstract term, it has little if any importance in the study of history by us ordinary folk. Very much to the contrary, for responsible adult citizens it is a *practical* subject of a great importance. Our economic circumstances are the background against which we live our lives and the single most important factor affecting us, whether we are rich or poor and whether we are in the upper or the lower levels of the society to which we belong.

Cobbett's *History of the Protestant Reformation* contains, therefore, in combination: in Lingard, an impressive scholar responsible for facts both full of interest and in many cases previously little known; in Cobbett, a justly renowned and even heroic defender of justice against injustice, as his political career showed; in Gasquet, another impressive scholar who took responsibility for checking and editing everything said by Cobbett; in Rogers, almost certainly the greatest English economic historian there has ever been; in Lingard and Gasquet, two authors representing the Catholic Church; and in Cobbett and Rogers, two authors representing the Church of England. Given the care and thoroughness that went into the book at each stage of its development, and the high degree of objectivity that can reasonably be supposed from its multiple authorship, it can perhaps be doubted whether, in all history, a single-volume book on history has comparable credentials for earning our close attention, our respect and our appreciation.

My other main source is simply some of the laws enacted by the various regimes that we shall be examining and which, being officially on record, cannot be successfully falsified. Of the available compilations of laws of England, I have found useful for our purpose Reeves's *History of English Law, From the Time of the Romans, to the End of the Reign of Elizabeth*, and in particular the edition by W. F. Finlason whose footnoted comments are important sources of information in themselves, as we shall be seeing.

~

I invite my readers, as they read what follows, to keep in mind the greatest crimes that are even only *alleged* of the thirteenth century's King John of supposed unparalleled wickedness. I invite them, further, to keep asking themselves whether his crimes, whether real or any alleged, do not pale into insignificance by comparison with those of the Tudor family's three Protestant monarchs, King Henry VIII, King Edward VI and Queen Elizabeth I, or vice versa.

CHAPTER TWENTY-SIX

'Bluff King Hal' Takes Spiritual Charge of His – Grateful? – People

King Henry VIII

Born 1491 and reigned 1509–1547. The second son of King Henry VII. The elder son, Arthur, having died, King Henry VIII succeeded to the throne on the death of his father.

(i) The main events of the reign in summary

1509. King Henry came to the throne. Immediately he had two of his father's chief ministers, Sir Richard Empson and Edmund Dudley, imprisoned in the Tower of London on the charge of constructive treason, and executed in the following year.

Constructive treason has been appropriately described as 'one of the law's most useful frauds', and surely there can be no other kinds of fraud that are as nauseating in their unscrupulous dishonesty. Since the word 'constructive' means 'treated as', 'constructive treason' does not mean genuine treason at all, which in turn means that it means whatever the authorities happen to want it to mean – making it a perfect instrument of oppression.

King Henry married his late brother's widow, Princess Catherine of Aragon, the fourth daughter of King Ferdinand and Queen Isabella of Spain. Catherine had already been briefly married to Henry's elder brother Prince Arthur, but Arthur had died less than a year after the wedding, at the age of only fifteen years. In order that

King Henry VIII

he could marry Catherine, Henry needed a dispensation from the Pope, because canon law forbade marriage to a brother's widow. On Catherine testifying that her marriage to Prince Arthur had never been consummated, Pope Julius II gave the necessary dispensation. King Henry remained married to Queen Catherine for twenty-four years.

1510. King Henry had Edmund Dudley executed.

1513. The Scots invaded England, and the English defeated them, inflicting terrible slaughter, at the Battle of Flodden Field, in which King James IV of Scotland was killed.

1515. Thomas Wolsey, whom Pope Leo X had earlier made Cardinal and was Archbishop of York, was appointed Lord Chancellor. In 1518 he became Papal Legate, and thus the most powerful man in the kingdom – even more so than the King, in that his decisive influence extended over both politics and England's Church. No English subject had ever been so powerful before.

1516. Queen Catherine gave birth to the future Queen Mary I.

1517. In Germany, Martin Luther, a Catholic monk, priest and professor of theology, who was later to break his freely taken vows of celibacy and to marry a nun whom he persuaded to break *her* vows, published what he called (translated) *Disputation of Martin Luther on the Power and Efficacy of Indulgences*, in which he alleged many abuses by the Catholic Church. This was to be known as *Ninety-five Theses*.

1520. King Henry and King Francis I of France met in an event known as the Field of the Cloth of Gold, renowned in history for its magnificence.

Henry entered into an alliance with the other great monarch of that time, King Charles V of Spain, who had recently also become the Holy Roman Emperor.

1521. King Henry VIII published a work, *Assertio Septem Sacramentorum* ('Defence of the Seven Sacraments'), in which he denounced Luther's *Ninety-five Theses* and defended the Church's seven sacraments against Martin Luther's attack.

Thomas More was knighted.

Pope Leo X conferred the title *Fidei Defensor* – 'Defender of the Faith' – on King Henry for having written the *Assertio*. Although British monarchs do not now recognise any authority in popes, they still officially use this title that was granted for the defence of the

Catholic faith. For instance, it appears in the 'FD' that is to be found on English coins as part of the monarch's title, under or next to the depiction of the king or queen.

1527. King Henry became enamoured of Anne Boleyn, the daughter of one of his courtiers, and applied to the then reigning Pope, Clement VII, for a declaration of the nullity of his existing marriage. Henry's argument was that, since Catherine was his brother's widow, his marriage to her had been invalid in the first place. (Catherine had by then, after no fewer than six pregnancies, given birth to only a single surviving daughter, Mary. No son had survived.) Since one of Pope Clement's predecessors, Pope Julius II, had *expressly* given the necessary dispensation to make the marriage of King Henry to Queen Catherine valid, Pope Clement was unable to give the decision that the King wanted.

1529. King Henry had Cardinal Wolsey indicted – officially accused – for failing to give him the support that he wanted in order to obtain the divorce. By then Wolsey had completed the building of the foundational stage of Hampton Court, situated in south-west London and later to be one of the world's greatest royal palaces. Wolsey resigned from four of his political offices and retired to his See at York. King Henry's close friend, Sir Thomas More, became Chancellor in his place.

Thomas Cromwell, who had been a member of Wolsey's household, started the meteoric rise that would lead to his controlling, under King Henry, all of King Henry's political affairs during the next decade.

1530. King Henry had Cardinal Wolsey arrested for high treason and committed to the Tower of London to await trial. On the way to the Tower, Wolsey died.

1532. Finding himself unable in conscience to support King Henry in the annulment of Henry's marriage to Queen Catherine, Sir Thomas More resigned from the Chancellorship. In the same year, King Henry secretly became betrothed to Anne Boleyn, bigamously.

1533. Determined to make his marriage to Anne Boleyn legitimate and valid, King Henry started a step-by-step programme to abolish the authority of the pope in England. His first steps were to outlaw all appeals to Rome, which until then could be made by anyone in the country, forbidding such appeals by Act of Parliament;

and then to arrange for the post of Archbishop of Canterbury to be filled by Thomas Cranmer, who was effectively his henchman. Cranmer at once annulled King Henry's marriage to Queen Catherine, whereupon King Henry married Anne Boleyn, who was half his age.

1534. As had been requested of him, Pope Clement finally pronounced his sentence on the claimed nullity of King Henry's first marriage. He declared the marriage lawful, and added that, if the King refused to take her back, he would be excommunicated.

An Act of Parliament, the First Act of Supremacy, was passed which (a) declared King Henry VIII, a layman with, at most, little ecclesiastical training, to be the Supreme Head of the Church of England, and (b) completely eliminated any authority of the pope in England.

The Act of Succession was then passed, pronouncing Princess Mary, Queen Catherine's daughter, to be illegitimate and thereby stripping her of the right to inherit the throne after her father's death. King Henry VIII's friend Sir Thomas More, the former Chancellor, refused to sign the Oath of Succession that confirmed Queen Anne's role as queen, because the preamble of the Oath repudiated the authority of the pope. Four days later, King Henry had More arrested and imprisoned in the Tower of London.

1535. Sir Thomas More, having been found guilty of treason for refusing to confirm his acceptance of the King's supremacy in the Church of England, was beheaded, as also, shortly afterwards, was Cardinal John Fisher, Bishop of Rochester, for the same reason. Both were later officially canonised by the Catholic Church as saints.

1536. In 1533, Queen Anne Boleyn had given birth to the future Queen Elizabeth, but, in three years of marriage, she had failed to produce a surviving son. King Henry had her beheaded on the grounds of adultery, treason and incest. *On the very next day*, he became engaged to Jane Seymour, one of the late Anne Boleyn's ladies-in-waiting, and ten days later married her. It is generally agreed by historians that there is insufficient reason to be certain that Anne Boleyn was guilty of the crimes of which she was charged.

1536–1539. All the monasteries and chantries in England, some 3,000 of them, were forcibly closed down. Their land, amounting to about a third of the acreage of England, was taken over by the King.

Some of this land he kept in his possession and the remainder of it he transferred to his principal supporters in this huge-scale robbery.

An immediate result of these unprecedented criminal activities that are tactfully referred to by historians as the 'dissolution' of the monasteries (the normal meaning of 'dissolution' is disintegration or coming-to-an-end, a *very* inadequate title for what took place) was that approximately 100,000 inhabitants of the monasteries – friars, monks and nuns – were left homeless and penniless. A further result was a massive destruction by fire of the books in all the monasteries' libraries, eliminating countless historical records as well as some of the most beautifully produced books that have ever existed.

The Reformation was often barbaric to an extent possibly without precedent. It was also oppressive to ordinary people. Prior to the Reformation a very large proportion of the land had been common land, where all could graze their animals and cultivate plots where they could grow their own vegetables. From the time of the Reformation until well into the eighteenth century, this land was gradually but systematically taken over by the rich landowners, in the process termed Enclosure. 'Enclosing' land was in reality stealing the use of it from everyone else and causing widespread abject poverty, including starvation. Between 1536 and 1650s, half of the peasantry of England was removed by enclosure from the land that was their livelihood and reduced to abject poverty and sometimes actual starvation. Furthermore, many of them were transported to the West Indies where they were worked as slaves on plantations and actually known as 'white slaves'.

1536. The separation of the English Church from Rome and what followed were deeply unpopular in England, and there were many risings of the people. The most threatening to King Henry was what is known as the Pilgrimage of Grace, in which the rebels who took part in it demanded the restoration of the traditional religion of England. This popular movement was initially so successful that those negotiating on behalf of King Henry promised in his name: a parliament to be held at York; suspension of the suppression of the monasteries; and a general pardon. Satisfied, the rebels then dispersed, but their decision turned out to be a naive one, since shortly afterwards the leaders were arrested and executed. The other undertakings were also breached as completely as though they had never been given.

1537. Jane Seymour died soon after giving birth to the future King Edward VI.

1540. On the advice of Thomas Cromwell, who had gained the King's confidence by being the official who took principal responsibility for destroying the monasteries, King Henry then married a German princess, Anne of Cleves. On meeting her, however, and at once disliking her appearance, he refused to consummate the marriage. In the same year he used his new authority as head of the Church of England to have their marriage annulled on the grounds of (a) non-consummation and (b) a previous engagement of hers to be married to Francis I, Duke of Lorraine. She did not contest the annulment, and King Henry was grateful and they became good friends. Within weeks of the annulment, he married Catherine Howard. He had Thomas Cromwell, because of his responsibility for the marriage to Anne of Cleves, charged with treason, condemned for treason without being allowed to speak in his own defence, and executed on the Tower of London's Tower Hill on the same day as his wedding to Catherine.

In the same year John Knox, originally a Catholic priest, introduced the new Protestant religion of Calvinism into Scotland and founded the Presbyterian Church of Scotland.

1541. At King Henry's command, the elderly Margaret Pole, Countess of Salisbury, was executed without her having known what crime she was accused of or in what manner the sentence had been passed. Because the main executioner was elsewhere, having been sent north to deal with rebels there, her execution was performed by 'a wretched and blundering youth' (as he was described by a diplomat Eustace Chapuys when giving an account of what took place to the Queen of Hungary) who hacked her head and shoulders to pieces. The reason for her execution was that her son, Cardinal Reginald Pole, who was forced to live overseas by King Henry's policies, had denounced both Henry's annulment of his marriage to Queen Catherine and his usurped supremacy in the Church. Unable to strike at Cardinal Reginald himself, King Henry vented his anger on the Cardinal's relations. (Considered a martyr, the Countess of Salisbury was beatified on 29 December 1886 by Pope Leo XIII.)

1542. War was declared against Scotland, which had been ravaging the English–Scottish border, and the Scots were quickly and thoroughly defeated. King James V of Scotland was so affected by the disaster for Scotland that he died, leaving his crown to his infant daughter Mary, who thus became Mary, Queen of Scots, with momentous results during the reign of Queen Elizabeth I.

1543. England and Scotland then entered into a treaty under which King Henry's son Prince Edward was to marry Mary, Queen of Scots.

King Henry married Catherine Parr, the daughter of a country squire descended from King Edward III. She had already been twice widowed.

1544. King Henry invaded France, and took possession of Boulogne.

1546. England and France entered into a treaty, the Treaty of Camp, in which France agreed to pay the huge sum of 2 million crowns within eight years, with Boulogne to be held as security until the payment was completed.

1547. King Henry VIII died. Catherine Parr, his sixth wife, survived him.

(ii) Of special interest

David Hume, the highly respected eighteenth-century philosopher, historian, economist and essayist, summarised his view of King Henry pithily as: 'A high-minded, magnificent, and generous prince.'

Can we lesser scholars accept that assessment?

A satisfactory appreciation of the many extraordinary events that took place in King Henry's reign would not be possible without some background knowledge of the state of English society at the start of the reign. For this purpose, I doubt if I can do better than quote directly from chapter 2 of Cobbett's *History of the Protestant Reformation*, both because his summary is succinct as well as excellent and because, a Protestant, he cannot be suspected of Catholic bias:

> Our ancestors became Christians about six hundred years after the death of Christ. And how did they become Christians? ... The work was begun, continued, and ended by

the Popes, one of whom sent over some monks who settled at Canterbury, and from whose beginnings the Christian religion spread, like the grain of mustard seed, rapidly over the land ... And in this religion with the Pope at its head, England continued to be firmly fixed for nine hundred years.

There never can have existed a state of society without an obligation on the land-owners to take care of the needy, and to prevent them from perishing for want. The landowners in England took care of their vassals and dependants. But when Christianity, the very basis of which is *charity*, became established, the taking care of the necessitous was deposited in the hands of the clergy ... The produce of where the priests officially resided was to be employed thus, as stated in a decree issued by a Bishop of York:

> Let the priests receive the tithes of the people, and keep a written account of all that have paid them; and divide them according to canonical authority. Let them set apart the first share for the repairs and ornaments of the church; let them distribute the second to the poor and the stranger with their own hands in mercy and humility; and reserve the third part for themselves ...

Thus the providing for the poor became one of the great duties and uses of the Church ...

Another great branch of the Catholic Church ... [was] the monasteries ...

The piety, the austerities, and, particularly, the works of kindness and of charity performed by the monks, made them objects of great veneration; and the rich made them, in time, the channels of their benevolence to the poor ...

The country people spoke of the monasteries with great reverence, and most grievously deplored the loss of them. They had large estates, were easy landlords, and they wholly provided for all the indigent within miles of their monastery.

England, more, perhaps, than any other country in Europe, abounded in such institutions ...

King Henry VIII succeeded his father, in the year 1509, to a great and prosperous kingdom, a full treasury, and a happy and contented people.

Here, now, is a summary of the most important details of King Henry's reign, as given by Cobbett, not all of which appear in most other works of history in which King Henry's reign is covered.

As soon as the new king came to the throne, he started undertaking what was necessary in order to marry his brother's widow Catherine. A dispensation from the Pope was needed, as prescribed by Church law, but it was easily obtained, and the marriage was celebrated less than two months after the King's accession.

Seventeen years later, having been suddenly 'taken' with one of the Queen's attendants, Anne Boleyn, he, as Cobbett puts it, 'affected' to believe that he was living in sin, in being married to the widow of his brother, and applied to the Pope for an annulment, though without remotely valid grounds, not least because the marriage had been *expressly sanctioned* by the Pope.

With the Pope obviously unable to grant the divorce, King Henry, as outlined in the introductory summary, resolved upon the extraordinary solution of eliminating the authority of the Pope in England and of making *himself* head of its Church. This meant, amongst other things, that he was suddenly in control of all the Church's property, including the monasteries, as well as of everything else relating to the Church.

The new 'Pope', as the King had now made himself, took the immediate step of making his henchman, Thomas Cranmer, Archbishop of Canterbury, the effect of which was that together they were the supreme judges in all Church matters.

In order to become Archbishop, Cranmer was consecrated in accordance with the usual form of such ceremonies, which included his having to swear obedience to the Pope.

'And here,' says Cobbett, 'a transaction took place that will, at once, show us of what sort of stuff the "Reformation" gentry were made.' Cranmer, immediately before being consecrated, went into a chapel where he declared on oath that he did not consider himself obliged by the oath that he was about to take, which he was doing only 'for the sake of form' to bind himself to anything that tended to prevent him from assisting the King in making any such 'reforms' as he might think useful in the Church of England.

At this point, I pause to invite my readers to wonder how it can be that the piece of alleged history that is now to follow, although to be found in several sources, never features in any other work of history dealing with King Henry's reign that they will have come across.

During the four years or so that the King and Cranmer were organising the divorce from Queen Catherine, the King had been keeping Anne Boleyn as his mistress for much of that period. Quoting Cobbett again:

> And here let me state, that, in Dr. Bayley's life of Bishop Fisher, it is positively asserted, that Anne Boleyn was the King's daughter, and that Lady Boleyn, her mother said to the King, when he was about to marry Anne:
>
> 'Sir, for the reverence of God, take heed what you do in marrying my daughter, for, if you record your own conscience well, she is your own daughter as well as mine.'
>
> To which the King replied:
>
> 'Whose daughter soever she is, she shall be my wife.'

Is it conceivable that this horrifying allegation is true? Certainly Cardinal Gasquet thought it worth examining the topic with considerable care, and, although he is restrained in his summing up, the fruits of his research leave no reasonable alternative to what Cobbett stated his belief to be. He says in his footnote that readers who consult the examination of the matter made by Mr. D. Lewis in his Introduction to Sander's *Anglican Schism* will find, on pages xxxi–xliv, Lewis's conclusion tellingly summarised as follows:

> We have now the confession of Cranmer, of the two Houses of Parliament, and of the King, that the impediments (*sc.* to his union with Anne) were not only diriment [impediments making a marriage null and void from the outset], but also unknown. Admitting, then, that the impediment was unknown, we must shut out from the question the relations of Henry with Lady Elizabeth Boleyn, and with her daughter Mary, for

they were *not* unknown, and nothing remains but to accept the fearful story told not by Dr. Sander only, nor by him before all others, and say that, at least by the confession of the King and both Houses of Parliament, Anne Boleyn was Henry's child.

I resume my summary of Cobbett's account.

Three years after becoming King Henry's mistress, Anne Boleyn became pregnant. This meant that matters had to be rushed. Monstrously, a private marriage took place in January 1533. King Henry was still married to Queen Catherine, however, and, as Cobbett put it, 'it might have seemed rather awkward, even amongst "Reformation" people, for the King to have two wives at a time!' Extraordinary manoeuvrings were therefore needed and took place. In April 1533, Cranmer wrote to the King begging him to give him, Cranmer, permission to hold a trial for a divorce so that the King might no longer live in danger of committing an 'incestuous intercourse' – the incest being because of his being married to his brother's widow.

As Cobbett relates the story, 'the King graciously condescended to listen to this spiritual advice of his pious primate'. Then Henry, *as Head of the Church*, gave this 'pious primate' a licence to conduct a trial for the divorce. After sending a citation to Queen Catherine to appear before him, which she treated with appropriate scorn, Cranmer then proceeded to declare the marriage null from the beginning, and made this known to the King, 'beseeching him to submit to the will of God'. King Henry did so submit, and Cranmer then held a court at which he declared, under his authority derived from the successors of the Apostles, that the King's marriage to Catherine had been unlawful.

Eight months after her marriage to King Henry, Anne Boleyn gave birth to a daughter, the future Queen Elizabeth. A further three months and sixteen days later, however, Anne was beheaded on a scaffold, on a death-warrant signed by King Henry after being charged with, as noted earlier, treason, adultery and incest.

Immediately before the beheading took place, King Henry, in his capacity of 'Head of the Church', had ordered Cranmer to go through the necessary procedure to *divorce* him from Queen Anne.

This was not an easy task for Cranmer, since it was he who had originally exercised his authority in Church matters to pronounce the marriage with Anne to be lawful and valid. Nevertheless, on 17 May 1536, two days before the execution on 19 May, he reversed that pronouncement with the words: 'In the name of Christ, and for the honour of God,' the marriage 'was, and always had been, null and void'. Once again in Cobbett's words: 'Thus was the daughter, Elizabeth, bastardised by the decision of the very man who had not only pronounced her mother's marriage lawful, but who had been the contriver of that marriage!'

The King, no doubt symbolically of something, dressed himself in white on the day of his former wife's execution. As we have seen, *on the following day*, he became betrothed to Jane Seymour.

All that was the origin of the Reformation.

I trust my readers have been gaping, at least metaphorically, at what they have been reading in the last several paragraphs. It is also surely worth asking ourselves: how do the worst crimes that are even only *alleged* of 'Bad' King John, compare, in their moral status, with the undoubted *conduct* of 'Bluff King Hal' – the king who, we are widely led to believe, freed his country from the 'tyranny' of Rome?

As we have also seen, King Henry's next important step in bringing about the Reformation was the *practical* suppression of the Pope's supremacy in Church matters. To deny the King's supremacy was made *high treason*, and, what is more, to refuse to acknowledge that supremacy *under oath* was legally deemed to be a denial of that supremacy. Sir Thomas More, the Lord Chancellor, and John Fisher, who was Bishop of Rochester, the two greatest and most popular public figures of the day, both of them faithful servants of both King Henry and his late father, refused to take the oath to accept the suppression of the Pope's supremacy, as they obviously could not in conscience. They were put to death.

After this horrifying beginning, judicial bloodshed was speedily multiplied. And it embraced a remarkably wide range of victims because in 1521 King Henry had written a book denouncing the new religion of Martin Luther, and, although he was now bent on destroying the Catholic Church as it had been, he was equally bent on eliminating Luther's followers and therefore sent both Catholics and Protestants to the stake – *both* those who rejected the fantastic new notion of his spiritual supremacy *and* those who preached against traditional Catholic doctrines.

~

Cobbett devotes space to the social effects of King Henry's policy of freeing his nation from the Church of Rome. Before the Reformation started, there belonged to the Church, he points out, 645 monasteries, 90 colleges, 110 hospitals, and well over 2,000 chantries and free chapels. All these were seized. As mentioned earlier, some of them the King kept for himself, and others he gave to those who had assisted him in his plundering. Thus came into existence the great majority of 'stately homes' that are one of England's great tourist attractions today. Shamelessly, those who became owners of the stolen property often did not even change the names of their plunder, so that, for instance, the house called Woburn *Abbey* is still the family seat of the Duke of Bedford.

In Cobbett's words:

> Observe that this property was not by any means used for the sole benefit of monks, friars, and nuns; that most of its rents flowed immediately back amongst the people at large; and, that, if it had never been an object of plunder, England never would, and never could, have heard the hideous sound of the words *pauper* and *poor-rate*. The 'Reformation' despoiled the working classes of their patrimony and robbed them of that relief for the necessitous which had been confirmed to them by the law of God and the law of the land.

~

I have saved until last an extract from a document of that period that is especially interesting reading. I invite my gracious readers to deduce its authorship:

> When Luther so impudently asserts (and that against his own former pronouncement) that the Pope has no kind of right over the Church ... I cannot but marvel that he should expect his readers should be so credulous and stupid ... Luther shows how void he is of charity by not only destroying 'himself' in his rage but, much worse, trying to draw everyone else into

destruction too, as he strives to dissuade them from their obedience to the chief bishop ... He considers not ... what horrible punishments are deserved by him who refuses to obey the highest prince of all and the supreme judge on earth ... He refuses to submit to the law of God, desiring to set up his own law instead ... Let us on the contrary, by hating and detesting his wickedness, sing with the prophet: 'I have hated the unjust and have loved thy law.'

Yes, that is a word-for-word translation from chapter 2 of King Henry's theological treatise, *Assertio Septem Sacramentorum*, which earned him from the Pope the title of 'Defender of the Faith'.

I take my leave of King Henry with this reminder of the assessment of him by the eminent historian David Hume: 'A high-minded, magnificent, and generous prince.'

CHAPTER TWENTY-SEVEN

Nine-year-old King Edward VI Exercises His Spiritual Charge Over His People

King Edward VI

Born 1537 and reigned 1547–1553. Third surviving child and only son of Henry VIII, by Henry's third 'wife' Jane Seymour (who died soon after giving birth to him).

(i) The main events of the reign in summary

1547. King Edward VI came to the throne aged nine. His uncle on his mother's side, Edward Seymour, Duke of Somerset, was at once appointed Protector of England, to be assisted by a council of sixteen, and was effectively the ruler of England in the first half of King Edward VI's reign.

In order to enforce the marriage treaty between King Edward and his first cousin Mary, Queen of Scots, that had been entered into by King Henry VIII in 1543, England, under Somerset, went to war with Scotland and defeated Scotland at the Battle of Pinkie. Mary escaped to France, where a new contract was entered into on her behalf, to marry the future King Francis II of France.

The Vagrant Act was passed, enacting that 'any determinedly idle and able-bodied vagrant might be adjudged by two magistrates, to anyone wanting him, as a slave, branded with a letter V, and kept in slavery for two years'.

1547–1549. The 'Reformation' initiated by King Henry VIII developed further, with the Duke of Somerset and Archbishop Cranmer carrying out many further *reforms*, as the drastic overturning of long-standing traditions of that time are sometimes called. These included the removal of images of saints and of paintings in churches, and, in the First Act of Uniformity in 1549, making illegal the celebration of the Catholic Mass that had been celebrated throughout England during the previous nine centuries, and introducing the First Book of Common Prayer and in doing so changing the language of the church services from Latin into English. His reign is perhaps best remembered for the production of the prayer books that were the forerunners of the Church of England's present-day Book of Common Prayer.

1550–1552. The Duke of Somerset was deposed as Protector, and replaced by John Dudley, Earl of Warwick, he being the son of the Edmund Dudley whom King Henry VIII had had executed for treason. Warwick then created for himself the title of Duke of Northumberland. The Duke of Somerset remained briefly in the council, but in 1552 Northumberland had him arrested and executed.

1553. Persuaded, in effect instructed, by the Duke of Northumberland, King Edward nominated as his heir to the throne Lady Jane Grey, the Duke of Northumberland's daughter-in-law.

(ii) Of special interest

I pose this question. Could there *conceivably* ever have been a reign in which the, up until then, record number of executions that took place in King Henry VIII's reign came anywhere near to being matched?

However unbelievably, there was in fact one reign in which that record was *exceeded* – indeed comfortably exceeded, if 'comfortably' is not too unsuitable a word in such a context. Exceeded, moreover, by one of King Henry's own children, and with the distinction of having appeared in the *Guinness Book of Records*.

By which of his children? Perhaps his eldest daughter Mary, to whom the label 'Bloody' is traditionally attached?

As readers will be realising because of the chapter in which these questions are asked, yes, it was in the reign of King Edward VI. I quote from the 1989 edition of the *Guinness Book of Records*, page 206: 'Capital punishment reached a peak in the reign of Edward VI (1547–53), when an average of 560 persons was executed annually *at Tyburn [in London] alone.*' (My italics.)

Annually – year after year after year.

~

This was the reign in which the *true* Reformation at last began, and in which Protestantism at last became *visible* in England, with the abolition of the Mass and other Catholic services, and the introduction of the new Book of Common Prayer composed by Archbishop Cranmer.

What I am now about to give are two facts that must surely be as difficult to believe as anything else in this book.

First fact: the boy-king was declared to be, in effect, the *Pope* of England. To him belongs the distinction of having been the first, and so far only, nine-year-old to be publicly acknowledged as, for practical purposes, the Vicar of Christ, possessed of the Keys given to St. Peter (Matthew 16:19), and England's spiritual head and leader.

Second fact: in the year 1547 of King Edward's reign, the law listed as 1 Edward VI c.12 was passed, making it *high treason* to deny this child's spiritual supremacy over all his subjects, either by word or in writing or in print.

These are the remarkable words with which the child-king-pope promulgated his first religious legislation:

> We would not have our subjects so much to dislike our judgement, so much to mistrust our zeal, as though we either could not discern what were to be done or would not do all things in due time. God be praised, we know both what by His word is meet to be redressed, and have an earnest mind, by the advice of our most dear uncle ['Protector' Somerset], and other of our Privy Council, with all diligence to set forth the same, as it may most stand with God's glory and edifying

and quietness of our people; which we doubt not but all our obedient and loving subjects will quietly and reverently tarry for.[4]

Slipping momentarily into twenty-first-century vernacular: you couldn't make it up.

Nor should it be thought that King Edward was a mere puppet, carrying out what was imposed on him. He was, genuinely, an ardent Protestant.

~

By comparison with the huge-scale robbery that now took place in Edward's reign, Henry had in fact been moderate, restricting his and his fellow gangsters' plunder to millions of acres of Church land and Church treasures of inestimable value. In the reign of Edward an Act was passed (1 Edward VI c.14) conveying to the young Pope all the possessions of the schools, colleges and guilds of England, excepting only those of the colleges of Oxford and Cambridge and the guilds of London.

Nor did King Edward's newly acquired possessions find their way to the poor, for their benefit. They quickly passed into the hands of his privy councillors. In doing so they created a new class of super-rich that had never existed before. And this was at great cost to the ordinary Englishman, since one consequence was that education was virtually extinguished in England – other than for the very privi-leged who could afford private tutors for their children – until some new schools and colleges were established about fifty years later.

CHAPTER TWENTY-EIGHT

The First Two Tudor Queens

Lady Jane and then Queen Jane Grey

Born 1536/1537, reigned 1553 and died 1554. She was the great-granddaughter of Henry VII and granddaughter of Henry VIII's youngest sister Mary. Although the period between the death of King Edward and the loss of the throne was thirteen days, she is known as 'the nine-days Queen' because it was supposedly three days after King Edward's death that she was informed (a) of the King's death and (b) of the intention to put her on the throne, and it was the day after the third day that she was proclaimed queen, which was nine days before Queen Mary took the Crown.

The main events of the reign in summary

1553. King Edward bequeathed his throne to his first cousin once removed, Lady Jane Grey, rather than to his Catholic half-sister, Mary. The Duke of Northumberland, England's Protector during the second half of King Edward VI's reign, had arranged for one of his sons, Lord Guildford Dudley, to be married to Lady Jane in order to maintain his position as the power behind the throne. When the Duke of Northumberland told her that King Edward VI, shortly before his death, had excluded both his half-sisters, the Princesses Mary and Elizabeth, from the throne on the grounds of their previously decreed illegitimacy and had named her as his successor, Lady Jane doubtless thought that she had no realistic choice other than to accept, even though she was only sixteen years old and had had no preparation of any kind for queenship. It was a strange situation, however, in that it was the first time in history that someone whom most people had never even heard of had become a reigning monarch.

She was exceptionally intelligent and well-educated, and even at her young age was regarded as one of the most learned women of her day. When only thirteen or fourteen, she had startled Roger Ascham, a notable English scholar of the time who was the tutor for Latin and Greek of the future Queen Elizabeth, when he came across her reading Plato's famous work of philosophy, *Phaedo*, in the original Greek and clearly relishing it. She was also an ardent Protestant, and went so far as to correspond with prominent fellow-believers both in England and overseas.

The fifth of Northumberland's eight sons, Robert Dudley, who was to have a considerable role during the reign of Queen Elizabeth, marched with a small army into Norfolk, where Mary was assembling her followers. His attempt to capture Mary was eventually unsuccessful, however, and it soon emerged that most people in the country with any influence were not prepared to support such a change in the right of succession and favoured Princess Mary, whereupon Northumberland's army deserted him, and both father and son surrendered. Northumberland, Robert Dudley and four of his brothers were convicted of treason and condemned to death, but the new Queen Mary was characteristically merciful and only Northumberland and one of his sons, Guildford Dudley, were executed.

The late King Edward's half-sister Princess Mary – a worthy granddaughter of Queen Isabella of Castile, who, with her husband King Ferdinand of Aragon, had set the stage for Spain to become a united country for the first time since the Muslim invasions in the eighth century – swiftly launched a counter-revolution that was widely backed by the 'common people'; and on the thirteenth day of her reign, the 'nine-days Queen' found herself Mary's prisoner in the Tower of London, with Mary, the rightful heiress, being proclaimed Queen. Northumberland was executed.

Queen Mary, at once showing herself to be by no means a typically blood-thirsty Tudor, made it clear that she intended to spare ex-Queen Jane and her husband, and she was even planning to set Jane free in due course. The Protestant ardour of Lady Jane, however, was so great that, writing letters from prison, she continued to oppose the restoration of the Catholic religion by Queen Mary. Eventually realising that some show of justice was needed if only to satisfy her supporters, Queen Mary sent her for trial. Four months later, Lady Jane was sentenced to death for high treason.

Queen Mary then refused to sign the execution warrant. In 1554, however, a large landowner, Sir Thomas Wyatt, led a Protestant rebellion aiming at replacing Queen Mary with her half-sister Elizabeth, the only daughter of Anne Boleyn. Lady Jane's father was one of the leading conspirators in the rebellion. With Queen Mary now having no reasonable alternative to agreeing to her execution, Lady Jane was at last beheaded.

Queen Mary I: 'Bloody Mary' or 'Good Queen Mary'?

Born 1516 and reigned 1553–1558. She was the eldest surviving child and daughter of Henry VIII, by his first wife, Catherine of Aragon.

(i) The main events of the reign in summary

1553. Nine days after Lady Jane Grey was proclaimed queen by 'Protector' Northumberland, Mary, whether Queen or Princess, arrived in London, had Lady Jane Grey arrested, and, shortly afterwards, was crowned queen. At once, all the statutes relating to religious matters passed in the reign of King Edward VI were annulled; married priests were dismissed from their livings; use of the new Prayer Book introduced by Archbishop Cranmer was forbidden; and the Mass was restored and enthusiastically welcomed in most parts of England.

1554. Mary declared her intention to marry Philip, the future King of Spain, as a step towards the restoration of the pope's authority in England. As noted earlier, one result was that Sir Thomas Wyatt led a rebellion in order to depose her. Thanks to Queen Mary's courage and leadership, the rebellion was crushed; and both Lady Jane Grey and her husband, Northumberland's son Lord Guildford Dudley, were eventually executed.

Queen Mary I

Queen Mary married Prince Philip of Spain. After the marriage, Parliament issued a decree that he should have no share in the government of England, to his displeasure at this indignity.

Cardinal Reginald Pole, the son of the Countess of Salisbury for whose execution King Henry had been responsible, and who had been living in Italy for many years, came to England as papal legate. On 30 November, all the members of the House of Lords and the House of Commons, assembled in Whitehall, went down on their knees and acknowledged their anti-Catholic errors and, still on their knees, begged to be received back into the bosom of the Church. Cardinal Pole granted absolution to all of them of all the sins of heresy and schism that they had committed during the reigns of Kings Henry VIII and Edward VI. All the statutes against the authority of the pope that had been passed in those two reigns were then repealed.

1555. The laws dealing with heresy were revived, and the nation of England became reconciled to the Catholic Church and to the pope.

Four Protestant clergyman who had been leaders in the Protestant revolt, John Hooper, Rowland Taylor, Nicholas Ridley and Hugh Latimer, were tried and convicted of heresy and burnt at the stake.

1556. Cardinal Pole was appointed Archbishop of Canterbury.

Thomas Cranmer, the Archbishop of Canterbury whom Cardinal Pole replaced, was convicted of heresy and burnt at the stake.

Queen Mary's husband became King Philip of Spain and left England to take up his position.

1557. King Philip visited England for the second and last time and persuaded Queen Mary to support Spain by declaring war on France. The war started well for England, with the comprehensive defeat of the French at the Battle of St. Quentin.

1558. England's success in the war was reversed, even to the extent that the French ended up taking possession of the port of Calais, which had been in English ownership for 210 years and by then was the last English possession in France.

Queen Mary died at St. James's Palace, London.

(ii) Of special interest

Queen Mary is typically referred to with such epithets as 'bigoted' and 'vengeful'.

In the words, once again, of William Cobbett, however:

Our deceivers have taught us to call Queen Mary's reign
the reign of 'Bloody Queen Mary'; while they have taught
us to call that of her sister, the 'Golden Days of Good
Queen Bess'. They have taken good care never to tell us
that, for every drop of blood that Mary shed, Elizabeth
shed a pint; that Queen Mary gave up every fragment of
the plunder of which the deeds of her predecessors had put
her in possession and that Queen Elizabeth resumed this
plunder again, and took from the poor every pittance which
had, by oversight, been left them; that Queen Mary never
changed her religion, and that Queen Elizabeth changed
from Catholic to Protestant, then to Catholic again, and
then back again to Protestant; that Queen Mary punished
people for departing from that religion in which she and
they and their fathers had been born, and to which she had
always adhered, and that Queen Elizabeth punished people
for not departing from the religion of her and their fathers,
and which religion, too, she herself professed and openly
lived in *even at the time of her coronation*. Yet, we have been
taught to call the former 'bloody' and the latter 'good'! How
have we been deceived!

Queen Mary's first political acts on coming to the throne were to
pay all debts owed by the crown and substantially to reduce taxation.
After that, most urgent in her mind was to restore the Catholic religion in every respect as it had been before the Reformation, from its
very outset the cause of such widespread misery. Here she faced
grave difficulties, arising from the massive plunder that had been
part of the Reformation and the number of plunderers who had
greatly profited from it. If Parliament were to organise the restoration of the pope's spiritual supremacy in the kingdom, the pope was
likely to insist on the stolen property being restored, since theft of
Church property was sacrilege. To give up their stolen riches was
unthinkable to the newly rich.

Faced with the alternative of remaining Head of the Church, as
she had suddenly become, which would be hateful to her, she decided

to compromise with the plunderers and to allow them to keep their stolen property.

With the robbers thus satisfied, another of the scarcely believable events of which there had already been so many took place.

Three years earlier, the two houses of Parliament had legally established Cranmer's Church and declared it to be 'the work of the Holy Ghost'. Now, the Queen having agreed that the plunderers could keep all their plunder, the two Houses, as noted in the introductory summary, confessed that they had been guilty of defecting from the true Church, said that they sincerely repented of this defection, and resolved to repeal all the laws that had removed the authority of the pope, and on 29 November Cardinal Pole, in the name of the pope, absolved the two Houses and the whole nation, whereupon the members of the two Houses, on their knees, said 'Amen' in unison.

~

Does Mary deserve the nickname 'Bloody' that is customarily attached to her?

She *opened* her reign with a *lack* of severity that could almost be considered criminal in itself. Here is *The Early Tudors* of the Oxford History of England series, which was certainly not written in order to defend the Catholic Church: 'The Queen of her own accord showed a mercy deemed excessive even by the imperial ambassadors [the ambassadors representing Spain and the Holy Roman Empire], themselves advocates of clemency. Only three men lost their lives.'[5]

The most prominent of these was of course the Duke of Northumberland, who had organised and led the attempt to make Lady Jane Grey Queen immediately after Edward VI's death. As we have seen, Lady Jane Grey was not executed then, even though she had been found guilty of high treason and sentenced to death. Nor was Cranmer executed then, despite his having been a party to the plot and who indeed had signed the treasonous document assigning the crown to Lady Jane, for which he could legally have been immediately hanged, drawn and quartered. And the long pardon rolls testify to Mary's complete forgiveness of scores of others.

Even to the Duke of Northumberland she could not restrain herself from showing what mercy she reasonably could. The sentence pronounced on him was that he should suffer the standard traitor's death – execution by being slowly hanged, disembowelled and then dismembered – but Mary commuted it to beheading, almost infinitely less painful.

The fact is that it was only after a *second* rebellion, that of Sir Thomas Wyatt in 1554, that Mary became convinced that there was no alternative to taking really severe measures to protect her throne against traitors and the Church against internal enemies.

For information about Queen Mary's reign, historians have tended to rely on John Foxe's voluminous *Book of Martyrs*, published in 1563 and one of the best-selling books in early English literary history. Made publicly available *by law* in every cathedral and in the most important churches, it is full of accounts of the supposed martyrdoms of Protestants in Queen Mary's reign, and, in the words of a modern author, Robert Tombs, in his *The English and Their History*, 'was, and still remains, the basis of much that we think we know about this time, because Foxe is the best, and often the only, source for many of its memorable episodes.'

Finlason, however, in his edition of Reeves's *History of English Law*, dismisses the *Book of Martyrs* as hopelessly unreliable, with Foxe being even 'so reckless as actually to record circumstantially the death of persons who lived until long afterwards'.

Does there yet remain any justification or excuse for referring to Queen Mary as 'Bloody'? If there does, it must be the penalty inflicted during her reign on four churchmen whose names have reverberated down through the centuries ever since: Hooper, Latimer, Ridley and Cranmer, widely revered as great martyrs for religion. To allow a fair comparison between this aspect of Queen Mary's reign and those of her non-Catholic predecessors and successors, we must have a quick look at the careers of these four clergymen, of whom only Cranmer has crossed our path so far.

The Protestant William Cobbett, in paragraph 250 of his book (the italics for emphasis are mine in every case):

> Hooper was a monk. He broke his vow of celibacy and married. He was the ready tool of the Protector Somerset, whom he greatly aided in his plunder of the churches. He was a cooperator in all the monstrous cruelties inflicted on the

people during the reign of Edward, *and was particularly active in recommending the use of German troops to bend the necks of the English to the Protestant yoke.*

Latimer began his career, not only as a Catholic priest, but as a most furious assailant of the Reformation religion. By this he obtained from Henry VIII the bishopric of Worcester. He next changed his opinions, but he did not give up his Catholic bishopric! *In the reigns of Henry and Edward he sent to the stake Catholics and Protestants for holding opinions which he himself had before held openly, or that he held secret at the time of his so sending them.*

Ridley had been a Catholic bishop in the reign of Henry VIII, *when he sent to the stake Catholics who denied the king's supremacy and Protestants who denied transubstantiation.* In Edward's reign he was a Protestant bishop; denied transubstantiation himself; and got the bishopric of London by agreeing to transfer the greater part of its possessions to the rapacious ministers and courtiers of that day.

A pretty trio of Protestant 'saints' ...

Then, of course, there was Cranmer, about whom we have already learnt much. Worth noting is part of the oath that he took when entering into England's most important ecclesiastical office.

I will be faithful and obedient to the Blessed Peter, the Holy Apostolic Church of Rome, and our Lord Pope Clement VII, and his canonical successors. I will not consent, either by advice or act, to any injury being done to them in any manner. I will not reveal to any one, to their disadvantage, any information with which they may have entrusted me. I will not consent to any injury being done to them in any way. I will not reveal their intentions to any one. I will assist in the preservation and defence of the Roman Papacy and the royalties of St. Peter against every one. I will carefully preserve, defend, increase, and promote the rights, honours, privileges, and authority of the Church of Rome, and of our Lord the Pope and of his successors. To the best of my ability I will persecute and assail all heretics, schismatics, and rebels against our said Lord and his successors. So help me God and these Holy Gospels.

Those promises were made with both hands on the open book of the Holy Gospels.

The period during which Cranmer kept his sacred oath was short. King Henry, England's 'Defender of the Faith', had required him to fulfil urgently the task of getting rid of Queen Catherine, who, as Dean Hook, a well-regarded nineteenth-century Protestant authority, says in his *Lives of the Archbishops of Canterbury*: 'had, for a quarter of a century, lived as an honest wife, a courteous queen, and a pious Christian, and was not to regard herself as a cast-off concubine, and her daughter – her only surviving child – as a bastard.'[6]

Still the 'bloodthirsty' queen would not sign the order for his execution.

Then came the Wyatt rebellion which, but for Mary's courage and resourcefulness, as to which most Protestant historians are agreed, would have cost her the throne. At long last she was persuaded that severe measures were necessary – and what sane person would not have been so persuaded?

Even so, she would not sign the order for Cranmer's execution. Instead, she had him arraigned on the charge of heresy, remaining consistent in her reluctance to visit the ultimate penalty on him for a crime against *her*, but no longer holding any such view in respect of his multiple and grievous treasons against God.

Should we deplore this treatment of heresy as a capital crime? Be that as it may: at the very least, it is surely not only wholly inappropriate that Cranmer should face trial for the *very same offence* as that for which he had consigned numerous people to death in the previous two reigns, and indeed, under King Henry, had *himself sent* others to the stake as heretics, for expressing *the very same Protestant opinions* as *he himself* undoubtedly held while he was condemning them.

~

There is another subject concerning which instructive comparisons can be made between conditions in Queen Mary's reign and conditions in the other reigns of the sixteenth century. I believe that what is to come, presented as it is by learned authors obviously unprejudiced in the direction of their findings, *does* need to be said, from which, however, it does not follow that everyone needs to read it. Readers who prefer to jump straight to the last paragraph of this chapter are welcome to do so.

For the purpose of introduction, here is the *Encyclopaedia Britannica*, 13th edition:

> [Mary's] name deserves better treatment than it has generally met with; for she was far from cruel. Her kindliness to poor people is undoubted, and the severe execution of her laws seemed only a necessity ... Her conduct as queen was certainly governed by the best possible intentions ...

'Her kindliness to poor people is undoubted ...' By contrast, here is how the treatment of the poor in the reigns of King Henry VIII and King Edward VI is summarised by a *non*-Catholic author, Brooks Adams, in his book *The Law of Civilization and Decay* published in 1895:

> In 1530, Parliament published the first of a series of Vagrant Acts (22 Henry VIII c.12). At the outset the remedy applied was comparatively mild, for able-bodied mendicants were only to be whipped until they were bloody, returned to their domicile, and there whipped until they put themselves to labour. As no labour was supplied, the legislation failed, and in 1537 the emptying of the monasteries brought matters to a climax. Meanwhile Parliament tried the experiment of killing off the unemployed; by the second Act vagrants were first mutilated *and then hanged as felons*. (27 Henry VIII c.25)

For further details of these products of remarkable Tudor inventiveness and resourcefulness in legislation, I turn once again to W. F. Finlason's edition of Reeves's *History of English Law*. After noting that the number of beggars and vagabonds increased markedly in the reign of Henry VIII, Reeves says: 'It has been a favourite opinion that the provision for the poor had never been an object of necessity till the abolition of religious houses had deprived many persons of a support from the gifts regularly made there; but the first statute we shall mention was passed before that event …'

'Not so', says Reeves's editor, in a footnote to that passage, and continues:

[Reeves] had forgotten that this Act was after the dissolution of many of the lesser religious houses in the fifteenth year; and after he had already plundered the clergy, under pretence of their having obeyed the authority of a papal legate licensed by himself; and moreover, it was after he had forced them to acknowledge him as supreme head of the church. Moreover, it was after he had resolved upon the dissolution of his marriage with Catherine, and after the friars (who were mendicants) had preached against these measures. [Reeves] had forgotten that the friars were mendicants, and might be called vagrants; and that the present statute was in reality directed against them is the more probable because there was a similar statute directed against the monks after the dissolution of the religious houses.

Now let us turn to another Act of Henry's reign, passed five years later, 27 Henry c.25. Reeves, page 259:

Public officers were to take up all children in every parish within their limits under fourteen and above five years of age, that were found begging and in idleness, and appoint them to masters of husbandry, or other crafts or labours, to be taught, and so be enabled to get their living; and they were to give them some of the charitable contributions to equip them for such service. Such as refused to go to service, or who departed from it without reasonable cause, being above twelve and under sixteen years, were to be publicly whipped.

Such legislation was never dreamt of in pre-Reformation England. Continuing with Reeves:

Once in every month the above public officers were to cause privy search to be made, by night or by day, as they thought proper, for vagabonds and suspected persons, and all persons were to assist in such search. Those found a second time in a state of vagrancy were not only to be whipped, but to have the upper part of the gristle of the right ear clean cut off. For a third offence he was to be committed to prison by a Justice, and then indicted for wandering and loitering; and if found guilty he was to suffer death as a felon and enemy of the commonwealth.

On this piece of legislation, Finlason comments in one of his footnotes: 'It may, it is believed, be safely said that this was the first time in the history of this or any other country in which the absence of regular employment (which might, it is obvious, be no fault of the party) was made punishable with death!'

Yes, in Reformation England, *inability to get work* was a crime worthy of the *death penalty*, for the first time in history in any country in the world. Why do we not read about this in other history books dealing with the period? Why is it *King John* who is called 'Bad King' and *Queen Mary* who is called 'Bloody'?

So much for Henry's reign. Here is Reeves's summary of a statute published in the first year of the reign of King Edward VI, 1547.

Vagrancy and begging seems to have become a greater grievance than ever; and in the solicitude to correct and suppress the effects of this evil, the parliament, during these two reigns, more than once changed its system of conduct. The first interposition was by statute 1 Edward VI c.3, which laments the increase of vagabonds and declares them to be more in number than in other regions.

What measures, do you suppose, good readers, were eventually taken in order to deal with the problem, the making of which had nothing to do with the vagabonds themselves?

The design now was to treat such offenders with extreme severity. This Act, therefore, begins with repealing all former laws for the punishment of vagabonds and sturdy beggars; it then ordains that any person may apprehend those living idly, wandering and loitering about without employment, being servants out of place, or the like, and bring them before two Justices, who, upon proof by two witnesses or confession of the party, were to adjudge such offender to be a vagabond, and to cause him to be marked with a hot iron on the breast with the mark of V, *and adjudge him to be a slave* ...

Yes, in the reign of King Edward VI slavery was reintroduced in England as the punishment for having been impoverished by the – what shall we call them? – 'domestic policies' of Bluff King Hal and of those who subsequently ruled in Edward's name. Continuing the sentence at the point at which I broke it off:

... to be a slave to the person who brought him and presented him for two years. This person was to keep him upon bread, water, or small drink, and refuse-meat, and cause him to work, by beating, chaining or otherwise, in any work or labour he pleased, be it ever so vile. If such slave absented himself from his master within the two years for the space of fourteen days, then he was to be adjudged by two Justices to be marked on the forehead, or the ball of the cheek, with a hot iron with the sign of an S, and further adjudged to be a slave to his master for ever; and if he run away a second time, he was to be deemed a felon.

No, this is not legislation belonging to pagan Rome at its cruellest and most degenerate. It is a not untypical law passed in England shortly after the Reformation had started to take hold and to bring about its inevitable effects and before Queen Mary had succeeded to the throne.

Queen Elizabeth I

CHAPTER TWENTY-NINE

'Good Queen Bess' or 'Bloody Queen Bess'?

Queen Elizabeth I

Born 1533 and reigned 1558–1603. The second daughter of Henry VIII, by his second 'wife' Anne Boleyn, and half-sister of Queen Mary.

(i) The main events of the reign in summary

1558. On the death of her half-sister Queen Mary, Queen Elizabeth came to the throne. She *immediately* made Lord Robert Dudley Master of the Horse – the Dudley who, for his part in the attempt of his father, the Duke of Northumberland, to make Lady Jane Grey Queen of England, had been imprisoned in the Tower of London and condemned to death, but then spared.

Dudley had been confined in the Tower of London by Queen Mary at the same time as the then Princess Elizabeth had been, and it was widely suspected that there was a more than casual relationship between them even though he was at the time married to the former Amy Robsart, the daughter of a large Norfolk landowner. From the beginning of Queen Elizabeth's reign he was known to be her 'favourite', and he was to be her suitor for many years.

1559. Queen Elizabeth was crowned at Westminster Abbey, and the third stage of the Reformation began. Within a year of her ascending the throne, the Protestant religion had been restored. The Second

Act of Supremacy – the first such Act had been passed in the reign of King Henry VIII – declared the Sovereign to be the Supreme Head of the Church.

A Second Act of Uniformity enacted that 'all persons inhabiting the realm should attend the Church of England, under penalty of a fine of one shilling for those who did not'.

The Revised Prayer Book was issued.

1560. Lord Robert Dudley's wife Amy was killed by falling down a flight of stairs, a sufficiently unlikely cause of death to cause a scandal which lasted for the rest of Dudley's life and made it, practically speaking, impossible for him to marry Queen Elizabeth.

1562. Queen Elizabeth fell ill with smallpox. Believing her life to be in danger, she asked the Privy Council to make Robert Dudley Protector of the Realm.

John Hawkins and Francis Drake, later to become Sir John and Sir Francis, made their first slave-trading voyage to America.

Queen Elizabeth, fully recovered, gave assistance to the Protestant Huguenots in the French Wars of Religion.

1564. Queen Elizabeth created Robert Dudley Earl of Leicester.

1568. Mary Stuart, Queen of Scots from 1542 to 1567, now began to feature prominently in England. On the death of Queen Mary, she had become the senior living descendant of an English monarch, since Elizabeth was the daughter of Anne Boleyn, whose marriage was not only null in the eyes of those – everyone holding the traditional religious beliefs – who held King Henry's marriage to Catherine of Aragon to be indissoluble, but also in the eyes of *King Henry himself*. Queen Elizabeth had no legitimate title to the throne other than what could be conferred by Parliament outside the traditional roles of the British monarchy.

Mary, Queen of Scots, had spent most of her childhood in France; had married the man who became King Francis II of France; had returned to Scotland on the death of her husband; had married her first cousin Lord Darnley, who in 1567 was mysteriously murdered; and had then married the man widely suspected of the murder, the Earl of Bothwell, which had caused some of the Scots noblemen to rebel. Defeated in the war that had ensued, she was captured, imprisoned and compelled to abdicate in favour of her son, who became King James VI of Scotland.

In 1568, she escaped from prison but suffered another military defeat and then took refuge in England, where she hoped for the protection of her cousin Queen Elizabeth. Since, however, Mary was thought by those who had remained with the religion of their ancestors to be the rightful queen of England, Queen Elizabeth, rather than offering her hospitality, had her taken prisoner and kept her in prison for eighteen years.

1568–1586. There were several plots and conspiracies, real or only apparent, organised by Catholics to rid England of Queen Elizabeth, none of them successful. The best known of these is the Babington Plot in 1586, thought by some to have been a fabrication by Queen Elizabeth's Secretary of State, Sir Francis Walsingham, to provide a pretext for the execution of Mary.

1569. There was a rising, known as the Rising in the North, under the Earl of Northumberland and the Earl of Westmorland, in an attempt (a) to bring back 'the old religion', which Queen Elizabeth had sworn at her coronation to uphold and protect, and (b) to secure the release of Queen Mary. The rising was brutally suppressed.

1570. Pope Pius V, whose authority Queen Elizabeth had accepted under a solemn oath when she came to the throne, excommunicated Queen Elizabeth, declared her to be no longer Queen of England, and released all her English subjects from allegiance to her. Pope Pius's bull opened with a long list of Elizabeth's crimes but based its sentence of deposition essentially upon her desertion of the Catholic Church. Profession of the Catholic faith had long been a recognised condition throughout Christendom of the right to rule a Christian nation. The bull made no direct allusion to her illegitimacy.

By now, at the age of thirty-seven, Queen Elizabeth had lost her hair and her eyebrows, and her teeth were yellow, and a little later were to become black. King Henry had been horribly diseased because of youthful dissipation and it is probable that this was the cause of the ill-health of his only three children who survived childbirth. Mary was constantly ill until she died aged forty-two, Edward even more so until swept away by consumption aged fifteen, and Elizabeth as above.

1578. A policy was initiated of torturing Catholics. This policy was executed by Richard Topcliffe, famed for his sadism and inventive cruelties, under the authority of the Queen, Lord Burleigh and, later, Lord Burleigh's son, Sir Robert Cecil.

1584. Sir Walter Raleigh established a colony in North America and called it 'Virginia', after Queen Elizabeth, the supposedly Virgin Queen.

1586. Mary, Queen of Scots, was sent to trial. She was found guilty of being involved in the Babington Plot.

1587. On 8 February Mary, Queen of Scots, was executed on the instruction of Queen Elizabeth for the supposed crime of treason. Queen Elizabeth hesitated long before signing the order for the execution, and then pretended that it had been executed contrary to her instructions.

1588. The mighty Spanish Armada, consisting of a fleet of 129 massive ships, launched an attack on England. The provocation was considerable. During his voyage round the world, Drake had committed several acts of piracy, plundering Spanish ships carrying gold to Spain, and, in the event known as 'Singeing the Beard of the King of Spain', even sailing into Cadiz harbour and, without any due cause, destroying forty Spanish merchant ships. England defeated the Armada.

1599. The Earl of Essex, one of Queen Elizabeth's favourites, led an expedition to Ireland.

1600. The First Charter was granted to the East India Company, which in due course was to lead to India becoming part of the British Empire.

1601. The Earl of Essex led a revolt against Queen Elizabeth to have her deposed, and was executed.

1603. Queen Elizabeth died.

(ii) Of special interest

Queen Elizabeth I is generally considered to come closest to Kings Canute and Alfred in deserving to be known as 'the Great'. A book about her published in 1958, by the historian the late Elizabeth Jenkins, is actually called *Elizabeth the Great*, and many other historians take much the same view of her. Here is what is said in three modern books.

The English and Their History by Robert Tombs (2014): 'Her virtues, and vices, did much to keep the country safe throughout her long reign. However one describes them, these characteristics – caution, cunning, cleverness, procrastination – give her some claim to be considered England's greatest monarch.'

A Short History of England by Simon Jenkins (2011): 'She had brought her nation glory and peace. Elizabeth was surely the greatest of England's rulers.'

From *Elizabeth the Queen* by Alison Weir (reprinted in 2009):

Queen Elizabeth was such a fascinating and charismatic character that her life as queen merits a book of its own ... This is a study of personal government at its best ... She would identify herself with her people and work for their common interests. She would bring peace and stability to her troubled kingdom. She would nurture it, as a loving mother nurtures a child ... The Queen ... also brought unity to her people by effecting a religious compromise that has lasted until this day, and making herself an enduring focus of their loyalty. She had enjoyed a unique relationship with her subjects which was never seen before and has never been since. Few Queens have ever been so loved ...

The most fitting epitaph to this extraordinary woman is to be found in the pages of Camden's biography: 'No oblivion shall ever bury the glory of her name; for her happy and renowned memory still liveth and shall forever live in the minds of men.'

Furthermore, by the name, Gloriana, which she bestowed upon herself, she is more honoured by today's Royal Family than are any of their other predecessors; since 'Gloriana' is the name of the royal barge, with its gilded prow, now used by the Royal Family on the Thames, and was, for instance, part of the celebration of Her present Majesty's Diamond Jubilee when, carrying the Royal Family, it led a flotilla of some fifty boats under Tower Bridge, where the Tower canon boomed the traditional sixty-two-gun salute.

A true successor to King Alfred the Great, it seems.

~

Sad to say, it does not seem possible to agree that those representations of Queen Elizabeth, which are similar to those of most historians, come within any distance of reality. Rather, a not-inappropriate question could even be: was Queen Elizabeth the single most evil woman in the whole of recorded history? I do not put that question lightly. Would anyone like to suggest any candidates, or even only a single candidate, for that terrible title who could be credibly considered to be her superior?

My first witness is, once again, the legal historian W. F. Finlason, in the edition of Reeves's *History of English Law* edited by him and published in 1869:

> The law and legislation of the present reign [Queen Elizabeth's] upon the subject of religion were based upon the principle of despotism, and in that respect were marked by the same spirit as that which had pervaded the reign of Henry VIII and Edward VI. In a word it was the spirit of tyranny. So the rapacity which characterised the previous reigns was equally characteristic of the present. *The conduct of Elizabeth with regard to the Church was worse than that of the worst tyrants of the Norman sovereigns.* During the whole of her reign the confiscatory laws passed under Henry VIII and Edward VI were rigidly enforced, *and all colleges, or hospitals, or charities which had escaped their rapacity were seized by the queen. The system of confiscation involved many charities that were not obnoxious to the law* [that is to say, were doing no harm].[7]

~

At her coronation, Queen Elizabeth took the ancient and customary oath – the same oath that Queen Mary had taken a few years earlier: to maintain 'the laws and customs granted to [the people of England] by the ancient kings of England, and especially the laws, customs and privileges granted to the clergy and people by the glorious King St. Edward [the Confessor] ... and towards God, Holy Church, and to clergy and people, peace and accord in God ...'

She kept that oath for just six weeks. What follows, in summary, is the relevant information provided by Cobbett, in paragraphs 267, 268 and 269 of his *History*.

In 1559, in the first year of her reign, Elizabeth enacted the Act of Uniformity. Attacking at the very root the consciences of all Catholics in her realm, more than half the English population in 1559, it directed that the Catholic Mass, the central part of the religion of England during over a thousand years, should at once be outlawed. The only church services that could legally be attended were the almost entirely new church services based on the government-ordered Protestant Book of Common Prayer, and attendance of these was *obligatory*, with huge penalties for those who refused, and the penalty of death for those who persevered in their refusal.

All her subjects were obliged, *on pain of death*, to take the oath of supremacy, acknowledging the Queen's supremacy in 'spiritual' matters and, in doing so, renouncing the pope and becoming apostates from the Catholic religion. In Cobbett's words: 'Thus was a very large part of her people at once condemned to death for adhering to the religion of their fathers, *and moreover for adhering to that very religion in which she had openly lived until she became queen, and to her firm belief in which she had sworn at her coronation.*'

It was made high treason for a priest to say Mass, or to come into the kingdom from abroad, and also for anyone to harbour a priest who said Mass.

Under such laws, continues Cobbett, 'hundreds upon hundreds were butchered in the most inhuman manner, being first hung up, then cut down *alive*, their bowels then ripped out, and their bodies chopped into quarters – *only* because the unfortunate persons were too virtuous and sincere to apostatise from that Faith which this queen herself had at her coronation, in her coronation oath, solemnly sworn to adhere to and to defend!'

Cobbett then asks:

Where are you to find persecution and cruelty like this inflicted by Catholic princes? Elizabeth put, in one way or another, more Catholics to death *in one year*, for not becoming apostates to the religion *which she had sworn to be hers, and to be the only true one*, than Mary put to death *in her whole reign* for having apostatised from the religion of her and her fathers, and to which religion she had always adhered. Yet the former is called, or has been called, 'Good Queen Bess', and the latter 'Bloody Queen Mary'.

Is not what Cobbett has just told us truly fantastic?

Nor can what Cobbett has just told us reasonably be doubted. I offer for confirmation the greatly respected Protestant constitutional historian Henry Hallam, in his *Constitutional History of England*:

> The Statute of Uniformity trenched [encroached] further on the natural rights of conscience; prohibiting – under pain of forfeiting goods and chattels for the first offence, of a year's imprisonment for the second, and of imprisonment during life for the third – the use by a minister, whether beneficial or not, of any but the established liturgy, 'and imposing a fine of one shilling *on all who would absent themselves from church on Sundays and holy days* [of which there were seventy-seven]'. Since a skilled craftsman, such as a carpenter, could expect to earn about ten-pence (less than a shilling) a day, even a fine of a shilling would have been crippling for a large family; but it was only the beginning. Later in Elizabeth's reign the head of a *non-conforming* family was subjected to a progressively accumulating monthly fine of £20 for the first month, £40 for the second, £60 for the third, up to a maximum of £200, when the *recusant* was bound over in the sum of £200 until he or she conformed – vast sums of money in those days.[8]

~

No fewer than seven Acts relating to treason were passed in Elizabeth's reign. Sufficient for our purposes will be to look at a representative four of them.

1. As may be remembered from the last chapter, the first Act of the first Parliament of so-called 'Bloody Mary's' reign *reduced* the number of offences constituting treason, so that the only ones remaining were those contained in King Edward III's Act of Treason 1 of 1352. These addressed genuine treason and were necessary for the safety of the realm and its ordinary citizens. Those of my readers who have been embracing the concept of 'Good Queen Bess' will surely have supposed that

the new queen, 'so loved' by her people, quickly set about out-doing Mary in liberalising the laws. Having recently looked at one of the first Acts of Mary's reign, let us now look at the very first Act of Elizabeth's, '1 Elizabeth c.1'. Under it, words spoken and written and actions done against the Royal Supremacy – Supremacy that was *spiritual* as well as temporal, let it be noted, since Queen Elizabeth was now grasping back what Mary had voluntarily abandoned – were punishable as follows:

For a first offence, all real and personal property was for-feited, real property being immovable property such as land and buildings.

For a second offence, the penalties of Praemunire were inflicted. These were loss of all civil rights, forfeiture of goods and chattels (movable property) as well as of land, and imprison-ment 'during the royal pleasure'.

For a third offence, *the penalties for high treason were inflicted.*

2. Two more Acts followed, '5 Elizabeth c.1' and '13 Elizabeth c.1'. Both of them drastically increased the scope of treason and changed its definition. Then, in 1581, a further Act made it *high treason* to 'reconcile or to be reconciled to 'the Romish Religion' (23 Elizabeth c.2) – that is to say, the religion to which St. Augustine had converted the English a thousand years before, and which had prevailed until the time of King Henry VIII and which Queen Elizabeth *had sworn to uphold.*

3. Perhaps most remarkably of all, in 1585 an Act (27 Elizabeth c.2) was passed which made it high treason *merely to have been ordained a priest* in the religion which Elizabeth *had sworn by solemn oath to uphold.* This applied to anyone ordained since the first year of her reign. Under this single statute alone 123 priests were hanged, drawn and quartered during the reign of Queen Elizabeth.

The fortunate people who harboured or gave comfort to priests were not in fact adjudged guilty of treason, but only of an *ordinary* felony. This meant that they were subjected *only* to hanging, rather than to hanging, drawing, cutting off the privy parts, and all the rest.

4. With Queen Elizabeth evidently not yet content with her efforts
    to be 'so loved' by her people, 35 Elizabeth c.2 enacted the
    following:

    • Anyone who during a month refused to attend public worship
      was committed to prison.
    • If those so committed should persist in their refusal for three
      months they were obliged to leave the country.
    • Those refusing this condition or returning after banishment
      were subject to capital punishment as felons.

This last Act, incidentally, was called 'An Act to retain Her
Majesty's Subjects within due Obedience'. *To retain within due
obedience!* What *kind* of obedience? *Religious* obedience was the
obligation of the 'loving' subjects of 'Good Queen Bess', under penalty
of imprisonment and then execution if their consciences forbade them
to abandon the religion that Queen Elizabeth had solemnly sworn to
uphold.

Queen Elizabeth's death was not a happy one. During her last
illness she recalled a prophecy that she would die naturally in bed,
and she refused to go to bed, instead stretching herself out on cush-
ions outside her bedroom. There she remained for ten days, fully
dressed, fasting and sleepless, with her eyes fixed on the ground and
a finger always in her mouth, and uttering no word of repen-
tance. When she was clearly close to death, the Archbishop of
Canterbury and other prelates approached her, but she told them to
be packing, declaring that she knew full well that they were 'hedge-
priests' – a colossal irony given that she herself had been responsible
for the creation of these 'ministers of God' whom she now denounced
as worthless.

~

So much for Queen Elizabeth I, revered as she is by most historians.
To those who think it an exaggeration to wonder whether she could
possibly have been the most evil woman that ever lived, I put the question: What more would she have needed to do in order to earn that
title?

PART VIII

AFTER THE REFORMATION: KINGS OF ENGLAND, WALES, IRELAND, SCOTLAND AND ELSEWHERE

CHAPTER THIRTY

The House of Stuart Comes South

King James VI of Scotland and I of England

Born 1566 and reigned as King of Scotland from 1567–1625 and as King of England, Scotland and Ireland 1603–1625.

King James I of England, the only son of Mary, Queen of Scots, and the great-great-grandson of King Henry VII, was the first of the Stuart monarchs of England. He was already James VI of Scotland when he succeeded to the English throne on the death of Queen Elizabeth, having reigned there as King James VI since 1567, when he came to the throne as a one-year-old infant, because of the deemed abdication of his mother Mary, Queen of Scots. He reigned as King of England, Scotland and Ireland from 1603 to 1625.

(i) The main events of the reign in summary

1603. King James VI of Scotland became King James I of England, Scotland and Ireland, uniting the crowns though not the countries. Immediately on his arrival in England, a plot to set Lady Arabella Stuart, a great-great-granddaughter of King Henry VII, on the English throne was discovered. Sir Walter Raleigh, who had achieved renown as a notable explorer of the distant world in Queen Elizabeth's reign, was implicated in it and committed to prison in the Tower of London, where he remained for thirteen years.

1604. A peace conference at Somerset House resulted in, at last, peace between England and Spain.

A conference at Hampton Court failed to resolve the differences in religious teaching between the Anglican Church headed by King James and the Puritan critics of the Anglican Church, those Puritans being the fore-runners of those who were to become politically dominant in the Oliver Cromwell era in the 1650s. The result was contests between King James and his Parliaments that gave rise to a struggle for authority and power which was to reach its climax with the judicial murder of King James's son, King Charles I, in the next reign. The purpose of summoning Parliaments was to provide King James with the money he needed to administer his kingdoms in addition to what he could already gain from customs and other duties.

1605. The Gunpowder Plot, appearing to be an attempt by Catholics to blow up the King and Parliament, was discovered in time to frustrate whatever would otherwise have happened. The plotters were executed in the following year, and severe laws were passed against the Catholics in England. Exactly what led up to this event in its final stages has always been a subject of debate. What is certain is that the Earl of Salisbury, the Secretary of State, knew of the plot more than a week before the attempt to carry it out took place, and yet did not mention it to the King for some days after learning of it. Many have supposed that he either invented the plot or, having learnt of it, infiltrated the plotters with his own agents and then allowed it to continue for the purpose of propaganda and an excuse to introduce the further anti-Catholic measures that were indeed instituted. As can be part of the very nature of conspiracies, no conclusive evidence exists either way. A result was greatly increased hostility towards Catholics.

1607. The Earls of Tyrone and Tyrconnel, who had been the leaders of the current opposition to the English rule in Ireland that had started with an invasion by the Normans in the twelfth century, ended their rebellion and fled to Europe. Ulster, two-thirds of which is today known as Northern Ireland, had recently been colonised by Protestant invaders from England and Scotland, resulting in an oppression of the native Irish there that was to continue for some three centuries.

The English Parliament rejected political union with Scotland. King James therefore continued to be king of two separate countries.

1610. The struggle between King James and the House of Commons became more severe, with neither side achieving a winning position. Eventually, King James dissolved the Parliament.

1611. The Authorised Version of the Bible, often known as the King James Version, was published.

Lady Arabella Stuart, his earlier rival for the throne, was imprisoned.

1612. King James's eldest son, Henry, Prince of Wales, died of typhoid fever, leaving his younger brother, Prince Charles, heir to the throne.

Heretics were burnt at the stake for the last time in English history. The particular crime held to be heretical by the Anglican Church, of which King James was the official head, and for which this punishment was inflicted, was denial of the doctrine of the Holy Trinity, and maintaining that Jesus Christ was *not* God as well as man.

1614. A Second Parliament was summoned, sometimes known as the Addled Parliament because it did not pass a single Act. King James dissolved it and summoned no further Parliaments for seven years.

1615. George Villiers became King James's favourite, nicknamed by him 'Steenie' and even 'Sweet Steenie', and was to become his constant companion, his closest adviser and his leading statesman. In due course he became Earl of Buckingham and then Duke of Buckingham.

1616. With King James much in need of money, Sir Walter Raleigh was released from prison and led an expedition to Guiana, in search of the legendary city, virtually synonymous with gold and wealth, known as El Dorado. He had already led one such expedition back in 1594. Part of Guiana was to become British Guiana in the nineteenth century.

1618. King James, when giving Sir Walter Raleigh permission to conduct a second expedition to Guiana, had also given him orders not to enter into any conflict with the Spaniards of that region. During the expedition, Raleigh disobeyed those orders, and on his return he was executed, allegedly for treason, in fact for disobedience to the orders that he had been given.

The terrible Thirty Years War began – the King of Spain and other Catholic princes on one side, and Protestants, mainly in Bohemia, now known as the Czech Republic, on the other. King James had an indirect involvement in it, in that his daughter Elizabeth had married one of the Catholic princes, but he refused to give assistance to his son-in-law.

1620. Negotiations with Spain were opened for a marriage between Prince Charles, King James's heir, and the daughter of the King of Spain, the Infanta Maria Anna.

The 'Pilgrim Fathers' set sail for America in a ship called the *Mayflower*.

The first titled newspaper, *Corante*, appeared for sale.

1621. A Third Parliament. Leading statesman Lord Bacon (Francis Bacon) was impeached by the Commons for bribery and corruption; was condemned; and was deprived of all his offices and heavily fined.

1623. Marriage negotiations between Prince Charles and the Infanta Maria Anna were broken off when, during a secret visit to Spain with Buckingham, Prince Charles refused to submit to the condition imposed by the Spanish King that he should become a Catholic.

1624. A Fourth Parliament. Supplies, the money needed in order to conduct a war, were at last voted, and war against Spain was declared.

(ii) Of special interest

Even during his reign King James I's reputation was attacked, but never more effectively than, some 200 years later, by the historian Lord (Thomas Babington) Macaulay in his *The History of England from the Accession of James II*. In the first chapter of the book, a strangely titled book in that, at least in outline, it covers Britain's history from earliest times, Macaulay first assails King James I's defence of the absolute rights of monarchs, and then proceeds:

By his fondness for worthless minions, and by the sanction he gave to their tyranny and rapacity, he kept discontent constantly alive. His cowardice, his childishness, his pedantry, his ungainly person and matters, his provincial accent made him an object of derision ...

Perhaps no less telling, in its influence in creating the generally unfavourable verdict on the first King of Great Britain, was the single phrase, often attributed to King Henry IV of France, with which an author contemporary to him, Sir Anthony Weldon, dismissed him as: 'The wisest fool in Christendom' or, correctly translated, 'the most learned fool in Christendom'.

King James was certainly ungainly in his behaviour – in speaking, eating, ordinary manners and with a strange and erratic way of walking. He had the misfortune, too, that his tongue was noticeably too big for his mouth, which interfered with his speech and caused him to look strange when he was drinking. There was, however, much more to him than this. Here is Roger Lockyer, in his *James VI and I* published in 1998: 'James is probably the best-educated ruler ever to sit on an English or Scottish throne, and the only one with any claim to be a political philosopher. He constructed a formidable theoretical justification of monarchy as the most valid form of government.'[9]

Lockyer accepts that he promoted favourites, and gave them too much influence and power. Undoubtedly, too, James sold titles. He even created an entirely *new* title, that of the baronet – what amounted to a hereditary knighthood – and offered this title to anybody who was prepared to pay the price at which he offered it. What, however, was ultimately behind his unpopularity with many historians is that he was a stout and genuinely convincing defender of the Royal prerogative, which is the customary authority and immunity that only a sovereign can possess. Nor, as Lockyer has pointed out, was there anything absurd about that. King James's interpretation of it was disputed in his reign; and in a court decision known as the Case of Proclamations in 1610, Sir Edward Coke and other leading judges insisted that the royal prerogative was limited, for instance stating that the monarch could make laws only through Parliament. In his recording of the final judgment, Coke first of all stated that 'the King cannot change any part of the common law, nor create any offence, by his proclamation, which was not an offence before, without Parliament,' and then concluded: 'It was resolved that the King has no prerogative but that which the law of the land allows him.'

Other than in Venice and the United Provinces (present-day Netherlands), monarchy, although admittedly in different forms, was the standard form of government throughout Europe, which indeed it had been for as long as monarchy had existed in Europe. Was King James objectively right in maintaining that there was no obvious really good alternative to monarchical rule? This is how the distinguished eighteenth- and early nineteenth-century politician the second Viscount Wentworth expressed his answer to a question such as that: 'The authority of a king is the keystone which closeth up the arch of order and government, which contains each part in due relation to the whole.'

In other words, take away the authority of a king or enfeeble it, and the whole construction, the work of many centuries, would come crashing to the ground.

And even Sir Edward and his fellow judges were not suggesting that the monarch's powers be abolished, or even much modified. Rather, Sir Edward was stating that there were limitations on the part of a monarch: that these powers only existed within the framework of the existing common law.

It is important that both the traditional theory of monarchy in England and the somewhat different position of King James I be understood.

Traditionally, monarchy was considered to be the best form of government, not least because the rich and powerful of the nation are inclined to oppress the poor, and a monarch is able to be the strongest check on this. Since, however, kings are themselves capable of being tyrants, acting unjustly and oppressing the poor, as did Henry VIII, instead of ruling for the benefit of their people, it was also important that there be checks on what the king could do to prevent him from abusing his power. The first check was held to be the Church, which was believed to be the depository of God's power and to possess the right, exercisable by the reigning pope, to excommunicate a king and even in extreme circumstances to depose him for grave offences. A second check was provided by the law of custom concerning the king, as expressed in the coronation oath. Thus, for instance, although it is true that the king is not subject to

conventional laws, of which he is the fount, and cannot be prosecuted for breach of laws that his subjects *can* be prosecuted for, it is
also true that he obtains the crown by customary law and is then
bound by customary law relating to kings, having the right to exercise his power only in accordance with the existing body of
constitutional custom.

In other words, in terms of the customary constitution of the
Kingdom of England, King James I was overstating his royal rights
and powers. In his book written when he was King of Scotland but
not yet of England, *The True Law of Free Monarchies*, which he liked
to quote in Parliament to remind its members what their place was,
he said:

> The State of monarchy is the supreme thing on Earth ... As
> to dispute what God may do is blasphemy, so is it treason in
> subjects to dispute what a king may do ... A good king will
> frame his actions according to the law, yet he is not bound
> thereto but of his own goodwill.

Thus for James the theologian and theorist, the king had a divine
'right to govern wrong', and could not be legitimately criticized or
challenged, let alone resisted, if he did. This contrasts sharply with
the more traditional view appealed to by Coke, according to which
the king's powers were limited by natural law and the unwritten constitution so that arbitrary royal Acts had no force in conscience and
could be disregarded by the courts, though resistance could not
extend to regicide or revolution.

~

On King James in general, well worth noting are the words of an
exact contemporary of his, the French ambassador M. de Fontenay,
whom King James's mother, Mary, Queen of Scots, had sent as her
agent to make an assessment of her son. (After Mary was forced off
the throne of Scotland in 1567, leaving him as king in her place
when he was only thirteen months old, they were never to see each
other again, and his mind was continually poisoned against his
mother by those surrounding him.)

He grasps and understands quickly; he judges carefully and with reasonable discourses; he restrains himself well and for a long time. In his demands he is quick and piercing, and determined in his replies. Of whatever thing the dispute, whether it be religion or anything else, he believes and maintains always what seems to him most true and just.[10]

And I recommend anyone who, influenced by such as Macaulay, doubts the justice of that description to read, as examples of James at his best, his published letter titled *Basilikon Doron* written to his son Henry (who, as we have seen, in fact died before succeeding his father), and especially the very first treatise he published as King of England, *A Counterblaste to Tobacco*. To many of his contemporaries who were both profiting from tobacco and addicted to it, the *Counterblaste* was embarrassingly unanswerable.

The reality is that the cause of much of the opposition to King James, some of it unscrupulous, during his reign was his whole-hearted support for the union of England and Scotland as a single kingdom with a single Parliament, as was eventually to happen, though brought about by shameless means as we shall be seeing. As he put it in a speech in the House of Lords directed at the Commons, it was his deepest wish to leave behind him at his death 'one worship to God, one kingdom entirely governed, one uniformity in laws'. He was opposed in this by strong vested interests, and was unsuccessful, and indeed to this day there is not 'one uniformity in laws' between the two countries. His arguments were powerful, however, and, as Lockyer pointed out above, it can be claimed on his behalf that – with, arguably, the exception of King Alfred the Great some eight centuries earlier – he was the only king or queen of England who can be rated as a genuine philosopher.

Although James was undoubtedly an accomplished scholar, he met his match in his pamphlet war with the phenomenally learned Cardinal (later Saint) Robert Bellarmine and was reduced to the ignominy of accumulating scriptural texts allegedly proving that the pope was the Antichrist. While his limitations as a constitutional lawyer were highlighted in his stand-off with Coke and his limitations as a theorist were highlighted in his debates with Bellarmine, my aim has been to make the point that much of the animosity of later writers against James was due not to his having defended monarchy *badly* but to his having dared to defend it at all.

~

One incident early in James's reign sheds light on the esteem in which Geoffrey of Monmouth was then held as a historical source:

In 1604 King James asked Parliament for the authority to assume the title of King of Great Britain, to replace his two titles of King of Scotland and King of England. The House of Commons refused. James could not understand why there should be any objection to a title which in law was already his – the isle was Brittany, he said, and therefore, being King of the whole island, he would be King of Brittany, as Brutus and Arthur were, who had the style and were the kings of the whole island.

Although the King's request was not accepted, it was *not* suggested that grounds for refusal should include any doubt that Brutus and Arthur had been kings of all Britain. The *only* reason given was that the moment that 'the Parliament gives the King the name of Great Brittany, there followeth necessarily … an utter extinction of all the laws now in force.'[11]

Thus in a dispute on the matter of the utmost gravity, which concerned the entire future of the country and involved scholars and statesmen of the calibre and renown of Sir Edward Coke, Sir Francis Bacon and Sir John Fortescue, and in which it would have suited almost everyone at least to call into *some* question the accuracy of the information provided by Geoffrey of Monmouth's *Historia*, *not one single person did*.

King Charles I: guilty as charged?

Born 1600 and reigned 1625–1649. Second son of James I, the elder son, Prince Henry, having died. Married to Princess Henrietta Maria of France, daughter of King Henry IV of France.

King Charles I

(i) The main events of the reign in summary

1625. King Charles's First Parliament was convened, mainly for the purpose of organising the money needed for the war with Spain that had been declared in the previous year. Parliament refused to grant what was needed without imposing conditions that were unacceptable to King Charles, who accordingly dissolved the Parliament.

1626. The Second Parliament met. It impeached the Duke of Buckingham, who had been one of King James I's favourites and was now the King's chief adviser, whereupon King Charles dissolved the Parliament in order to save him.

1627. War was declared between England and France.

1628. The Third Parliament met and what is called the Petition of Right, a declaration of 'the rights and duties of the subject', was drawn up and presented to the King. In fact it amounted to an unprecedented reduction of the authority of kings. King Charles first protested and then reluctantly agreed to it.

The Duke of Buckingham, while preparing for a campaign overseas, was stabbed to death in Portsmouth by an officer in the army who believed that he had been passed over for promotion by him.

1629. After an extraordinary tumult in Parliament, during which, amongst other dramatic events, the Speaker was forcibly held down in his chair, King Charles dissolved the Parliament and proceeded to rule without a Parliament for the next eleven years, exercising his authority through the Star Chamber. He became increasingly unpopular because of being forced to raise money by means that had never been used before.

1637. On the advice of William Laud, Archbishop of Canterbury, King Charles attempted to enforce the English church liturgy in Scotland. This was opposed, everyone in Scotland of any importance signed the National Covenant, and an official declaration of opposition. The 'Covenanters' formed an army to defend their rights.

1639. King Charles advanced with an army to invade Scotland, but found himself compelled to abandon the invasion and sign a treaty with the Scots.

1640. By now in grave financial difficulties, King Charles summoned the Fourth or Short Parliament. Once again Parliament refused to grant him a subsidy without conditions that were unacceptable to him and was dissolved after only three weeks.

The Scots invaded England and defeated the royal forces at the Battle of Newburn. At the Treaty of Ripon that followed, it was agreed that the Scots would cease all hostility on condition of receiving a monthly payment of £40,000. By now in even graver financial difficulties, King Charles summoned his Fifth or Long Parliament, which was to last for twenty years, until 1660.

Archbishop Laud was impeached by the Long Parliament for supposed high treason and imprisoned in the Tower of London. In 1644 he was tried, with no verdict being reached because no specific action of his that was treasonable could be pin-pointed. Almost unbelievably, Parliament took over the matter and passed a 'bill of attainder', under which the Archbishop was beheaded in 1645 even though King Charles tried to rescue him by granting him a royal pardon.

1641. Further impositions were made on King Charles. These included: the passing of a Bill which enacted that Parliament could not be dissolved without its own consent; the abolition of the Star Chamber through which he had been governing the country; and the passing of the Grand Remonstrance. The Grand Remonstrance contained 204 clauses listing (a) Acts done by King Charles since the beginning of his reign that were alleged to be unconstitutional, and (b) good work that Parliament had done during the same period, and demanded that, from then on, Parliament should have the right to appoint ministers.

1642. King Charles attempted to arrest Hollis, Hamden, Hazlerig, Pym and Strode, the five ringleaders of what amounted to a revolution against the monarchy, by, in real effect, transferring the monarch's traditional authority and powers to Parliament. When King Charles failed, he at once left London. Both the King and Parliament now prepared for what was to be the First Civil War. Thus came into existence what are known to history as the Roundheads and the Cavaliers. The Roundheads were the supporters of Parliament, and maintained that Parliament had the right both to limit the power of the king as it chose and also to impose 'puritanical' rules on the nation, which amounted to supreme control over the administration of the nation, which in turn meant reducing the king to little more than a figurehead. The Cavaliers, who were the Royalists, were defending the principle of a king who really *was* king, by God-given right.

1642–1644. There were several battles, with the Royalists usually victorious. The King's chief officer was his nephew, Prince Rupert of the Rhine.

1645. Parliament brought into existence Britain's first standing army, to be called the New Model Army. At the Battle of Naseby, this army, led by Parliamentary commander-in-chief Sir Thomas Fairfax and Lieutenant General Oliver Cromwell, effectively destroyed the royalist forces, which were half its size, and at once brought the civil war to an end. Fairfax, as a result, became effectively the ruler of the republic that came into being in 1649. Eventually he was replaced by his subordinate, Oliver Cromwell.

1646. King Charles surrendered himself to the Scots, who handed him over to the English Parliament, which took and kept him prisoner.

1648. King Charles succeeded in engaging in a conspiracy with the Scots, of whom he was also King, which resulted in the Scots invading England and the start of the Second Civil War. The Scots were defeated by Cromwell at the Battles of Preston and Warrington. Cromwell's army, clamouring for the execution of King Charles, had him taken to Whitehall in London. A meeting of Parliament followed. One hundred Members of Parliament, who were of the Presbyterian religion, refused to sit in judgement on the King, maintaining that no such trial could be valid because kings, by the very nature of the institution, were above the law; but, in what became known as 'Pride's Purge', Colonel Thomas Pride, the commander of the New Model Army, forcibly removed all of them from Parliament, leaving only fifty-three Members, who called themselves Independents. These then voted that the King should be tried.

1649. The House of Lords was abolished by the House of Commons. The members of the House of Commons that still remained, who were a mere forty-six, carried the following motion: all power originates from the people; the Commons represents the people; the Commons is therefore invested with authority to pass any laws without the consent of king or lords. King Charles was then tried by a High Court of Justice, found guilty of having levied war against his kingdom and the Parliament, sentenced to death and beheaded.

(ii) Of special interest

The reign of King Charles I, including of course how it came to an end, was the most dramatic in England's history. It is perhaps the most romantic as well. One reason is that, as were all of the descendants of King James I, King Charles was a man of appealing personality: when he had the leisure, he was cultured, as the several portraits by the magnificent artist Sir Anthony van Dyck testify, and also modest and even gentle. For whatever reason, he was, as historians agree, much loved everywhere in the country. It was indeed his great popularity which made it necessary for his conquerors to have him put to death.

My principal clash with many other historians on the subject of King Charles is on what I believe to be an incorrect representation of a crucial feature of his conduct. This is the attitude that he displayed to the *status* of his trial.

His single argument at the trial was that, irrespective of any innocence or guilt on his part, those trying him lacked the necessary authority for the purpose. Relatively few historians discussing him support his position fully in this matter. Many criticise him, whether directly or by implication. For instance, David Starkey says in *Crown & Country* (2010):

> On 20 January 1649, King Charles was brought to Westminster Hall to be tried for high treason. According to the indictment, Charles was 'a tyrant, traitor, murderer and a public and implacable enemy of the Commonwealth of England'. The unthinkable act of killing the King was drawing even closer. Charles's strategy, which he stuck to with remarkable persistence, was to refuse to recognise either the authority or the legality of a court ...[12]

The implied accusation of stubbornness is simply not valid. Even with his life at stake, King Charles could not, morally, have acknowledged the authority of the court. It would have been a betrayal of the very nature of monarchy, as it had been accepted by virtually everyone up to that time. Once again: the very *basis* of monarchy is that it is the fount of law and therefore of all enacted legislation. And a *fount* of law can only be *superior to* the law. For a fount of law to be subject to its own laws would be a self-contradiction – as indeed is recognised even today, when a monarch committing a crime could not be tried in any court of law.

The same quotation's use of the word 'strategy', therefore, misses the point. It was *not* a matter of strategy, but, rather, one of clear and inescapable *duty*. As far as King Charles I was concerned, he had no alternative. To admit that he could be tried would be to imply that the claims on which monarchy had always been based were illusions, and indeed fraudulent ones.

~

What must be stressed is that the execution and the trial leading up to it had nothing to do with the wish of the people. King Charles was popular with the masses, and it was never denied that they were opposed to his trial and execution. What took place was a bid for power by a tiny minority, not revolution for the betterment of ordinary people.

This is not to say that his conduct had been always satisfactory before then. He had, for instance, married his wife under false pretences, having undertaken to her father, the King of France, to allow religious tolerance to Catholics and to have their own children brought up as Catholics until the age of twelve. He had betrayed his greatest supporter and chief adviser Thomas Wentworth, Earl of Strafford. Strafford had constantly tried to strengthen the royal position against Parliament, but, when Parliament condemned him to death, King Charles had signed the death warrant for his execution, giving rise to the words of Wentworth, quoting Psalm 145 or 146 (according to which version of the Bible you use), on being told that he had been thus betrayed, 'Put not your trust in Princes', that have reverberated ever since. And there had been many other falsehoods and deceptions in his statecraft.

~

Eleven years later, in 1660, King Charles I's eldest son became King Charles II.

PART IX

NO KINGS, AND THEN THE KINGS OF ENGLAND, WALES, IRELAND, SCOTLAND AND ELSEWHERE AGAIN

CHAPTER THIRTY-ONE

Between Two Reigns: the Commonwealth and the Protectorate

Oliver Cromwell: 'A king in all but name'

Born 1599, a member of a land-owning family in Cambridgeshire, and 'reigned' 1657–1658.

(i) The main events of Cromwell's life and 'reign' in summary

1629. Oliver Cromwell became a Member of Parliament.

1630 or soon after. Cromwell adopted, to an extreme extent, a new version of Christianity: Puritanism. Puritanism, it should be noted, was never intended to imply anything to do with moral purity. It referred to the desire to 'purify' the Church of England from bishops.

1645. In the First Civil War, Oliver Cromwell first fought as Lieutenant General, second-in-command to Lord Fairfax. He then organised the New Model Army, which was unique in all English history up till that time in being a standing army, an army that was permanent rather than raised for a special purpose. He filled its ranks with 'men of religion', members of the new 'Puritan' religion. At the Battle of Naseby this army destroyed King Charles's troops and his prospects of survival as a ruling king.

1649. Cromwell was one of the signatories of King Charles I's death warrant. England was then proclaimed a Commonwealth and a Free State.

1652. Cromwell's New Model Army conquered Ireland and was responsible for horrifying atrocities there.

1652–1654. The refusal of the Dutch to enter into an alliance with the Commonwealth and salute the English flag in the English Channel led to the First Dutch War. This was concluded in 1654 with conditions agreed by the Dutch that included the promise that they would give no support to English Royalists.

1653. The former offices and responsibilities of the now-abolished, as 'useless and dangerous', monarchy and the House of Lords were gradually taken over by what came to be known as the Rump Parliament, a 'Council of State' consisting of forty-one members.

A little later, the Rump Parliament was itself abolished by Cromwell, and replaced by the Barebone's Parliament, so called after a junior member for London whose enthusiastically Puritan name was Praise-God Barebone. (He is said to have been christened even more enthusiastically as Unless-Jesus-Christ-Had-Died-For-Thee-Thou-Hadst-Been-Damned Barebone.) This Parliament was summoned by Cromwell, who selected its members from a list of men who were 'faithful, fearing God and hating covetousness'.

Once again not satisfied with what he had just created, Cromwell had the 'Instrument of Government' drawn up. This stated that the supreme authority should be vested in a man with absolute authority and power, the Lord Protector, who should be assisted by a Council of State, and that the office of Protector should be for life, under the title His Highness by the Grace of God and Republic, Lord Protector of England, Scotland and Ireland. It soon followed that the three countries were subject to the rule of the Lord Protector only.

1654–1655. According to Hyamson in chapters 16 and 17 of his *History of the Jews in England*, representatives of Jewish merchants in Amsterdam, acting as an ambassadors for Jewry, paid visits to England petitioning for the readmission of the Jews to England on terms of equality with its Christian inhabitants. Although Cromwell was on both occasions in favour of granting the petitions, the Council of State consistently rejected them. Cromwell proceeded to, as Hyamson puts it, 'connive at a Jewish settlement', and King Charles II adopted the same policy when he came to the throne; but no equivalent petition on behalf of the Jews was made at any time in the future, and it is an interesting anomaly that, even though Jews have been prominent members of both Houses of Parliament and there has even been a Jewish Prime Minister, technically the expulsion enacted by King Edward I in 1290 remains legally in force.

1655. There was opposition to Cromwell, whereupon he dissolved this constitution that he had created, divided the country into twelve military districts, and appointed to each district a major general with absolute power subject only to him.

1656. Needing money in order to keep and exercise power, Cromwell summoned his Second Parliament, from which, however, he excluded a hundred of its representatives who would have opposed him.

1657. This new Parliament 'presented' to Cromwell what it called its 'Humble Petition and Advice': (1) that the Protector should take the name of King; (2) that he should have the power to nominate his successor as King; (3) that a second House of Parliament should be brought back into being.

1658. *Both* Houses of this Third and Last Parliament met. After sixteen days, both were dissolved by Cromwell, who ruled for the rest of his life, which ended on 3 September of that year, in effect as an absolute monarch, although not officially as king. His son Richard Cromwell was declared Protector in his place.

(ii) Of special interest

When Cromwell received his appointment as Lord Protector of England, Scotland and Ireland, he did so dressed in a simple black suit, and, on the face of it, had to be voted into his new status. By the end of his political career, he had undergone everything relating to a coronation but the wearing of the crown. He even held a sceptre and sword as symbols of his power. Furthermore, although 'Lord Protector' had not been intended to be a hereditary title, he eventually nominated his son Richard as his heir. Step by step, he had indeed become what he has been commonly called: 'a king in all but name'.

~

After the death of Elizabeth, persecutions of Christians whose beliefs, both Catholic and of some Protestant sects, the monarch reigning at the time did not share, had continued in the reigns of King James I and King Charles I. During the period of the Commonwealth and of Cromwell's Protectorate, the persecutions increased, now being directed not only at Catholics, but also at Protestants who did not submit to the now dominant creed of Puritanism. Included in this new policy:

- The celebration of Christmas and other festivals actually became *illegal* throughout the country.
- In 1645 an ordinance was issued by which any person using the Book of Common Prayer was punished as follows:
  - For the first offence a fine of £5.
  - For the second offence a fine of £10.
  - For the third offence a year's imprisonment.

Thus in the *early* part of the Reformation it had been *legally obligatory* to use the Book of Common Prayer, under severe penalties for those who did not; while now, almost exactly a century later, the use of the same book was *legally forbidden*, under pain of similar penalties.

~

However astonishingly, posterity has provided Cromwell with some enthusiastic supporters. For John Milton, Thomas Carlyle and Samuel Rawson Gardiner, he was a hero of liberty and in 2002 a poll carried out by the BBC that was sponsored by the military historian Richard Holmes selected him as one of the ten greatest Britons of all time. Judicial murder, regicide, mass murder, mass murder amounting even to near-genocide in Ireland are perfectly good qualifications for the highest praise among serious thinkers, it is clear.

In my submission, this adds support to what we have been learning about the limits to the trust that we can dare to give to experts. Let us hypothesise that we could bring ourselves to regard judicial murder, near-genocide and the rest as relatively harmless foibles. As we have seen, there still remains his *continual* self-contradiction in his public actions, during the course of little more than a decade. No crimes were too extreme for him; and even more extreme than extreme, on the hypothesis that such be possible, were the crimes that he invented in order to oppose his own earlier crimes.

~

As already noted, the Third and Last Parliament lasted a full sixteen days before both of them were dissolved by Cromwell, who ruled, in effect as an absolute monarch, for the rest of his life. On his death on 3 September of that year, his son Richard Cromwell was declared Protector in his place.

Richard Cromwell

Born 1626 and reigned as Lord Protector 1658–1659. Died in 1712.

(i) The main events of his 'reign' in summary

1658. Richard Cromwell was declared Protector.

1659. The new Protector soon became unpopular with everyone, including the army, acquiring such unflattering nicknames as Tumbledown Dick, Queen Dick and Hickory Dick. After a few months he resigned from the Lord Protectorship, retired into private life, and in doing so closed down the short-lived institution of Lord Protectorship for ever.

(ii) Of special interest

It is thought that he left behind an enduring social effect in the nursery rhyme 'Hickory Dickory Dock', in which 'the mouse runs down' when 'the clock strikes one', reflecting his abandonment of his reign within a single year.

King Charles II

CHAPTER THIRTY-TWO

The House of Stuart Restored

King Charles II, 'the Merry Monarch'

Born 1630 and reigned in Scotland from 1651 and in England also 1660–1685. Elder son of Charles I. Married to Princess Catherine of Braganza.

(i) The main events before and during the reign in summary

1645. Aged fourteen, Prince Charles took part in the military campaigns of his father.

1646. Fearing for his safety, he left England and, in 1648, moved to The Hague, where his sister Mary and his brother-in-law William II, Prince of Orange, were ruling. There, a brief relationship between him and Lucy Walter resulted in a son, later to be both Duke of Monmouth and Duke of Buccleuch, the first of Charles's many illegitimate children who were to become prominent in British society.

1649. On England's becoming a republic, the Covenanter Parliament of Scotland proclaimed Charles II 'King of Great Britain, France and Ireland' – the English Crown had not yet abandoned its claim to France – but refused to allow him to enter Scotland unless he accepted Presbyterianism throughout Britain and Ireland, which he declined to do. The Marquess of Montrose invaded Scotland on King Charles's behalf, but was captured and executed.

1650. Charles became party to a treaty with the Scottish Covenanters, agreeing under oath to uphold in Scotland both the Covenant and the new Presbyterian religion that was based on the teachings of the French theologian John Calvin and had become Scotland's national religion in the sixteenth century. This agreement made him unpopular in England.

1651. King Charles was crowned King of Scotland at Scone Abbey. The Scots, led by King Charles, mounted an attack on England that ended in defeat at the Battle of Worcester. With a reward of £1,000 on his head and notwithstanding the risk of death for anyone caught helping him, he escaped to Normandy in France.

1658. On the death of Cromwell, King Charles's chances of regaining the crown remained slender, with Cromwell being succeeded by his son Richard.

1659–1660. Richard Cromwell abdicated and the Protectorate was abolished. An English soldier, George Monck, now entered the English political arena. Having first taken Prince Charles's side when the Prince was proclaimed King of Scotland, then fought on Cromwell's side and with him achieved a resounding Roundhead victory at the Battle of Dunbar in 1650 that had resulted, he was made commander-in-chief in Scotland by Cromwell and completed the subjugation of Scotland. From then on, he appeared to alternate between King Charles's side and the Parliamentary side in England. Now, in full communication with King Charles, he accepted King Charles's Declaration of Breda, in which, amongst much else, King Charles undertook to forgive all those who had been in opposition to the monarchy, with the exception of fifty expressly named men who had been involved in the judicial murder of his father, including the three people most directly involved in the murder. These – Oliver Cromwell, Henry Ireton and John Bradshaw – were by then dead but were subjected to the posthumous indignity of being dug up from their graves and decapitated.

With Monck's agreement the New Model Army was disbanded completely, with the single exception of the regiment of which he was Colonel.

Amongst the gifts with which King Charles showed his gratitude to General Monck were a number of peerages including the dukedom of Albemarle and some land in North America. The land, in fact a very large tract, became the American states of North Carolina and South Carolina, named after King Charles ('*Rex Carolus*' in Latin).

1660–1665. On 1 May 1660, the new Convention Parliament in England formally invited King Charles to become the reigning King, in what became known as the Restoration. Monck's army, with Monck at its head, made a famous march from Coldstream, a town situated on the borders of England and Scotland, to London, after which Monck was instrumental in restoring King Charles to the throne. After Monck's death his regiment was given the name of the Coldstream Guards and it has survived to the present day, behind only the Grenadier Guards in the Guards Regiments' order of precedence.

The Convention Parliament was dissolved in December 1660 and, shortly after the coronation, the second English Parliament of the reign assembled. It was to be known as the Cavalier Parliament because it consisted mostly of old Cavaliers.

The new Parliament passed several Acts in order to establish the dominance of the Church of England, and one of those Acts, the Act of Uniformity of 1662, made the use of the Anglican Book of Common Prayer once again compulsory and forbade the public practice of any other religion. The various Acts became known as the Clarendon Code, named after Edward Hyde, the first Earl of Clarendon and King Charles's chief minister, although Lord Clarendon was not in fact responsible for the Acts in question nor even fully in favour of them.

1662. A substantially revised edition of the Protestant Book of Common Prayer was published, and has remained the official prayer book of the Church of England up to the present day.

1664. War broke out between England and the Dutch again. This time the cause was that the English naval squadron had sailed into the harbour of the Dutch settlement, originally called New Amsterdam by the Dutch, in Manhattan Island on the east coast of America.

1665. New Amsterdam was incorporated under English law as an English colony, and given a new name, New York City, after the Duke of York, the future King James II.

The Great Plague, which had been raging on the Continent, broke out in London. Lasting from May to September, and with a death toll of 7,000 in a single week at its worst, it is believed to have killed between 60,000 and more than 100,000 people, out of a population of only about 300,000 people.

1666. In September, the Great Fire of London started in a bake-house in Pudding Lane near London Bridge, and raged for three days and three nights, reducing a full two-thirds of the city of London to ashes. More than 13,000 houses were destroyed, and 87 churches, including, most notably of all, St. Paul's Cathedral, which was later rebuilt by Sir Christopher Wren. King Charles and his brother the Duke of York were both active in directing the fire-fighting.

1667. To the horrified dismay of everyone in England, Dutch ships sailed up the River Thames and blockaded London for several weeks. Lord Clarendon was impeached in the House of Lords for the incompetence of his handling of opposition to this invasion, and, on the advice of King Charles, fled overseas, never to return to England.

1667. A Parliamentary committee was formed to help run the country: Lord Clifford, Lord Arlington, the Duke of Buckingham, Lord Ashley and the Duke of Lauderdale – to be known by the acronym Cabal and introducing into the English language the word 'cabal', meaning a secret intrigue or a clique. For the first time in English history, the king officially had a group of men to advise him rather than a single 'favourite'.

1670. The Secret Treaty of Dover was established between King Charles and King Louis XIV of France. It included an undertaking by King Charles to declare himself a Catholic within six months. King Charles did not keep that solemn undertaking.

1672. King Charles showed his true beliefs relating to religious freedom, very different from those of Parliament, by issuing his first Declaration of Indulgence. This repealed all previous acts that had outlawed either Catholicism or the Nonconformist religions.

1673. Not prepared to risk his throne for the sake of religious freedom, King Charles found himself forced – *by Parliament* – to withdraw the 1672 Declaration and to pass the Test Act, which made Catholics ineligible for any public office. One result of this was that the Duke of York had to resign both from the King's Privy Council and from the post of Lord High Admiral that he had held with great success.

1677. The Duke of York's daughter, Mary, married the Protestant Prince William of Orange, a powerful opponent of King Louis XIV. King Louis justifiably regarded this as an act of treachery on the part of King Charles, who had given the marriage his full support.

1678. The so-called 'Popish Plot' took place. A man plainly without any credibility, Titus Oates, who had earlier been gaoled for the particularly grave offence of perjury in Hastings in Sussex, escaped from gaol, fled to London, where he was received into the

Catholic Church, and shortly afterwards alleged that there was a Catholic plot to murder the King and restore the Catholic religion, and also that the Queen was involved in this and was working with the King's doctor to poison the King. Although virtually no one who gave the allegations any consideration believed them, acceptance of them somehow took hold of the uncritical populace at large – it has been said that the nation went mad – and 2,000 completely innocent people were imprisoned and 15 of these put to death before opinion started to turn against Oates. After being convicted of a second charge of perjury, Oates was stripped, tied to a cart and whipped from Aldgate, at the east of the London Wall, to Newgate, at its west. (Shockingly, when William of Orange and Queen Mary came to the throne in 1689, Oates was pardoned and given a pension of £260 a year. His reputation did not recover, however.)

The Disabling Bill was passed, 'disabling' Catholics, with the single exception of the Duke of York, the King's brother, from sitting in either House of Parliament. This was to continue to exclude Catholics from Parliament for a further *150 years* into the future.

1679. The Habeas Corpus Act was passed, outlawing imprisonment either without due cause or indefinitely. This was not a new legal principle – indeed the writ of *habeas corpus* had already existed in various forms in England for at least five centuries – but a strengthening and confirmation of traditional legislation that had long been part of the English common law. This Act is still in existence today.

The House of Commons put forward the Exclusion Bill, intending its effect to be the exclusion of the Duke of York from succession to the throne because of his membership, owing to his conversion in 1668 or 1669, of the Catholic Church – the religion that had been England's for some nine centuries until King Henry VIII found himself wanting to divorce his wife Catherine in order to be able to marry Anne Boleyn. To save his brother from this monstrous injustice, King Charles dissolved the Parliament.

1680. The Exclusion Bill was reintroduced, passed by the House of Commons, but thrown out by the House of Lords.

King Charles, now feeling more secure on the throne, used the King's dispensing power, the traditional the right of a monarch to set aside penal laws in particular cases, to restore the Duke of York to the King's Privy Council and the post of Lord High Admiral.

The party system came into existence for the first time, with Whigs and Tories the first two political parties.

1681. The Exclusion Bill was put forward for the third time. Again King Charles dissolved Parliament in order to prevent it from being passed. He never summoned another Parliament but ruled as absolute monarch until his death in 1685.

1683. The Rye House Plot for the murder of King Charles during his journey back to London from racing at Newmarket was frustrated by the King setting off for London earlier than expected.

(ii) Of special interest

Perhaps as renowned as anything for his wit, King Charles is known to history as the Merry Monarch. As we have seen, the difference between his court and that of Cromwell could not have been more extreme, with both rulers going much too far in opposite directions.

By his wife he had no children, but, astonishingly, there are today more royal descendants of his mistresses and their illegitimate offspring, many of whom he ennobled, than legitimate royal descendants of all the monarchs who have reigned since him. Some of his descendants of the male sex only:

- By Lucy Walter: a son, James Scott, whom he made Duke of Monmouth, who was to try to overthrow King James and become King of England himself, for which, when the rebellion failed, he was beheaded for treason. His wife Anne, however, was created Duchess of Buccleuch in her own right, and her title passed to the descendants of Monmouth and her.
- By Catherine Pegge: a son, Charles FitzCharles, whom he made Earl of Plymouth. A gallant soldier, Plymouth met his death aged twenty-three while campaigning.
- By Barbara Villiers: three sons whom he ennobled – Charles FitzRoy, whom he made successively Lord Limerick, Earl of Southampton, Duke of Southampton and Duke of Cleveland; Henry FitzRoy, whom he made successively Earl of Euston and Duke of Grafton; George FitzRoy, whom he made successively Earl of Northumberland and Duke of Northumberland.
- By Nell Gwyn: a son, Charles Beauclerk, whom he made Duke of St. Albans.

- By Louise de Kérouaille: a son, Charles Lennox, whom he made Duke of Richmond.

Of these, there are today still ducal descendants of the Dukes of Buccleuch, of Grafton, of St. Albans and of Richmond.

Once King, Charles was determined that, as he put it, he would not go on his travels again, and he compromised on his principles on virtually every matter except one. He never succumbed to constant pressure on him to betray his brother James, who had been his devoted friend and supporter, whenever needed, throughout their lives.

The scene of King Charles's death was as dramatic as any in his life.

On his deathbed he was surrounded by his Protestant friends and officials. The Duke of York approached him outside the hearing of the others and asked him if he would like him to find a Catholic priest to receive him into the Church and hear his confession. 'With all my heart,' was King Charles's earnest response. The Duke left his side and was able to find a priest, Father Edward Petre, who, it turned out, had helped King Charles during his flight in 1651. The Duke brought Father Petre to the King's bed, where, shortly before the King's death, the ceremonies at last bringing him into the Catholic Church took place.

~

During the reign of King Charles a social change took place that was as dramatic as the Puritan one had been. The theatres that had been closed during Cromwell's Protectorship reopened, and Restoration Comedy, a completely new kind of theatrical production, became dominant, as also did Restoration Literature. And although at one extreme what was published included *Paradise Lost* and *Pilgrim's Progress*, at the other extreme the restoration material was more vulgar and unseemly than had ever been seen before in England. The Earl of Rochester was the most notorious of the latter extreme's proponents.

The Royal Society, the oldest learned society still in existence, and still enjoying the greatest prestige worldwide, was founded, being granted a royal charter by Charles II.

King James II

CHAPTER THIRTY-THREE

Dethroned – and Good Riddance?

King James II:

Born 1633 and reigned as King of England, Scotland and Ireland 1685–1688. Died in 1701. Charles I's second son and Charles II's younger brother.

He was Duke of York from 1644; Earl of Ulster from 1659; Duke of Albany as well from 1660; then, succeeding King Charles II, was King James II of England and Ireland and King James VII of Scotland from 1685. He married, first, Anne Hyde, and, secondly, after Anne Hyde's death, Princess Mary of the Duchy of Modena in Italy.

(i) The main events of the reign in summary

1685. The Earl of Argyll led a rebellion in Scotland, to put the illegitimate son of Charles II, the Duke of Monmouth, on the throne. The rebellion was crushed and Argyll was executed. The Duke of Monmouth then rebelled against King James II in his own name, and was defeated by King James at the Battle of Sedgemoor.

1686. King James claimed the right of monarchs to use the traditional 'dispensing power', by which a king could set aside penal laws in particular cases, and used this right to promote Catholics as well as non-Catholics to important positions in Oxford and Cambridge universities, at that time legally barred to Catholics, and to the command of regiments in the army.

In the same year, he set up near London a standing army consisting of 13,000 troops.

Still in the same year, two papers were found in King Charles II's strongbox, written in his own handwriting, setting out the arguments of Catholicism over Protestantism. Lord Macaulay relates in chapter 6 of the first volume of his *History of England to the Death of William III* that King James published these papers and challenged the Archbishop of Canterbury and all the other bishops in England to refute King Charles's arguments, with the words: 'Let me have a solid answer, and in a gentleman-like style; and it may have the effect, which you so much desire, of bringing me over to your Church.'

The Archbishop said that it could be done 'without much difficulty' but refused – claiming to do so on the grounds of 'reverence for the memory' of the late King Charles. In the words of Macaulay: 'This plea the King considered as the subterfuge of a vanquished disputant' – a piece of cunning dishonesty by someone who had lost the argument but was not prepared to admit that he had.

1687–1688. King James issued two Declarations of Indulgence, also known as Declarations for Liberty of Conscience, suspending all the laws against both non-Catholics and 'Nonconformist' Protestants. When, in 1688, King James ordered the English clergy to read the second Declaration of Indulgence on an appointed day, many refused and seven of the bishops officially requested King James that they be excused. He rejected their petition, and on their then refusing to comply with his instruction, he had them sent to the Tower of London and brought to trial for rebellion against the King's lawful authority. Even though the case against them was straightforward, the jury acquitted them.

1688. King James's wife, Mary of Modena, gave birth to a son, in due course to succeed to the titles of King James III of England and Ireland and James VIII of Scotland, and to be referred to by his enemies as 'the Old Pretender'. (A pretender is someone who makes a claim to an official title, such as, in this case, those three thrones.) The future King James would be brought up as a Catholic.

Seven leaders of the two main political parties, the Whigs and the Tories, sent an invitation to King James's son-in-law, Prince William of Orange, Orange being then an independent state in the south of present-day France, to come over with an army to, as they put it, 'defend the rights and liberties of the people of England'. Prince William landed at Torbay in Devonshire, from where he proceeded towards London. At that point King James was betrayed by his close friend John Churchill, the future Duke of Marlborough, who owed to him every single step of his advancement to the rank of lieutenant general. Only minutes after professing to undying loyalty to James, Churchill deserted, together with the troops under his command, to Prince William. Thereupon James left the country for France, and William arrived in London and was proclaimed sovereign jointly with his wife Mary, King James II's daughter.

(ii) Of special interest

As a useful sample of what is said about King James, here is some of what Macaulay had to say in the second volume of his *History of England*, first published in 1848:

> Obstinate and imperious … Of small understanding … Not to be dislodged by reason … His mode of arguing, if it is to be so-called, not uncommon among dull and stubborn persons – he asserted a proposition, and, as often as wiser people ventured respectfully to show that it was erroneous, he asserted it again, in exactly the same words, and conceived that, by doing so, he at once disposed of all objections.

Winston Churchill, in his biography of the most famous of his ancestors, titled *Marlborough: His Life and Times*, goes even further than Macaulay, depicting King James as a cruel, intolerant, dour, half-hearted 'papist'.

Other authors add other unpleasant features. These include allegations: that he was a fanatic and especially in the direction of religious intolerance; that he was determined to impose popery on everyone by force; that he was tyrannical, foolish, incapable of logical discussion, vengeful, unforgiving by nature, sullen, humourless and apt to be consumed with anger; and in general that he was a man whom it was impossible to like.

In short, we are led to believe, first, that he was, in his character and in his actions, entirely responsible for the loss of his throne, and secondly, that the country was very much better off without him.

~

It can, however, be conclusively shown, first, that those allegations include scarcely anything with any semblance of truth; and secondly, that, measured against any reasonable yardstick, King James II can fairly and accurately be described as, in political terms, one of the half-dozen or so greatest men in *any* country *in the whole of recorded history*. By that I mean 'right up there' with Alexander the Great, who conquered the whole known world and was responsible for Greek being the *lingua franca* throughout the Roman Empire; with Julius Caesar, who was responsible for the present division of the calendar into twelve months and the names of the month of July and, indirectly, of the month of August as well; with Emperor Charlemagne, founder of the Holy Roman Empire; and in our own country, with King Alfred the Great. It can also be shown that, far from being sullen, humourless, apt to be consumed with anger, and impossible to like, he was attractive as a person and time spent in his company was thoroughly enjoyable.

Against such an apparently extravagant claim, it is as well to look at aspects of him in some detail.

Military. During his period, long before he came to the throne, in exile from England after his father King Charles I had been subjected to judicial murder, and wishing to occupy himself as usefully as he could, he at once embarked on soldiering. In 1652, when only eighteen years of age, he joined the French army, and was so successful and impressive in acquiring military knowledge and skills that the greatest soldier in the world of his era, Vicomte de Turenne, Marshal of France, promoted him to the rank of lieutenant general when he was *only twenty*. In that rank, he continued to impress, and, when he was twenty-four, Turenne *put him in charge of the entire French army* when he, Turenne, had to leave it for a short period.

A few years later, one of the terms of a treaty that King Louis XIV entered into with Oliver Cromwell's England forced James to leave the French army. With, now, a magnificent international reputation as a military leader, he transferred his services to the Spanish army.

As it happened, not long previously a Frenchman who was second only to Turenne as a great soldier of his time had been put in charge of the Spanish army. This was Louis II of Bourbon, Prince of Condé, who because of political difficulties with Louis XIV had been left with no alternative other than to leave the French army.

Condé was given charge of the Spanish army, and under him James was made Captain General, the equivalent today of a general or a field marshal, and in due course was put in charge of the Spanish infantry; and at one point, when Condé went down with a life-threatening fever, James, still only in his mid twenties, *was put in charge of the entire Spanish army.*

In 1660, and still only in his twenties, the Duke of York was offered both a military command *and* a naval command. King Philip IV of Spain invited him to command the Spanish army against Portugal and at the same time to accept the office of High Admiral of Spain, with the title 'Principe de la Mare', an appointment never before held by anyone other than a member of the Spanish Royal Family, and including in it, not only command of all the Spanish ships, but the automatic status of Viceroy of any country where the High Admiral landed, and for as long as he remained there.

With the agreement of his brother Charles, the Duke of York was very pleased to accept the appointment, but in the same year, the Restoration of the monarchy in England at last became a real possibility, and he had to withdraw his acceptance of it.

The Duke of York's naval career did not remain still-born for long. Immediately after the Restoration of the monarchy in England, the new king, Charles II, appointed him to the position of Lord High Admiral in England, and in this position he served his king and his country in two capacities, as we shall be seeing.

As an administrator. With the able help of Samuel Pepys:

He organised the English fleet into – for the first time in England's history – proper existence as an institution, so that the British navy was no longer hastily assembled whenever there was an external threat, but was transformed in its entirety into a solid and permanent institution.

Of highest importance, he instituted the rank of midshipman (at first called King's Letter Boys), which was to play such an important role in training naval officers from then on, and thus in creating the greatest navy the world had ever seen.

He was also the principal author of, and responsible for, the naval regulations that existed relatively unchanged until well after the Second World War.

In other words, he was one of the principal founders of the Royal Navy, which eventually dominated all the oceans of the world and was of course indispensable to the gradual building up of the vast British Empire. According to historian Sir Arthur Bryant, in his Introduction to his *Memoirs of James II*: 'With the help of his lieutenant, Samuel Pepys, he did more personally for the Royal Navy than any other English Sovereign, past or future.' And had there not existed the British navy, as brought into being by James, there could never have been the Empire, controlling and administering a quarter of the world, that was still in existence during the first half of the twentieth century.

As Lord High Admiral. In those days England was often at war with the Dutch, then a great nation, both in Europe and in America. James commanded the Royal Navy during both the Second Anglo-Dutch War in 1665 to 1667 and the Third Anglo-Dutch War in 1672 to 1674, and in the course of those wars the Navy was victorious in the two most important sea battles. The decisiveness of those battles made James arguably England's most important naval commander from that time until Nelson. Sir Arthur Bryant again, in the same book:

> With his ancestor, Edward III, he shared the unique privilege for a king of England of commanding her Fleet in action. He not only took part in one of the major battles of British sea history, but he directed it victoriously as Commander-in-Chief.

In duties attached to kingship. In 1679, Charles appointed him Viceroy of Scotland, and there James ruled, in effect as king, for several years. Those in Scotland had nothing but praise for him and, as the fact of the later Jacobite movement bearing his name (*Jacobus* being the Latin for James) would tend to confirm, he was evidently both efficient and personable.

In the field of politics. As already noted, so respected and liked was James in Scotland that his popularity was an important factor in the long-enduring Jacobite movement to restore the Stuart Royal Family after the loss of the monarchy due to treason, and to the extent of his being honoured by a political movement being named after him.

Arguably most remarkable of all ... In 1663, his brother King Charles made a gift to him of a stretch of land, Long Island, in what was known in those days as the 'West Indies'. Charles had the right to do this, because, in the words of the gift, 'the tract of land between New England and Mary Land had always belonged to the Crown of England since it was first discovered'.

At the time the gift was made, it was of doubtful value because the Dutch in the meantime had built a town and several fortresses there. On James sending two warships to reclaim England's property, however, the Dutch submitted without firing a shot, and many of them remained peacefully there.

Not at the Duke of York's request but in his honour, the town, up until then called New Amsterdam, was renamed 'New York' after him; the countryside surrounding it, New Netherland as it had been called under Dutch rule, was renamed the province of New York; and the fortress up the river from New York was named Albany after his Scottish title, Duke of Albany; and Albany is now the capital city of New York state. Thus, scarcely mentioned by any of the historians who make reference to him, what is generally recognised as being one of the three greatest cities in the world today – London and Paris being the other two – was named after him. In fact, surely uniquely, a great city, and an American state, and that state's capital are *all* named after him.

~

As to the allegations against him that are used to deny him the right to his good name, although not all of them melt under careful examination, most of them do.

The 'Bloody Assize'. The so-called 'Bloody Assize' (Assize sometimes incorrectly called 'Assizes'), perhaps the most renowned event of his reign, was a series of trials instituted by him and presided over by Judge (George) Jeffreys after the Duke of Monmouth's treasonous rebellion. The courts of assize were courts held in England and Wales at various times during the year until 1972, when they were abolished and replaced by a single permanent Crown Court.

According to H. E. Marshall, in her book *Our Island Story,* on which all English children used to be brought up:

> A man called Chief-Justice Jeffreys by his cruelties made for himself a name which has never been forgotten. He was a monster; an ogre more fierce and terrible than in any fairy tale … Judge Jeffreys did not do justice. He did wrong and murder, and King James praised and rewarded him for it.[13]

But …

In the first place, there need not have been an Assize at all. Traditionally, and reasonably, the summary execution of traitors caught *in flagrante delicto*, with their weapons in their hands, was legitimate and normal. It was only out of a characteristic urge to bend over backwards to be fair that James made an exception in this case.

Secondly, the so-called 'Bloody Assizes' were not 'Bloody'. Scholarly biographies of both James and Jeffreys have made it clear that James's choice of Judge Jeffreys for the job was perfectly sound, and that Jeffreys did the job competently and fairly.

Thirdly, those trials at the time drew no criticism of either James or Jeffreys from contemporaries. Indeed Parliament officially referred to the convictions and sentences that emerged from the trials as 'punishments rejoiced at by all good men'.

The cause of King James's loss of the throne. Historians tell us that King James's first legal action on becoming king was to release thousands of men and women, Catholics *and* Protestant Nonconformists, who were imprisoned solely on account of their religion, and to inform the lawyers that his government intended to discourage prosecutions related to religious issues. Then in 1687 he published, both in England and in Scotland, his Declaration of Indulgence, 'establishing the equality of all before the law, irrespective of creed, and giving liberty of conscience to every Englishman and -woman' – the Declaration being a temporary measure – and the very opposite of tyrannical – which he hoped to make permanent by confirmation of Parliament. Hard though James tried, he never obtained Parliament's agreement to this legislation before he was forced off the throne by people less enamoured of the principle of religious liberty.

It is dismaying that King James's Declaration of Indulgence is seldom actually quoted from by standard historians. Here is a sample of it, from near its end:

> We do hereby give our free and ample pardon unto all nonconformists, recusants and our other loving subjects for all crimes and things by them committed or done contrary to the penal laws formerly made relating to religion and the profession or exercise thereof, hereby declaring that this our royal pardon and indemnity shall be as good and effectual to all intents and purposes as if every individual person had been therein particularly named, or had particular pardons under our great seal.

In 1688 King James reissued the Declaration and required the bishops and clergy to read it out in England's churches. William Sancroft, Archbishop of Canterbury, and six other bishops presented a petition to the King declaring the Indulgence illegal and refused to publish it. Since the Declaration is very obviously reasonable throughout, James could hardly have foreseen that the bishops would act towards it in such flagrant bad faith; and when they did so act, he had no choice but to initiate legal action against them and to have the seven bishops tried. No king who hopes to reign well, justly and for the common good can afford to have his legitimate orders successfully defied, no matter by whom. The bishops were acquitted even though clearly and flagrantly guilty.

His conduct at the Battle of the Boyne. The Battle of the Boyne took place across the River Boyne in the east of Ireland in 1690, two years after he had lost the throne to his daughter and son-in-law, Mary and William. His aim in fighting the battle was to regain the thrones of England and Scotland. He was defeated by King William.

He is accused of cowardice in the battle, actually running away. Something of a byword is the alleged exchange between him and the

Countess Tyrconnel – a prominent figure in his court and the elder sister of the Sarah Jennings who was to wield great political influence during the reign of Queen Anne – on his arrival in Dublin following the Boyne defeat. 'Your countrymen, madam, can run well,' James is supposed to have said. 'Not quite so well as Your Majesty, for I see you have won the race,' is supposed to have been her rejoinder.

There is no contemporary evidence whatever of any such conversation, and no contemporary evidence whatever that anyone thought his conduct at the tail-end of the Battle of the Boyne cowardly, or anything other than in accordance with common sense.

His character as a person. Remarkably, against the background of the description of him by Churchill and other authors given earlier in this chapter, the evidence is strong that he was cheerful, charming and in general delightful company. For instance:

His two appointments to take charge of an entire army, one in France and the other in Spain, at an extraordinarily young age are compelling evidence that he had the respect and liking, not only of Turenne and Condé, the two greatest commanding officers of their day, but also of his brother officers of various nationalities, most of whom of course were much older than he.

As already indicated, his period as Viceroy of Scotland earned him not only the greatest respect but an enduring affection that can be fairly called romantic. His elder brother Charles, undoubtedly shrewd and a good judge of character, greatly liked and respected him, as well as always trusting him.

King Louis XIV, another shrewd judge of men, was King James's host during the last few years of James's life, and he very much liked and respected him.

~

None of this is to deny that James made occasional blunders. Even so, there could scarcely be a more dramatic example of the contrast between 'generally received' history and the factual reality. Given what I have outlined above, can he not indeed be justly rated as 'up there' along with the 'greats' of past history? Is not the prostitution of the talents of the superb writer and scholar, Lord Macaulay, actually horrifying and odious?

A further point worth noting is this. It is in fact not even true that James was not appreciated in his own country. After his two victories against the Dutch and his superb administration during the Great Fire of London of 1666, when King Charles put him in charge of handling that crisis, he was, understandably, the most popular man in England. Contrary to what is generally assumed, it was not the ordinary English who wanted him off the throne and out of the country, but a group of powerful people who wanted control of the affairs of the country for their own benefit. We shall be seeing more of these people 'in action' in future reigns.

King James III ('The Old Pretender')

Born in 1688, the only son of King James II, and reigned *de jure* – by right though not in actuality – 1688–1766. In 1719 he married Maria Clementina Sobieska, granddaughter of the King of Poland. He was never crowned king and did not rule, but he was acknowledged as king by many people in England and outside England, and his seventy-eight years were arguably the longest reign of any monarch in England's history.

(i) The main events of the reign in summary

1701. On his father's death in 1701, he was recognised by King Louis XIV of France as the rightful heir to the English and Scottish thrones, King James III of England and VIII of Scotland. Spain, the Papal States and Modena also recognized him and refused to recognise William III, Mary II or Anne as legitimate sovereigns. As a result of his claiming – justly claiming, of course – his late father's lost thrones, James was attainted – sentenced to death – for treason in London on 2 March 1702, and his titles were forfeited under English law.

1708. James attempted an invasion of England, but failed to achieve a landing at the Firth of Forth.

1713. At the Treaty of Utrecht between Britain and France, one of the conditions insisted on by England and submitted to by the French was that the French should exile James from their country.

1714. Queen Anne, who was reigning in England in James's place, died. Leading members of her administration, Robert Harvey and Lord Bolingbroke, entered into correspondence with James and both of them made it clear to him that his restoration would be helped if he were to convert from his Catholic position to the Protestant religion. Indeed the Bill of Rights of 1689 and the Act of Succession of 1701 had excluded Catholics from the British throne though not from the Scottish throne. James refused to convert from the religion that, with the single exception of King Edward VI, every single English monarch from King Ethelbert to Queen Elizabeth had sworn to uphold and protect. His second cousin, George, the Elector of Hanover, a German-speaking Protestant who never learnt to speak English, became King George I.

1715. The 'Fifteen' Jacobite rising in Scotland, designed to put James on the thrones of Scotland and England, after early successes ended in defeat. From then on James lived first in Avignon and then in Rome.

1745. James's eldest son Charles – known to history as both 'Bonnie Prince Charlie' and 'the Young Pretender' – led a second attempt to gain the throne for James, 'the Forty-five'. After initial successes it too failed, ending any real likelihood that the Stuarts would regain the thrones, and indeed on James's death in 1766 the pope of the day, Clement XIII, accepted the Hanoverian family as legitimate rulers of Britain and Ireland.

(ii) Of special interest

Never in human history was there a more romantic political movement than the Jacobite movement, for most of its existence centred on and personified by King James II and his eldest son, and made all the more memorable by some of the most beautiful popular romantic songs ever composed.

PART X

KINGS OF ENGLAND, WALES, NORTHERN IRELAND, SCOTLAND AND ELSEWHERE

CHAPTER THIRTY-FOUR

The House of Stuart Concluded

King William III and Queen Mary II

William was born in 1650 and Mary in 1662. They reigned jointly 1689–1694, when Queen Mary died, after which King William ruled alone until his death in 1702. Mary was James II's eldest daughter, and did not in fact *rule* as well as reign. William of Orange was Charles I's grandson and therefore James II's nephew.

(i) The main events of the reigns, both joint and individual, in summary

1688. Seven leaders of the Whigs and Tories jointly sent a signed invitation to the Dutch prince, William of Orange, to 'come over with an army and defend the rights and liberties of the people'. Thus began the event known to historians as 'the Glorious Revolution' and sometimes as 'the Bloodless Revolution'.

1688–1691. The Irish invited King James II to bring an army from France to take possession of his lawful kingdom. It took nearly three years of almost continual fighting, including the battle at the River Boyne, the defence of Limerick, the siege of Athlone and the battle at Aughrim – some of the best-known military engagements in Irish history – and several smaller battles as well, before the Irish were subjugated and forced to sign the Articles of Capitulation of the Treaty of Limerick on 3 October 1691. Under this treaty the Irish soldiers were offered the opportunity to take service with the King of France, and the civilians were promised, in exchange for taking an oath of allegiance to William and Mary, 'not less toleration' than they had enjoyed prior to the accession of James II.

As soon as the great Irish military leader, Patrick Sarsfield, had sailed off to France with upwards of 20,000 Irish soldiers, leaving the rest of Ireland to rely upon the security of the solemnly pledged word of King William, the Treaty of Limerick was immediately broken by William and his Irish Parliament, and wholesale slaughter and dispossession of the native Irish followed.

1689. The Scots rebelled against their new king and queen. This started with Highland clans rising up under the leadership of John Grahame of Claverhouse, Lord Dundee – known as 'Bloody Clavers' or 'Bonnie Dundee' according to whether we read the history books written by the winners or the losers – and achieving one of the most extraordinary military victories in history. In a battle lasting no more than *ten minutes*, some 2,000 untrained, primitively armed, bare-footed, half-starving Highlanders completely routed about 5,000 fully trained, well-armed and properly fed English and Lowlanders at the Battle of Killiecrankie. Sadly for the Scots, Dundee was killed in the battle. With him dead, the Jacobite cause largely petered out.

1692. The Macdonalds of Glencoe had fought under Dundee at Killiecrankie, and, like most of the other Highland clans, had afterwards resisted both bribes and threats to induce them to break their allegiance to King James. In 1691 a government proclamation stated that the members of any clan whose chief did not take the oath of allegiance to William on 1 January 1692 would be declared outlaws and therefore subject to military execution and stripped of all their lands. To save their peoples from extermination, the chiefs of the clans, still unshakably loyal to King James, wrote to him in France asking for his permission to take the oath. James granted it and all took the oath, and, as had been demanded, gave up their weapons and their right to keep weapons. The Macdonald chief of Glencoe, a clan consisting of some 200 people, was, however, hampered by heavy snow and the fact that he was an old man, and, arriving a few days late, did not take the oath until 6 January.

King William sent a decree to the commander of the forces in Scotland, signed by him, unusually, both at the top and the bottom, as if to emphasise his authority behind it. The decree included this:

'As for MacIan [the clan chief] and that tribe, it will be proper for the vindication of public justice, to extirpate that gang of thieves.'

There followed bloodshed of the most terrible kind of all: mass murder under trust. Nine hundred of King William's soldiers were commissioned to accomplish the 'extirpation', by which was meant the killing of every single clan member under seventy years of age. Twenty of those 900 soldiers appeared at Glencoe, asked for hospitality and were graciously accommodated and entertained by the Macdonalds until all the pre-arranged components of the plan were coordinated. At that point the twenty soldiers would rise up in the early hours of the morning and, with all the other soldiers placed so as to bottle up in the valley any Macdonalds who tried to escape, they would slaughter their trusting hosts in cold blood.

About three-quarters of the Macdonalds did in fact escape, crawling – many of them women, children and wounded – through appalling winter conditions, twenty-two miles to Appin, the home of the nearest neighbouring clan, and safety; and 'only' thirty-eight people, including the old chief, as he was getting out of bed, and his equally old wife, were murdered.

1693. The National Debt, indebtedness of the *whole country*, instituted by its government, was introduced for only the second time in any country in all history, the first time having been a few years earlier in Holland, which had been William's home before he invaded England in 1688.

1694. The Bank of England was established, bringing into being another institution that had never existed anywhere before.

Queen Mary died, leaving King William to reign alone until his death in 1702.

1698. The posting by the broker John Castaing of lists of share prices and commodity prices marked the beginning of the London Stock Exchange.

1700. An attempt by the Scots to found a colony at Darien, near the present-day Panama Canal, came to a disastrous end. Because it was backed by a large proportion of Scotland's financial resources, its failure left the entire lowlands of Scotland ruined, an important factor in weakening their resistance to the eventual 1707 Act uniting England and Scotland.

1701. The Act of Settlement or Succession Act was passed. Its most important feature was that it finally ended any possibility of England returning to the Catholic form of Christianity that had been its religion for nine centuries.

(ii) Of special interest

The massacre of the Macdonalds of Glencoe could well be history's single most loathsome piece of treachery. In this manner was carried out, in part, William's response to the invitation by the seven Whigs and Tories to 'come over with an army and defend the rights and liberties of the people'. It is tenable that this 'mini genocide' symbolises as well as anything what that invitation and the response to it amounted to in human and moral terms.

Can it be supposed that such an action would have been *imagined* by King John?

The reality is that William of Orange was not summoned over and offered the crown by the *nation* but by a *faction*, a small group of extremely rich men who wanted to become much richer.

~

Excuses in plenty for the massacre have been advanced by Whig historians. For instance, Bishop Gilbert Burnet, who was William's close confidant and, clearly, his propaganda mouthpiece, on page 703 of his *History of My Own Time* goes so far as to say of William of Orange that 'after all the abatements that may be allowed for his errors and faults, he ought still to be reckoned among the greatest princes that our history or indeed that any other, can afford' and maintained that William was so busy that he did not know what he was signing – an order to commit mass-murder of innocent and harmless people.

That, however, is flatly contradicted by the remarkable fact that, quite contrary to custom, William both signed and countersigned the document; and all the other excuses offered can be similarly exposed, even if they did not *already* lack credibility simply from the fact that they vary from historian to historian.

CHAPTER THIRTY-FIVE

Absolute Monarchy Versus Constitutional Monarchy: a Fundamental Turning-point and Some Consequences

ONE RESULT OF the usurpation of the throne by King William at the invitation of a handful of subjects of the legitimate king was that monarchy as it had been known in England throughout its history had come to an end. The form of monarchy existing in England up until then had been replaced by what is commonly called constitutional monarchy. That was a dramatic change indeed, because constitutional monarchy in this sense is not truly monarchy at all, but, rather, a deceptive *appearance* of monarchy, masking government by others, who in the late seventeenth century were, as we have been seeing, a group of powerful people more interested in furthering their own interests than the interests of the country. Kings and queens were ceasing to be kings and queens as traditionally defined, and on the way to becoming little more than figureheads.

In the history recounted so far, the history of the monarchs and the history of England have inevitably been almost completely the same because it is part of the very nature of monarchy that monarchs represent their country in the fullest sense.

From this point on, that is no longer so. Post-1688 British monarchs have retained some influence on events, but that influence has in general been slight and decreasing. Events are no longer subject to the decisions of monarchs.

CHAPTER THIRTY-SIX

The Last Member of the House of Stuart to Reign

Queen Anne

Born 1665 and reigned 1702–1714. James II's second daughter, Queen Mary's sister and King William III's sister-in-law, and married to Prince George of Denmark.

(i) The main events of the reign in summary

1702. The War of the Spanish Succession began. John Churchill, at that time the Earl of Marlborough, but not yet the Duke of Marlborough, was appointed commander-in-chief. He achieved a series of victories of which the most important was at the Battle of Blenheim, for which he was rewarded with the magnificent estate and house, the only non-royal house in Britain to have the status of Palace, which he named Blenheim, and is still owned and occupied by the ducal family of Marlborough.

1703. Buckingham House was built in Westminster for the Duke of Buckingham, to be acquired in 1761 by King George III and, by then enlarged, converted to a palace for the reigning monarch on Queen Victoria's accession in 1837.

1704. Gibraltar was captured from Spain.

1707. The Act for the Union of England and Scotland was passed, creating the new United Kingdom of Great Britain, from then on to be governed by a single Parliament in London, but with Scotland retaining her own Church, laws and courts of justice.

1711. Churchill, by then Duke of Marlborough, was accused of embezzlement and other financial fraud on a large scale, and dismissed from his command.

1713. The Treaty of Utrecht involving Britain, France and Spain was signed. Under this treaty, Gibraltar, Minorca, Hudson's Bay, Nova Scotia and Newfoundland became part of the British Empire. Gibraltar is still a colony – now called a British Overseas Territory – today. England was given the exclusive right to import black slaves into its colony Virginia, in America, for thirty years. France acknowledged the Protestant succession to the throne in England, ceasing to support 'the Old Pretender', whom up until then France had recognised as King James III.

1714. The two parties, the Whigs and the Tories, became more firmly established in opposition to each other, and the basic two-party system of British politics became consolidated.

The entire reign was remarkable for the fierce contests that took place between the two political parties.

(ii) Of special interest

Queen Anne, the last monarch of the House of Stuart, gave birth to no fewer than seventeen children, and lost every single one of them from miscarriages, still-births and post-birth illnesses. Had all or most of them survived, almost certainly there would still be a reigning Stuart monarch today.

~

Two women, at different points during her reign, strongly influenced Queen Anne.

The first was Sarah Jennings, the wife of the vile traitor, the Duke of Marlborough. A great beauty of her day and a woman of extraordinarily powerful personality, she was one of the Queen's Ladies of the Bedchamber and her closest friend – they called each other by pet names, 'Mrs. Morley' being the Queen's, and 'Mrs. Freeman' Sarah Jennings's.

Eventually, however, the Queen became resentful of her and affronted by her political views and her interference in politics, and turned to another of her Ladies of the Bedchamber, Abigail Hill, whose influence grew until she had completely replaced Sarah Jennings in the Queen's affections even though this new favourite was much less impressive in looks and personality.

In her old age, Sarah Jennings took dramatic and long-lasting revenge. She wrote a book of memoirs, *An Account of the Conduct of the Dowager Duchess of Marlborough from her first coming to Court to the year 1710*, which included a grossly unflattering depiction of the Queen, who amongst other unattractive features grew enormously fat as she grew older. Until well into the twentieth century this book strongly influenced what was written about Queen Anne by historians.

When close to death Queen Anne actually nominated her half-brother, James Francis Edward Stuart, the future rightful King James III, as her successor. The Protestant Whig Privy Councillors succeeded in being present when she was dying, however, and in preventing the Tory Lord Bolingbroke (pronounced 'bullingbrook') from declaring him king. Thus can small details have dramatic and long-lasting effects on future history.

~

The names of the two political parties, Whig and Tory, were both of them originally insulting names that somehow became adopted by the respective parties – Whig an abbreviation for Whiggamore, a name given to the rebellious, anti-royalist Presbyterians of Scotland, and Tory the nickname given to the outlawed Catholics in Ireland. The Tories upheld 'the divine right of kings' without, however, accepting it in practice, and represented, and of course favoured, the interests of the 'landed gentry'. The Whigs were aligned with commercial interests and considered the monarch to be, in practice, of no greater status than 'an official' responsible to the people for what he did, rather than responsible only to God, and to be capable of being dethroned if he acted unconstitutionally. In religion, the Tories were staunch supporters of the Established Church of England, while the Whigs, although themselves usually members of the Church of

England, leant theoretically in the direction of the Nonconformists, the Protestant 'dissenters'. Socially, there was no difference between them, and both were to be found in every class of society.

~

The union in 1707 of the two countries of England and Scotland, which from then on not merely shared the same monarch but were ruled through and by a joint Parliament based in London, was surely, in its effects, one of the most world-changing events in history. Before the union, Scotland was an insignificant country in the context of the world as a whole, and overseas its very existence would have been unknown to many. United with England, she could arguably be described as the engine of the Empire; and countless Scots were to have dramatic effects of all kinds worldwide. Indeed, sixty years later, the famous 'Enlightenment' French writer François-Marie Arouet, commonly known as Voltaire, was to say: 'There come to us from Scotland rules of taste in all the arts, from epic poetry to gardening; we look to it for all our ideas of civilisation.'

And that was only a small part of the influence that Scotland was to exercise worldwide.

CHAPTER THIRTY-SEVEN

The House of Hanover and Brunswick-Lüneburg Opens Its Reign

King George I

Born 1660 and reigned 1714–1727, although James III and James III's son Charles Edward ('Bonnie Prince Charlie') were still alive. Son of Ernest-Augustus, Duke of Brunswick-Lüneburg, and Princess Sophia of the Palatinate, and great-grandson of King James I.

(i) The main events of the reign in summary

1715. A Jacobite rebellion was launched in Scotland led by the Earl of Mar. Jacobites were supporters first of King James II, then of his son King James III – as many, including King Louis IV of France, officially accepted him to be – and finally of James III's son Prince Charles, 'Bonnie Prince Charlie'.

At the Battle of Sheriffmuir, near Stirling in Scotland, the Scottish rebels failed to defeat the Duke of Argyll and his army, and on the same day the English Jacobites, also in arms, surrendered at Preston in Lancashire.

1720. The first of many Stock Exchange scandals to come exploded. Known as the South Sea Bubble, it is still the most famous of them all.

1721. Sir Robert Walpole, later the first Earl of Orford, became First Lord of the Treasury, to be known afterwards as Britain's first Prime Minister ('First Minister'). He held that position for a remarkable twenty-one years, for the most part in the reign of King George II. One of the very few to benefit from the South Sea Bubble, in 1742 he was forced to resign on account of alleged corruption and self-enrichment on a massive scale

(ii) Of special interest

With shameless dishonesty, the legally established laws of succession were overridden in order to manipulate on to the throne a distantly related German princeling who could not speak English and, preferring the home of his birth to his new kingdom, could not be persuaded to spend more than about six months each year in England. He was of course unable to make even a pretence of governing the country, but the flagrant unscrupulousness on which his entire reign was based seems never to be noticed by historians.

That was truly the end of the monarchy as a monarchy, 'government by one person', and its replacement by an oligarchy, 'government by the few' – the few craftily concealing their existence by keeping the monarch as a figurehead with no power.

~

In theory the South Sea Company, after which the 'South Sea Bubble' is named, was created as a partnership between the government and the public for the purpose of reducing the ever-expanding national debt. To give it extra credibility, the company was granted the monopoly to trade with South America, in the 'South Seas'. In practice, there was never any realistic prospect that the company would engage in any profitable trading, and the rise in value of its shares was as unsupported by reality as any of the booms followed by busts since then have been. In the public excitement at the apparent prospect of making huge sums of money without effort that followed, other companies were swiftly floated on the Stock Exchange to tempt gamblers, one of which was described in its prospectus as 'a company for carrying out an undertaking of great advantage, but nobody to know what it is'.

The shares of the South Sea Company peaked in 1720 and then collapsed to the value at which they had originally been floated on the

Stock Exchange, with 'inside traders' having profited all the way up and many 'outsiders' being ruined on the way down. A Parliamentary enquiry resulted. Many Members of Parliament were disgraced.

King George II

Born 1683 and reigned 1727–1760. Son of King George I.

(i) The main events of the reign in summary

1738. John Wesley founded the Methodist religion, intended by him to be an 'evangelical' movement within the Established Church of England.

1739. A war with Spain broke out, called the War of Jenkins's Ear because an English sea captain testified before Parliament that his ear had been cut off by the Spaniards back in 1731. It started in North America, but from 1740 onwards it became part of a wider war in Europe, the War of the Austrian Succession of 1740 to 1748, which involved most European countries.

1743. King George II took part in that war at the Battle of Dettingen as head of the army of English and Hanoverian soldiers, and became the last British monarch to lead an army in battle.

1745. At the Battle of Fontenoy, the English and their allies were defeated by the French, who were led by the famous and justly admired Marshal Saxe.

The Scots, goaded beyond endurance by what they had been subjected to by the English, rose one last time. Prince Charles Edward – variously known as 'Bonnie Prince Charlie' and 'the Young Pretender' – landed in Scotland accompanied by only seven followers, raised his father's standard, soon found himself head of a Scottish army, entered Edinburgh and proclaimed his father king, comprehensively defeated the English forces at the Battle of Prestonpans, and gained complete control of Scotland.

He then marched into England, to the general rejoicing of many of the English who wholeheartedly believed King James III to be the rightful king; reached Derby; and marched onwards, victoriously at every point, to within ninety miles of London. As at least the majority of historians dealing with that period agree, Prince Charles could almost certainly have achieved a second Stuart restoration, and surely the most remarkable political turnaround in history, if he had continued his march. Mysteriously, however, instead of marching to London, where victory was now considered to be so probable that King George had hastily left the city, the Highland army suddenly turned round and retreated back to Scotland instead of continuing forward.

1746. Back in Scotland, the clans were defeated, with huge loss of life, at the Battle of Culloden, which brought to an end what was either a gallant rising or a rebellion, according to one's viewpoint. It was one of the most terrible battles ever fought, and the Jacobite troops were no match for government troops schooled at Dettingen and Fontenoy. What followed was even worse: a catalogue of atrocities all over the Highlands that earned for the English military leader, King George II's son the Duke of Cumberland, the enduring nickname 'the Bloody Butcher' and achieved the effective destruction of the Highland clans as any sort of political force.

The flight of Prince Charles after Culloden, commemorated in one of the most beautiful folk songs ever composed, the 'Skye Boat Song', quickly became legendary. Pursued over the mountains of western Scotland, with a reward of £30,000 on his head but never betrayed by any of the many Highlanders who saw him, he had many narrow escapes and eventually boarded a French frigate which transported him to France, where, with the Jacobite cause now completely lost, he spent most of the rest of his life, finally to be buried in St. Peter's in Rome, next to his brother and his father.

Since Prince Charles left no legitimate children and his by-now-elderly brother, Cardinal Henry Stuart, Duke of York, was also childless and had abandoned hope of a restoration, thus came to an end the Stuart dynasty of Britain's rightful kings. Britain under the victorious Hanovers, now secure at home, turned its attention to fighting for and gaining its first empire, in both North America and India. The British army incorporated its former foes and sent them to every corner of the earth to fight for king and country.

The composer John Bull wrote the tune of 'God Save the King [*or* Queen]' to help counter public enthusiasm for the Jacobite rising.

1748. The annual parade known as Trooping the Colour, celebrating the monarch's official birthday on Horse Guards Parade in London, was instituted.

1751. The Gin Act was enacted, imposing heavy duty on gin and restricting the sale of it to licensed dealers, in response to the effects of the excessive gin consumption that had taken hold, made famous in the prints of William Hogarth.

1752. The long-overdue adoption by Britain of the Gregorian Calendar took place, with the removal that year of eleven days in the then existing calendar and 2 September being immediately followed by 14 September – in the face of opposition by rioters in London shouting for the return of 'our eleven days'. At the same time, the beginning of the year in Britain changed from 25 March, as it had been up until then, to 1 January.

1756. Yet another war, and another terrible one, started: the Seven Years War, which was to continue until 1763, with England and Prussia, in Germany, on one side and France, Russia, Austria and Saxony, also in Germany, on the other.

In India, where the British, attracted by its wealth, were becoming increasingly involved, an incident that was to become famous, and even to feature frequently in popular culture, was that of the Black Hole of Calcutta. The Bengali army, led by the Nawab of Bengal, captured a fortress, Fort William, to which British troops had retreated, and held them there overnight in a dungeon as prisoners of war. By the following morning 123 of the 146 in the dungeon had died of suffocation and heat exhaustion in the cramped conditions.

1757. The British defeated the French at the Battle of Plassey, finally gaining the rich province of Bengal. This was to lead to Britain, through the East India Company, controlling most of India.

1759–1763. The Seven Years War came to an end in 1763, but a colonial war between England and France started in both India and North America. In India, where first the Portuguese and then the French had been the dominant foreign powers until then, the foundation of England's Indian empire was laid, largely thanks to the military genius of Major General Robert Clive, who was to be known as Clive of India. In North America, in 1759, which became known as the *annus mirabilis* – the 'wondrous year' – British forces under General Wolfe captured Quebec in Canada and Guadeloupe in the West Indies; and, at the First Treaty of Paris in 1763, British possession of the vast territory of Canada and several important islands in the West Indies was recognised.

(ii) Of special interest

Why did Prince Charles in 1745 suddenly abandon his march to London at a point when success and a restoration of the Stuarts had become likely to the extent of being almost certain? The extraordinary, even outrageous, decision was taken on the insistence of Prince Charles's military council, and in particular of his general, Lord George Murray, and was taken despite Prince Charles's frantic objections to what was clearly a ridiculous course of action. Only one historian that I know of, Jane Lane (in her authentic historical novel *The March of the Prince*), has produced a convincing solution: that Lord George Murray was a traitor deliberately planted in the Jacobite army. Indeed there seems to be no alternative realistic solution other than collective insanity.

~

Perhaps the single most famous event in the Seven Years War was the execution of Admiral Byng. Having failed to relieve a besieged British garrison during the Battle of Minorca in 1756, Byng decided to return to Gibraltar to repair his ships, which were indeed in very poor condition when put under his charge, rather than continue the battle. On his return to England he was tried for desertion by court martial, as military courts are called, sentenced to death and subjected to a firing squad. He was the last admiral to be executed in this manner. The event was satirised by Voltaire in his novel *Candide*, in which the hero, Candide, witnesses the execution of an officer in Portsmouth and, after asking for the reason, is told: 'In this country, it is good to kill an admiral from time to time, in order to encourage the others ('*pour encourager les autres*').' Here, more seriously, is Byng's epitaph in the church of All Saints in Southill, Bedfordshire, in which he was buried:

To the perpetual Disgrace
of PUBLICK JUSTICE

The Honble. JOHN BYNG Esqr
Admiral of the Blue
Fell a MARTYR to
POLITICAL PERSECUTION
March 14th in the year 1757 when
BRAVERY and LOYALTY
were Insufficient Securities
For the
Life and Honour
of a
NAVAL OFFICER

King George III ('Farmer George')

Born 1738 and reigned 1760–1820, as Elector and then King of Hanover in 1760–1820. Grandson of King George II and son of King George's son Frederick of Hanover. His son, then Prince of Wales, ruled as Prince Regent from 1811 to 1820.

(i) The main events of the reign in summary

1763. By the First Treaty of Paris between England, France, Spain and Portugal, England kept under its control Canada, some of the most important islands in the West Indies, and all its conquests in India.

1765. The Stamp Act was passed, making all legal documents in the North American colonies subject to a tax, as such documents already were in Britain.

1770. All the duties levied by the British on imports into America were abolished except on tea, which brought in only a negligible amount of revenue.

1772. The Royal Marriage Act was passed, under which no member of the Royal Family under twenty-five years of age could marry without the consent of the sovereign.

1773. In an extraordinary incident known as the Boston Tea-Party, a number of men dressed and painted to resemble Native Americans boarded the tea-ships, moored in Boston harbour, that belonged to the

East India Company, a corporation that had received a Charter from Queen Elizabeth I back in 1600, and emptied all the tea chests into the sea. The British government, clearly unable to ignore this contempt for authority, declared the port closed and abolished the colony's charter. The episode was gradually to escalate into revolution.

1776. The so-called American War of Independence, in fact a rebellion amounting to treason by the Americans against their lawful sovereign, broke out, to last until 1783. George Washington, a landowner and slave-owner in Virginia, the colony in America that had been named after the supposed 'Virgin Queen', was appointed commander-in-chief of the rebel forces.

On 4 July, and on that day commemorated ever since, the American Congress drew up, passed and published what, as will be explained shortly, is surely a strong contender for the title of the most ludicrous, hypocritical and dishonest document ever composed, and yet was revered at the time and has been influential ever since: the Declaration of Independence, signed by delegates from all thirteen British states.

1778. The Roman Catholic Relief Bill was passed, repealing some of the most repressive laws against Catholics.

1780. Lord George Gordon, an anti-Catholic fanatic, led a riot in opposition to those concessions, in which 60,000 Londoners marched to the Houses of Parliament to present a petition against Catholic Emancipation (the removal of many restrictions on Catholics), and tried to force their way into the House of Commons. After dispersing, the rioters reassembled shortly afterwards and over a period of several days broke open every single prison, burnt down Catholic chapels and pillaged the private dwellings of Catholics, and attacked the Bank of England and other public buildings. Order was eventually restored by 70,000 British troops. The episode was to provide the background to Charles Dickens's first historical novel, *Barnaby Rudge*.

In the same year, the Earl of Derby inaugurated at Epsom Downs the race, the most prestigious of all horse races, known as the Derby Stakes.

1783. The Treaty of Versailles between England, France, Spain and the new United States was signed. Amongst other provisions, it formally recognised the independence of the United States.

William Pitt 'the Younger', Prime Minister of England, was responsible for the India Bill being passed, giving the Privy Council supreme authority over the administration of the East India Company, which from then on was popularly known as John Company.

1787. Britain's First Fleet of eleven convict ships set sail for Botany Bay, to found Sydney, New South Wales, the first European settlement in Australia. The last convict ship to sail to Australia arrived in Western Australia in 1868.

1789. The French Revolution broke out and, after countless executions of innocent people and massacres, resulted in the abolition of the traditional rights of the French monarchy, the nobles, the clergy and all the other classes. It was to lead to the Napoleonic Wars.

1797. The Spithead Mutiny by sailors protesting over pay and working conditions was for a short time a threat in the war against the French. Conditions for sailors were improved.

1798. The Irish rebelled against British rule, which included continual injustice on the part of the British. At Vinegar Hill, near Wexford in the south-east of Ireland, the rebels were defeated and the rebellion was crushed.

At the Battle of the Nile, Horatio Nelson's fleet destroyed the French navy.

1799. Income tax was levied for the first time.

1800. Prime Minister William Pitt was responsible for the passing of the Bill for the Union of Great Britain and Ireland, under which there was one Parliament for the whole of the new United Kingdom, as it was now called, and which included, on behalf of Ireland, four Protestant bishops in the House of Lords, twenty-eight other peers in the House of Lords, and one hundred commoners. In consequence the Union Flag ('Union Jack'), dating back to 1603, was redesigned into its present form.

1803. War with France, now ruled by Napoleon as First Consul and soon to be ruled by him as Emperor, broke out.

1805. Napoleon made extensive preparations to invade England. Admiral Nelson, after being misled into going to the West Indies in pursuit of the French and Spanish fleets, returned and was responsible for England's most famous naval victory, at the Battle of

Trafalgar, in which he was killed and for which he was commemorated by Nelson's Column in the newly named Trafalgar Square.

1806. Napoleon issued the Berlin Decree, declaring the British Isles blockaded and forbidding France and her allies to trade with them, and also put his brother Joseph on the throne of Spain. Portugal refused to obey the Decree, and Portugal and Spain appealed to England for help, which was to lead to the Peninsular War.

1807. Thanks mainly to the efforts of William Wilberforce, an Act outlawing the slave trade anywhere in the British Empire was passed. Since the foundation of the British colonies in America and the West Indies, there had been an extensive trade and transport of Africans from Africa to the American plantations, with many undergoing great suffering during the journey, and some dying, and those who survived becoming slaves on their arrival.

1808. In response to Napoleon's putting his brother Joseph on the throne of Spain, the Peninsular War started, to last until 1814, and in which Arthur Wellesley, the future Duke of Wellington, was to distinguish himself.

(ii) Of special interest

Facts that do not appear in most books dealing with the history of England and America include:

- Although it is often claimed that all the northern states in America had abolished slavery by 1804, that is incorrect. For instance, New York state did not abolish slavery until 1827, and 'bondage' remained legal in Delaware, Maryland, Kentucky and Missouri until 1865.
- The War of Independence was not the event that its title would indicate. During the war, at least 50 per cent of the population remained loyal to the crown, and no fewer than 35,000 colonists fought on the British side.
- At the end of the war, which had ostensibly been about unacceptable taxation, taxes actually *increased* under George Washington's administration. A tax on alcoholic spirits provoked a rising of enraged citizens known as the 'Whiskey Rebellion'.

The rebellion in America that started in 1776 prompted a government mobilization of 17,000 armed militiamen who turned weapons upon their fellow citizens and by force of arms put down what was a clearly justifiable protest against the very species of tyranny that had been so recently alleged of the British. It was the first time that the United States government turned the military loose on dissident citizens, but it would not be the last.

Within twenty years of its inception the new United States government had accelerated government power, produced tyrannical policies, put into place onerous taxes, embarked upon unprecedented government spending, and stifled free speech by imposing fines and gaol terms for up to five years for those citizens who criticised the government or its officials.

Worthy of note, and of shame, is the effect of the original colonisation of North America by the British. Native Americans had dominated North America, and more than 500 tribes from Canada to Mexico had enjoyed limitless freedom, food, clean water and wildlife. Although there had been warfare between them and the French and Spaniards, this had made relatively little difference to their numbers. The British and other European immigrants, however, used their superior weapons to slaughter them on a vast scale and placed the few survivors into 'reservations' that were in reality internment camps. There the Native Americans lost their languages, their cultures and their way of life; and the tendency today is for them to suffer from illiteracy, alcoholism, poverty and to lead wretched lives – a strong contrast with the lives available to the native Americans in most of Spanish and Portuguese South America.

Equally worthy of note is that George Washington, Benjamin Franklin, Alexander Hamilton and Thomas Jefferson all owned slaves, and shamelessly treated them as slaves. Indeed when Pennsylvania passed a law emancipating slaves after six months' continual residence in the state, Washington went so far as to move his enslaved cook from Philadelphia to Mount Vernon just before the cook would have been eligible for his freedom.

Against that background, these are the famous opening words of the 1776 Declaration of Independence: 'We hold these truths to be self-evident: that all men are created equal ...'

Could any collection of a dozen words or so be more flagrantly untrue or more pernicious – as well as grossly hypocritical – coming as they did from slave-owners? Could anything be more self-evident that all men are *not* created equal in *any* respect, not even in the ability to breathe, think and communicate, let alone in more demanding activities, mental and physical?

Prince George, Prince of Wales, the Prince Regent

Born 1762 and ruled as Prince Regent, able to exercise in full the powers of a king, such as they were by then, from 1811 to 1820.

(i) The main events of the reign in summary

1810. King George III had his first bout of insanity, and from then on his eldest son ruled in his place, officially as Prince Regent from 5 February 1811.

The barbaric 'Highland Clearances' in Scotland started. With the full cooperation of the English, some of whom profited greatly from what took place, the chiefs of the Highland clans, until then leaders and protectors of their clans but now corrupted, ruthlessly evicted the families who had been farming the land since time immemorial, causing starvation and homelessness. The result was to be mass emigration to North America and Australia.

1811. In Leicestershire, Ned Ludd smashed one of the newly invented textile machines that were threatening the livelihoods of the traditional hand-labourers, starting the Luddite movement directed against such machines.

1814. The allies, with Britain still led by Arthur Wellesley, were victorious in the Peninsular War. Wellesley was made Duke of Wellington, and Napoleon abdicated and went into exile on the island of Elba off the west coast of Italy.

1815. Napoleon escaped from Elba, gathered old comrades round him, marched on Paris, and for three weeks was Emperor again, with King Louis XVIII, who had replaced him as head of France, fleeing from the country. At Waterloo, nine miles from Brussels, Napoleon and the Duke of Wellington faced each other in battle for the first time. Napoleon was defeated and this time condemned to exile on the British island of St. Helena in the South Atlantic, where he died in 1821.

1816–1819. A series of riots broke out. These sometimes included massacres, the most notable of which was the Peterloo Massacre in which a peaceful meeting in Manchester was broken up by armed soldiers. This led to demand for reform, which was, however, resisted in Parliament, partly because of the recollection of some of the terrifying consequences of the 1789 revolution in France.

1819. John Loudon McAdam, a Scottish engineer, introduced the use of broken stones for making roads that has been used – in due course worldwide – ever since.

(ii) Of special interest

The Regency styles of architecture are named after the Prince Regent and in his honour. They include London's Regent's Park, Regent Street and Regent's Canal, the last of which the Prince Regent commissioned. Indirectly named after him is the Royal Crescent in the city of Bath.

~

The Regency period was the period during which fashion was 'everything' in High Society, with the consequence that the period has been favoured ever since by historical novelists. The most notable figures of that time were the Prince himself, known as 'the Prince of Pleasure', and the iconic George Bryan 'Beau' Brummell, a friend of the Prince Regent's and the founder of what quickly became known as dandyism. His sole claim to the immense admiration he enjoyed at the time and the fame he has enjoyed ever since is his dictate on what good fashion must consist of – which, for whatever this information is worth, was garments that are understated and fitted to the highest degree of perfection.

King George IV

The former Prince Regent reigned as King 1820–1830. His only legitimate child, Princess Charlotte, predeceased him.

King George IV

(i) The main events of the reign in summary

1825. On 27 September, the first ever passenger locomotive on a public rail line, designed by George Stephenson, ran from Darlington to Stockton, preceded by a man on horse carrying a flag reading *Periculum privatum utilitas publica* ('The private danger is the public good'). Once the horseman was out of the way, Stephenson opened the throttle and pulled his train of wagons carrying 450 persons at a speed of fifteen miles per hour. Within twenty years all the principal towns of Great Britain were connected by rail. This development, together with mechanical inventions such as Kay's Flying Shuttle, Hargreaves's Spinning Jenny and Cartwright's Power Loom, dramatically speeding the process of weaving wool and cotton respectively, and the development of the steel industry, were the main initiators of the Industrial Revolution that was to transform the world more radically than any wars had done.

1828. The Duke of Wellington became Prime Minister, with Sir Robert Peel as Home Secretary.

1829. A long-drawn-out struggle for the emancipation of Catholics ended with the Roman Catholic Relief Act being passed, after difficulties which at one point made civil war appear to be inevitable.

There were reforms to criminal law. Starting at the time of the Reformation, some 200 crimes had become punishable by death, including stealing, forging, shoplifting and pocket-picking. About a hundred of these had had the death penalty for them removed in 1823 by Sir Robert Peel and in this year many more of them ceased to be capital.

The new profession of 'policeman' was introduced by the Home Secretary Sir Robert Peel, after whose name the police were for some time known as 'peelers', and indeed also as 'bobbies'.

(ii) Of special interest

Although it was widely supposed that King George IV was married to the widow Mrs. Fitzherbert, as was indeed the case, for two reasons this had to be kept officially a secret. One was that she was a Catholic, and a known marriage to her would have cost him the throne because of the laws of England at that time. The other was that in 1795, on the insistence of his father, who had not known about the existing marriage, he had bigamously, in a relationship which had lasted less than a year, become married to Princess Caroline of Brunswick.

King William IV ('The Sailor King')

Born 1765 and reigned in England and as King of Hanover from 1830 to 1837. Son of King George III, brother of King George IV.

(i) The main events of the reign in summary

1832. The Third Reform Bill, known as the Great Reform Bill, became law after two previous attempts at much the same legislation had failed, its strongest opponent having been the Duke of Wellington, who had become Prime Minister in 1828.

1833. The Factories Act was passed, thanks mainly to the efforts of the Earl of Salisbury, designed to protect workers from the tyranny that they had been subjected to and, for instance, making it illegal to employ children under nine years old in factories or children under thirteen for more than eight hours a day. In the same year, an Act for the Abolition of Slavery outlawing slavery was passed in all the dominions of the British Empire.

(ii) Of special interest

The Third Reform Bill made more people eligible to vote at elections and therefore the House of Commons more directly representative of the people, but there is no good reason to suppose that the United Kingdom was better governed as a result.

PART XI

MONARCHS OF ENGLAND, WALES, NORTHERN IRELAND, SCOTLAND AND ELSEWHERE, AND EMPERORS OF INDIA

CHAPTER THIRTY-EIGHT

Concluding the House of Hanover and Opening the House of Saxe-Coburg-Gotha

Queen Victoria

Born 1819 and reigned 1837–1901. Empress of India 1877–1901. She was the daughter of the Duke of Kent, who was the fourth son of King George III. In 1840 she married Prince Albert of Saxe-Coburg and Gotha, to whom she gave the title Prince Consort.

(i) The main events of the reign in summary

1837. There was a rebellion in Canada caused by the preponderance of the original French settlers in Lower Canada. Lord Durham was sent by England to restore order and quickly suppressed the rebellion.

1839. England's invasion of Afghanistan, because of fear that Russia would invade British India through Afghanistan, started the first of three Afghan wars (1839–1842, 1878–1880 and 1899) fought between England and Russia. In this year the British forces occupied Kabul, the capital of Afghanistan. In 1842 an uprising was to force Major General Sir William Elphinstone, the commander, to conduct a retreat of some ninety miles, with about 4,500 soldiers and nearly 10,000 camp-followers and other civilians, to the nearest garrison, at Jalalabad. Only a single Englishman, Dr. Brydon, survived to tell the

Queen Victoria

terrible tale, the rest dying from frostbite, starvation and constant attacks by Afghan tribesman.

Also in 1839 was the start of the first of the two Opium Wars with China, Britain officially declaring war in 1840. Opium is a herb, inducing sleep and reducing pain, that can be valuable if administered in suitable doses by competent practitioners, but when used for pleasure soon becomes a poisonous and addictive drug and indeed is the source from which heroin is derived. Early in the nineteenth century, merchants had started profiting by selling chests of opium for up to £100, with 24,000 chests of it being imported annually from India, and, very understandably, the Chinese government had become alarmed by the ever-increasing use of opium by the Chinese. In 1842 peace was concluded to British advantage, with five ports being officially opened to British trade, which included continuing to sell opium to the Chinese.

1840. Thanks primarily to the persistent efforts of Rowland Hill, an English teacher, preacher and social reformer, a new postage system, together with the first postage stamp, was introduced which was to be adopted worldwide. At the time the rates had varied between six and eighteen pennies according to the distance. The new standard one penny per half-ounce for all letters going anywhere in the United Kingdom dramatically increased the postal income because of the much greater number of letters sent.

1842. Income tax was reintroduced. Sir Robert Peel imposed a tax of seven pennies in the pound on all those who had incomes of more than £150 per annum. Assurances were given that this tax would last for only three years, but by the 1860s it had become part of the English fiscal system.

When Chinese authorities, very understandably, resisted the trade of opium and forbade its importation, a Scotsman, William Jardine, lobbied for military support. Shockingly, he was successful in his efforts. Parliament sent 4,000 troops to China to assist in waging what has been called the first Opium War. The British forces attacked China; established Shanghai and four other coastal cities – Canton, Amoy, Foochow and Ningpo – as the Treaty Ports; and forced treaties on the Chinese which granted British citizens immunity to Chinese law and ceded the island of Hong Kong and nearby territories to Britain.

1846. After many years of struggle, and notwithstanding many years of lobbying by farmers, Sir Robert Peel successfully achieved the abolition of the Corn Laws, which had long been levying heavy duties on corn imported into England to protect landowners from competition from foreign corn.

1851. On the inspiration of, and largely organised by, Prince Albert, the Great Exhibition 'of the Industries of All Nations' was held in London at the Crystal Palace. Britain showed its superiority in almost every field of industrial design and technology.

1853–1856. A dispute between Russia and Turkey about the guardianship of the Holy Places in Jerusalem gradually led to the outbreak of the Crimean War, during which took place, at the Battle of Balaclava, the Charge of the Light Brigade, to be immortalised in the poem of that name by Alfred Lord Tennyson.

1856. The Second Opium War broke out. By the time this war reached its conclusion, again to British advantage, in 1860, a further eighty trading ports, open to all foreign traders, had been established in China.

1857–1858. The British penetration of India, which had started back in 1612 with the establishment there of the East India Company, and had developed into rule by the East India Company in 1757, reached a critical stage. The Indian Mutiny, caused by Indian resentment at some of the British reforms and taxes and treatment of some of the Indian princes, now took place. (Many Indians took no part in the mutiny, and some even fought on the British side.) After the eventual British victory, the authority of the East India Company in India was transferred to the Crown, with India from then on ruled by a Viceroy, in theory directly responsible to the Queen. Rule by the British Crown, known as the Raj, a Hindustani word meaning 'rule', lasted from 1858 to 1947.

1861–1865. The American Civil War took place. During the course of it, an almost incredible 620,000 men died on the battlefield and tens of thousands sustained horrendous wounds.

1874. The islands of Fiji became part of the British Empire, on the direct request of the inhabitants of Fiji, such a request being possibly a unique event in the long history of empire-building by nations.

The Prime Minister Benjamin Disraeli persuaded the House of Commons to agree to the purchase of the major shareholding of the Suez Canal from the Khedive, a Turkish official, for £4 million.

1884. Greenwich Mean Time was established internationally, with times all over the world being calculated on the basis that Greenwich Park, one of the Royal Parks of London and overlooking the River Thames, was taken as nought degrees (0°) longitude.

1885. General Charles 'Chinese' Gordon, renowned for his exploits in China and in the Sudan, where, as Governor General, he had eliminated the flourishing slave trade, was murdered during the siege of Khartoum by the fanatical Sudanese leader the Mahdi. Lord Wolseley had been sent to relieve him but reached Khartoum too late.

1887. Queen Victoria's Golden Jubilee was commemorated with a thanksgiving service at Westminster Abbey, attended by the Queen, members of the Royal Family, many European monarchs, princes, Indian potentates and other people of distinction, and was enthusiastically celebrated worldwide.

1890. The City and South London electric underground railway, the first underground electric railway in the world, opened in London. The London underground railway had begun in 1863, but with trains powered by steam.

1895. Sir Henry Wood organised the first of the now world-famous Promenade concert seasons, known as the Proms. Originally they took place at Queen's Hall in Langham Place, London, which had opened two years earlier. In 1941 they were transferred to the Royal Albert Hall, which had been built as a memorial to the late Prince Albert, and where they have been held ever since.

1897. Queen Victoria's Diamond Jubilee was celebrated, in every part of what by then was much the biggest empire – 'on which the sun never set' – that the world had ever known.

1899–1902. The Boers in South Africa, the original settlers, demanded the abolition of British rule that the British had recently established because of the wealth being produced by gold-, diamond- and other mines. The British refused and war broke out, with Britain sending a large number of reinforcements to the Southern Cape of Africa. A famous event was the Relief of Mafeking, which Colonel Baden-Powell, to be the founder of the Scout Movement, had managed to defend for a period of 215 days. The Boers were eventually vanquished by the British, after it had taken three years and 450,000 Imperial troops to subjugate 60,000 Boer soldiers.

(ii) Of special interest

Reigning for 63 years and 216 days, Queen Victoria was the longest-reigning monarch, apart from the *de jure* King James III, until she was overtaken by Queen Elizabeth II in 2016. Many of the nine children of the royal couple made important diplomatic marriages, with the result that most of the present Royal Houses of Europe are in some way descended from Queen Victoria.

It is said with some justification that the modern world that we live in has its roots in the decade which began in 1850, with the invention in Britain of the railways and telegraphic communication, which between them shrank time and space so dramatically that every aspect of human life was transformed.

Unfortunately, this extraordinary and indeed unprecedented amount of progress in such a short time came at an unacceptably heavy cost. For instance, the Native Americans of North America, the Aboriginal people of Australia, and particularly in Tasmania, and the Maoris in New Zealand ceased to exist other than in the form of scattered remnants here and there.

King Edward VII

Born 1841, the eldest son of Queen Victoria, and reigned 1901–10. He married Princess Alexandra, daughter of King Christian IX of Denmark.

(i) The main events of the reign in summary

29 December 1902 to 10 January 1903. With the glory of the British Empire at its height, the celebrations of the King's coronation known as the Delhi Durbar or the Imperial Durbar took place in India, attended by the Duke of Connaught, King Edward's brother. A *durbar* was an Indian imperial-style mass-assembly organised by the British in Delhi to mark the succession of an

Emperor or Empress of India. The programme of events, lasting a fortnight, was on a scale that had never before been attempted anywhere.

A new day of celebration, to take place annually on 24 May, was inaugurated. Each Empire Day, millions of school children from all walks of life across the length and breadth of the British Empire would typically salute the union flag, sing patriotic songs such as 'Jerusalem' and 'God Save the Queen', hear inspirational speeches and listen to tales of 'derring-do' from across the Empire.

It is something of a pleasure to be able to say that the reign of king Edward VII was freer from disagreeably momentous events than most of the reigns that have had to feature in this book.

(ii) Of special interest

King Edward VII had been a scandalous Prince of Wales (his many mistresses included the American actress Lillie Langtry), but as king he became an able diplomatist and substantially redeemed himself.

King George V

Born 1865 into the House of Saxe-Coburg-Gotha (renamed the House of Windsor, due to anti-German sentiment, in 1917), the second son of King Edward VII. Reigned 1910–1936. Married Princess Victoria Mary of Teck, who would become Queen Mary.

(i) The main events of the reign in summary

1911. Another spectacular royal event took place, the Great Coronation Durbar in Delhi, in this case to mark the succession of King George.

The Parliament Act was passed, ensuring the predominant legislative power of the House of Commons. Specifically, the Act deprived the House of Lords of the power to reject what were called 'money bills'; laid down that a Bill passed three times by the House of Commons in a single Parliament should become law without the assent of the House of Lords; reduced the life of Parliament from seven years to five years; and granted Members of Parliament an annual salary of £400.

1914. On 28 June 1914, Archduke Franz Ferdinand and his wife Sophie, Duchess of Hohenberg, were both assassinated in Sarajevo, in the Austro-Hungarian country of Bosnia. The result was that, in quick succession, Austria declared war on Serbia; Russia declared war on Austria in support of Serbia; Germany declared war on France and, in order to invade France via the north, violated Belgian neutrality; and, in support of Belgium, Great Britain declared war on Germany. *Why* that assassination should have had that extraordinary series of effects, some of them apparently unrelated, most historians do not satisfactorily explain, though countless theories have been put forward, some of them with great thoroughness.

1917. The Russian Revolution brought about the destruction of the rule of the Russian Czars; and the Bolsheviks signed an armistice – a cessation of hostilities – with Germany. The Communists, at first under Vladimir Ilyich Ulyanov – Lenin – and then under Joseph Stalin, then proceeded to perpetrate mass murder of Russian Christians in vast numbers.

On 2 November the British government published the Balfour Declaration, which included: 'His Majesty's Government view with favour the establishment in Palestine of a national home for the Jewish people, and will use their best endeavours to facilitate the achievement of this object' – a contentious undertaking given that (a) Palestine already had a large indigenous population (of Muslims, Christians and Jews) and (b) at the time Britain had no political relationship with Palestine. Amongst much else, the Declaration was to lead to the establishment of the State of Israel in 1948.

British Lieutenant General Edmund Allenby and his forces captured Palestine from the Turks.

The United States declared war on Germany on the grounds that German submarines had started sinking American merchant ships which Germany maintained should not enter a designated war zone.

1918. In November, the Austro-Hungarian Empire and Germany both agreed to an armistice, bringing the war to what appeared to be an honourable end, with the Allies – the British Empire, France, Italy and Japan – the victors but Germany and the Austro-Hungarian Empire by no means completely defeated. The treatment of the defeated nations by the winning Allies was brutal to the extent of being unreasonable, however. The German Empire, the Russian Empire, the Austro-Hungarian Empire and the Turkish Ottoman Empire all ceased to exist, and war reparations imposed at the Versailles Conference were so severe that they bankrupted the nations, including Germany, that were subjected to them.

The League of Nations was established, supposedly to eliminate the possibility of future wars.

Under the Representation of the People Act 1918, voting rights were given to women for the first time, although until 1928 only to women aged over thirty. Interestingly, opinion polls taken during the period consistently found that most women did not want the vote, and the Women's National Anti-Suffrage League even conducted an active campaign to prevent the legislation.

1926. There was a general strike in England by no fewer than 2.5 million men, organised by the trade unions. The unions were easily defeated.

1933. Adolf Hitler and the National Socialist Party came to power in Germany.

1935. The Silver Jubilee of King George V was celebrated throughout the British Empire.

(ii) Of special interest

King George was king during the First World War, the General Strike, and also the Great Depression that began in 1929 with the stock-market crash in the United States in that year and affected the economies of most of the world's nations. It lasted until the beginning of the Second World War. He was regarded as a valuable political adviser during these crises.

CHAPTER THIRTY-NINE

The House of Windsor

King Edward VIII

Born 1894, the eldest son of King George V. Reigned in 1936 only and died in 1972.

The main event of the reign in summary

The main event was simply the drama of his determination to marry the American divorcee Mrs. Wallis Simpson. He was told that he could not do this if he wished to remain King. After less than a year on the throne, he abdicated and became Duke of Windsor, they married, and it is to be feared that they lived together unhappily ever after.

King George VI

Born 1895 and reigned 1936–1952. Second son of King George V and brother of King Edward VIII. Married Lady Elizabeth Bowes-Lyon, youngest daughter and ninth child of the Scottish peer Lord Glamis, who was later to become, by inheritance, the Earl of Strathmore and Kinghorne.

(i) The main events of the reign in summary

1938. Adolf Hitler's Germany annexed neighbouring Austria.

English Prime Minister Neville Chamberlain negotiated with Hitler the Munich Agreement which gave Germany control of Czechoslovakia, a highly industrialised country the factories of which, ironically, made it possible for Germany to fight the war which started in the following year.

1939–1940. Germany attacked and conquered Poland, Denmark, Norway, Holland, Belgium, France and Greece. Italy joined Germany.

1941–1942. Germany invaded Russia and attempted to make preparations to invade Britain, but failed to defeat the British air-force, the RAF, in the Battle of Britain. Japan launched a sudden attack on American shipping in Pearl Harbor, the American naval base in Hawaii, and this brought America into the war.

1945. On 7 May Germany surrendered unconditionally to the Allies – the British Empire, Russia and the United States of America. On 2 September Japan surrendered unconditionally to the Allies.

1947. To the dismay of a large proportion of its population, independence was granted to the Indian sub-continent, divided for that purpose into two countries: predominantly Hindu India and predominantly Muslim Pakistan. Quoting the learned Indian author Nirad C. Chaudhuri, in a letter by him published in the *Daily Telegraph* of 8 September 1992:

I have long been of the opinion that the abandonment of India in 1947 is to be regarded as the most shameful act in British history ... The massacre of nearly 1,000,000 Indians and the ruin of many more Indians that followed justifies my view. All of it was avoidable, and I have made the government of the day responsible for it.

Over the next few decades, the rest of the British Empire was wound up, often against the wishes of the inhabitants of its colonies. At the time of publication of this book, the British Overseas Territories, as the remains of the empire are now called, consist only of Gibraltar, the British Antarctic Territory, and a few islands and groups of islands with small populations, mostly in remote parts of the world.

(ii) Of special interest

During the Second World War, the King and his wife Queen Elizabeth were inspirational figureheads. After King George's death, his Queen was, and was referred to as, the Queen Mother for over fifty years, a title that was invented for her in place of the usual title of Dowager Queen, which would have led to confusion while Queen Mary, her mother-in-law, was still alive.

Queen Elizabeth II, Queen of Great Britain and Northern Ireland, and Head of the Commonwealth of Nations

Born in 1926, started reigning in 1952 and, at the time of going to press, still reigning. Eldest daughter of King George VI and Lady Elizabeth Bowes-Lyon. Both Queen Elizabeth II and her husband, Prince Philip, the Duke of Edinburgh, are great-great-grandchildren of Queen Victoria.

(i) Introductory

We have now reached the reign of Her Majesty the present monarch.

This book is intended to be purely a work of history. Current events therefore do not belong to it, and indeed little purpose would be served by relating facts that many readers can know simply by consulting their memories. Nor, for that matter, would I think it seemly to include the sort of judgements that I have made on other reigns, since it follows from what I have said about monarchy as such that Her Majesty's role is more to be the judge of her subjects than that of being judged by them, and all the more so given that, by the nature of things, she could make no reply on her own behalf to whatever I might say.

Accordingly, I do not think it the place of this book to include a treatment of this reign so far, and I therefore limit myself to a very few uncontentious facts and one reflection of some interest.

Queen Elizabeth II

(ii) Of special interest

In October 2016 Queen Elizabeth overtook Queen Victoria's tally of 63 years and 216 days to become the longest-serving British monarch in history. By then, incidentally, her eldest son and her heir Prince Charles, the Prince of Wales, already held a world record of his own: four years earlier he became the longest-waiting heir apparent, surpassing the fifty-nine years spent by his great-great-grandfather Edward VII as heir apparent to Queen Victoria. Other records that had been broken by the end of 2017 include: the Queen had become Britain's oldest ever monarch; she and her consort Prince Philip had become the longest-living royal couple; Prince Philip had become the longest-living consort of either sex; and she and Prince Philip had been enjoying the longest-ever royal marriage.

Because Queen Elizabeth's mother was a commoner (Lady Elizabeth Bowes-Lyon), Prince Philip has more royal blood running through his veins than does the Queen.

In 1960 Queen Elizabeth's sister Princess Margaret married the first male commoner – neither royal nor a peer – to marry into the Royal Family for 450 years, Antony Armstrong-Jones. In 1978 they became the first royal couple ever to be divorced as opposed to their marriage being annulled. (An annulment is an official judgement that there has been no valid marriage. A divorce takes place when two surviving spouses of a valid marriage are declared to be no longer married.)

I think it worth closing with an observation that makes an important point about monarchy as a system for running a country. I myself have had the opportunity to observe all fifteen Prime Ministers, starting with Winston Churchill and Clement Attlee, who have served during the reign of Queen Elizabeth. There is not one of them that I should prefer to have had in charge of the country's affairs, both domestic and overseas, than the Queen or the present Prince of Wales. It is, after all, ordinary sanity to expect that someone born to and educated for the role, with a long-term interest in it, and under no financial pressure, would be more suitable in every way for it than politicians whose qualifications for it need be no more than ambition and the ability to sell themselves, unscrupulously if necessary, to an all-too-often gullible public.

PART XII

CHAPTER FORTY

Concluding

WHAT IS THERE left to say, as I take my leave of my gracious readers?

I believe that, at the very least, I have shown that history, and especially the history of one's own country, is an important subject for all of us to study, from our earliest years onwards; that it can be perhaps the most difficult subject of all in which to arrive consistently at the truth; but that, nevertheless, consistently arriving at the truth in it very much matters.

To those who doubt, or even deny, that history and identifying reality in history are as important as I have been maintaining, it is surely sufficient to point out that such doubts have not been shared by those many who undertook the task of falsifying our history drastically in the past. On the contrary, their respect for the power of truth, and therefore for the desirability of falsification in many circumstances, was such that they left no stone unturned in their efforts to blacken the good names that monarchs such as King Richard III and King James II deserved and to prevent us from arriving at a just judgement of such monstrosities as Queen Elizabeth I and King William III.

I think it reasonable, perhaps even imperative, to urge that we should take such historians – the falsifiers of the past – extremely seriously. *They* recognise the importance of true history. *That* is why they take so much trouble to conceal, distort, falsify and eliminate this history. I greatly hope that this book will be of some help in the direction of reversing the destruction in which they have been so consistently successful.

FAMILY TREE

(Where dates are not given, they are unknown.)

ANCHISES – A prince of Troy
|

1. Unnamed = KING AENEAS = 2. LAVINIA (daughter of KING LATINUS – he
| (1104–1081 BC) | was king of the territory that would become Rome)

KING
Unnamed = ASCANIUS   SILVIUS AENEAS
|

KING SILVIUS = Unnamed NIECE OF LAVINIA
|

KING
BRUTUS (1104 BC) = IGNOGE (who may have been related to Brutus)

LOCRINUS = 1. GWENDOLEN   ALBANACTUS   KAMBER
2. ESTRILDIS
|

KING MADAN (1056–1016 BC)
|
KING MEMPRICIUS (1016–996 BC)
|
KING EBRAUCUS (996–957 BC)
|
KING BRUTUS II (first king of the Britons) (957–945 BC)
|
KING LEIL (945–920 BC)
|
KING HUDIBRAS (920–881 BC)
|
KING BLADUD (881–861 BC)
|
KING LEIR (861–801 BC)

GONERIL   REGAN   QUEEN CORDELIA (801–794 BC)
= HENWINUS (Duke of Cornwall)
|

KING CUNEDAGIUS (794–761 BC)
|
KING RIVALLO (761–743 BC)
|
KING GURGUSTIUS (743–723 BC)
|
KING SILICIUS I (723–683 BC)
|
KING KIMARCUS (683–663 BC)
|
KING GORBODUC (663–643 BC)
|
KING FERREX (643 BC)
|
(200 years of civil war, during which there are no surviving records)
|
KING PINNER (440–430 BC)
|
KING CLOTEN (King of Cornwall) (430–420 BC)
|

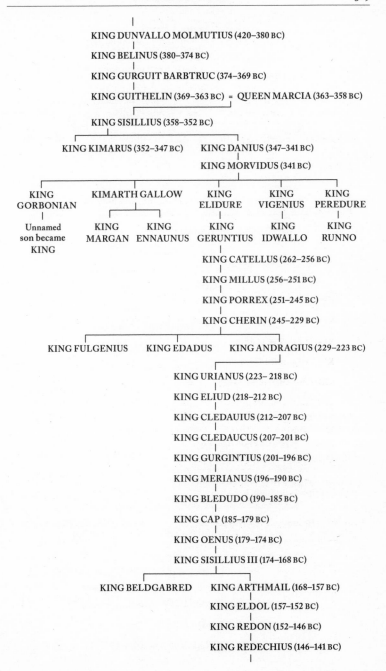

KING DUNVALLO MOLMUTIUS (420–380 BC)

KING BELINUS (380–374 BC)

KING GURGUIT BARBTRUC (374–369 BC)

KING GUITHELIN (369–363 BC) = QUEEN MARCIA (363–358 BC)

KING SISILLIUS (358–352 BC)

KING KIMARUS (352–347 BC)   KING DANIUS (347–341 BC)

KING MORVIDUS (341 BC)

KING GORBONIAN   KIMARTH GALLOW   KING ELIDURE   KING VIGENIUS   KING PEREDURE

Unnamed son became KING   KING MARGAN   KING ENNAUNUS   KING GERUNTIUS   KING IDWALLO   KING RUNNO

KING CATELLUS (262–256 BC)

KING MILLUS (256–251 BC)

KING PORREX (251–245 BC)

KING CHERIN (245–229 BC)

KING FULGENIUS   KING EDADUS   KING ANDRAGIUS (229–223 BC)

KING URIANUS (223– 218 BC)

KING ELIUD (218–212 BC)

KING CLEDAUIUS (212–207 BC)

KING CLEDAUCUS (207–201 BC)

KING GURGINTIUS (201–196 BC)

KING MERIANUS (196–190 BC)

KING BLEDUDO (190–185 BC)

KING CAP (185–179 BC)

KING OENUS (179–174 BC)

KING SISILLIUS III (174–168 BC)

KING BELDGABRED   KING ARTHMAIL (168–157 BC)

KING ELDOL (157–152 BC)

KING REDON (152–146 BC)

KING REDECHIUS (146–141 BC)

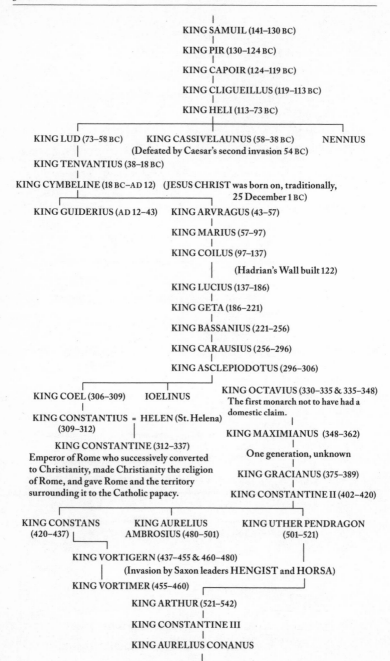

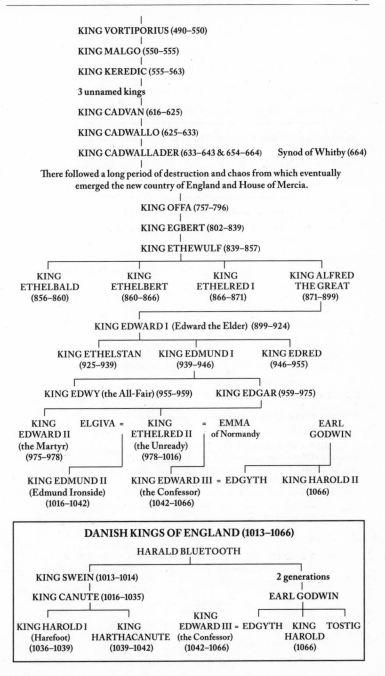

KING VORTIPORIUS (490–550)

KING MALGO (550–555)

KING KEREDIC (555–563)

3 unnamed kings

KING CADVAN (616–625)

KING CADWALLO (625–633)

KING CADWALLADER (633–643 & 654–664)   Synod of Whitby (664)

There followed a long period of destruction and chaos from which eventually emerged the new country of England and House of Mercia.

KING OFFA (757–796)

KING EGBERT (802–839)

KING ETHEWULF (839–857)

KING ETHELBALD (856–860)	KING ETHELBERT (860–866)	KING ETHELRED I (866–871)	KING ALFRED THE GREAT (871–899)

KING EDWARD I (Edward the Elder) (899–924)

KING ETHELSTAN (925–939)	KING EDMUND I (939–946)	KING EDRED (946–955)

KING EDWY (the All-Fair) (955–959)   KING EDGAR (959–975)

KING EDWARD II (the Martyr) (975–978)	ELGIVA = KING ETHELRED II (the Unready) (978–1016)	= EMMA of Normandy	EARL GODWIN

KING EDMUND II (Edmund Ironside) (1016–1042)	KING EDWARD III (the Confessor) (1042–1066) = EDGYTH	KING HAROLD II (1066)

DANISH KINGS OF ENGLAND (1013–1066)

HARALD BLUETOOTH

KING SWEIN (1013–1014)	2 generations
KING CANUTE (1016–1035)	EARL GODWIN

KING HAROLD I (Harefoot) (1036–1039)	KING HARTHACANUTE (1039–1042)	KING EDWARD III (the Confessor) (1042–1066) = EDGYTH	KING HAROLD (1066)	TOSTIG

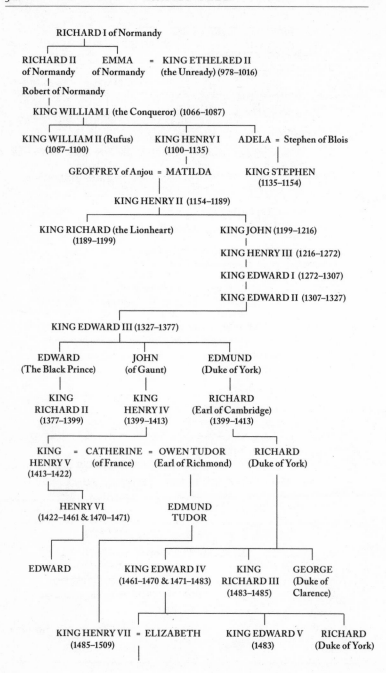

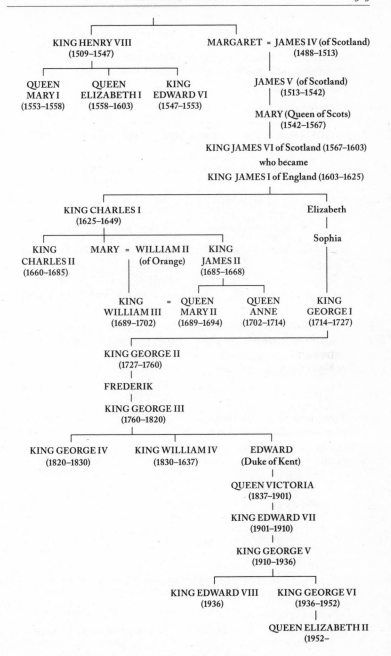

Notes

1. The document in question is listed at the Bodleian as *Jesus College MS LXI* – short for 'Welsh manuscript number LXI of Jesus College, Oxford' – and was originally known as the *Brut Tysilio* or *Tysilio Chronicle*.
2. Quoted in Beatrice Adelaide Lees, *Alfred the Great: Maker of England, 1848–1849* (New York and London: G. E. Putnam's Sons, 1915).
3. Gurdon, *History of the High Court of Parliament*, vol. 1, p. 37.
4. Heylin, *Ecclesia Restaurata, or the History of the Reformation*, vol. 1, p. 120.
5. Mackie, *The Early Tudors, 1485–1558*, p.530.
6. Hook, *Lives of the Archbishops of Canterbury*, vol. 6, p. 472.
7. Finlason (ed.), *Reeves's History of English Law*, vol. 3, p. 583.
8. Hallam, *Constitutional History of England*, vol. 1, p. 113.
9. Lockyer, *James VI and I*, p. 200.
10. Fontenay to the French secretary of Mary Queen of Scots, 15 August 1584.
11. Recorded by Sir Francis Bacon, a member of the House of Commons at the time. See Spedding (ed.), *The Works of Francis Bacon*, vol. 10, p. 94.
12. Starkey, *Crown & Country*, p. 346.
13. Marshall, *Our Island Story*, pp. 394, 399.

Bibliographical

1.

The following are books that I believe to be, as well as – I hope – this book, indispensable to anyone studying or writing about England's history. Remarkably, at least the great majority of them make no appearance in any bibliography that I have ever come across.

General (in alphabetical order of author)

George Carter (a schoolmaster), *Outlines of English History: Dates, Facts, Events, People* (London: Ward Lock, originally 1962 and regularly kept up to date until 1987).

William Cobbett, *A History of the Protestant Reformation in England and Ireland*. I recommend only the edition edited by Cardinal (Francis Aiden) Gasquet (Cobbett's original edition published in instalments 1924–1926; edition edited by Cardinal Gasquet, New York: Benziger, undated).

W. F. Finlason (ed.), *Reeves's History of English Law from the Time of the Romans to the End of the Reign of Elizabeth* (London: Reeves & Turner, 1869).

Sir John Fortescue, *In Praise of the Laws of England* and *The Governance of England*, fifteenth century, various editions in print.

J. A. Giles, *The British History of Geoffrey of Monmouth in Twelve Books, translated from Latin by A. Thompson Esq, and revised and corrected* (London: James Bohn, 1842).

Acton Griscom, *The* Historia Regum Britanniae *of Geoffrey of Monmouth with contributions to the study of its place in early British history* (London: Longmans, Green, 1929).

Peter Heylin, *Ecclesia Restaurata, or the History of the Reformation*, first published in 1661 (Cambridge: Cambridge University Press for the Ecclesiastical History Society, 1849).

Albert M. Hyamson, *A History of the Jews in England* (London: Jewish Historical Society of England and Chatto & Windus, 1908).

Jane Lane, various. Popular during her career as an author during the 1930s, 1940s, 1950s, 1960s and 1970s, but almost unknown today, she is the only historian I know of who, in my judgement, consistently gets history right in the many periods that she covers. Most of her books are in the form of historical novels. Generally speaking, I have reservations about historical novels as sources of history, because their authors tend to be prepared to sacrifice strict historical accuracy in the interests of a good story when they think this necessary. Jane Lane never did that, however, and, with very rare exceptions, her books are both reliable in that respect and wonderfully well-constructed and well-written. I have compiled a 143-page document listing her books, fifty-one in all, and giving descriptions of each of them which include indications of those which are suitable for adults only, those which are suitable for children as well as adults, and those, less than half a dozen, which I am unable to recommend at all. I am making it available, as an attachment to an email, for £5 to anyone who contacts me and asks for it.

Professor James Edwin Thorold Rogers, *History of Agriculture and Prices in England from 1259 to 1793* (London: Henry Frowde, 1866). Not as essential as the others in this list because the most important parts of it are reproduced in the Gasquet edition of Cobbett's *History of the Protestant Reformation*.

Of special usefulness for individual monarchs and dynasties (in the monarchs' date order)

John Morris, *The Age of Arthur: A History of the British Isles 350 to 650*, 3 vols. (London: Phillimore, 1973).

Leslie Alcock, *Arthur's Britain* (London: Allen Lane, 1971).

Alfred George Knight, *The Life of King Alfred the Great* (London: Burns and Oates, 1880).

Alan Lloyd, *The Maligned Monarch: A Life of King John of England* (New York: Doubleday, 1972).

Desmond Seward, *Henry V as Warlord* (1987), republished as *The Warrior King and the Invasion of France* (New York: First Pegasus, 2014).

Paul Murray Kendall, *Richard III* (London: George Allen, 1955).

V. B. Lamb, *The Betrayal of Richard III* (London: Research Publishing, 1959).

Jeremy Potter, *Good King Richard?* (London: Constable, 1983).

Josephine Tey, *The Daughter of Time* (London: Peter Davis, 1951).

Piers Compton, *Bad Queen Bess* (London: Alexander Ouseley, 1933).

2.

The following are books that I have come across during the course of many decades of studying English history, surely one of the most interesting and difficult of all subjects. That a book features in these two lists should not be considered to be any indication of whether I consider it to be very helpful, reasonably helpful, unhelpful or extremely unhelpful. The part of this book relevant to any particular period or monarchs covered should provide sufficient guidance. No completeness of any kind is aimed for in what follows, and all the more is this true of the period following the end of the Stuart dynasty.

General (in alphabetical order of author)

Lewis Broad, *Crowning the King: An Account of the Coronation Ceremonies, of King George VI's Life, His Homes and Palaces* (London: Hutchinson, undated); deals with coronations from Saxon times onwards.

Arthur Bryant, *A Thousand Years of British Monarchy* (London: Collins, 1975).

John Cannon and Ralph Griffiths, *The Oxford Illustrated History of the British Monarchy* (Oxford: Oxford University Press, 1988).

Richard Cavendish, *Kings & Queens: The Concise Guide* (Ohio: David & Charles, 2007).

Edward Coke, *Institutes of the Lawes of England*, 4 vols. (seventeenth century).

Eamon Duffy, *The Stripping of the Altars: Traditional Religion in England, 1400–1580* (London: Yale University Press, 1992).

Plantagenet Somerset Fry, *Kings & Queens of England and Scotland* (London: Dorling Kindersley, 1999).

Gildas, edited and translated by Michael Winterbottom, *The Ruin of Britain* (London: Phillimore, 1978).

Andrew Gimson, *Gimson's Kings & Queens* (London: Square Peg, 2015).

J. M. Golby, *Kings & Queens of Empire: British Monarchs 1760–2000* (London: The History Press, 2000).

Thornhagh Gurdon, *History of the High Court of Parliament* (London: R. Knaplock, 1731).

Henry Hallam, *The Constitutional History of England* (New York: W. J. Widdleton, 1877).

Walter Hook, *Lives of the Archbishops of Canterbury* (London: Richard Bentley, 1868).

John Lingard, *The History of England from the Invasion by the Romans to the Accession of William and Mary in 1688*, 12 vols. (London: Nimmo & Bain,

1883). It could be argued that this belongs to section 1 above, but all the most important facts in it are to be found in William Cobbett's *History*.

_____ and Hilaire Belloc, *The History of England from the Invasion by the Romans to the Accession of William and Mary in 1688*, vol. 11, a supplementary volume to the above (London: Sands; and New York: Catholic Publication Society of America, 1915).

H. E. Marshall, *Our Island Story: A History of England for Boys and Girls* (London: Thomas Nelson & Sons, undated, around 1905).

Nennius, edited and translated by John Morris, *British History and The Welsh Annals* (London: Phillimore, 1980). Written in the ninth century.

Matthew Paris, *Chronica Majora* (around 1250).

Jeremy Paxman, *On Royalty* (London: Viking, 2006).

'Penguin Monarchs' series (London: Penguin, 2015–).

Nicholas Sander, *The Rise and Growth of the Anglican Schism* (London: Burns & Oates, 1992).

James Spedding et al. (eds), *The Works of Francis Bacon* (New York: Houghton Mifflin, 1900).

David Starkey, *Monarchy: England and Her Rulers from the Tudors to the Windsors* (London: Harper, 2007).

_____, *Crown & Country* (London: Harper, 2010).

Agnes Strickland, *Lives of the Queens of England* (London: Henry Cockburn, 1848).

Dr. J. S. P. Tatlock, *The Legendary History of Britain* (Berkeley: University of California Press, 1950).

Robert Tombs, *The English and Their History* (London: Allen Lane, 2014).

Individual monarchs and dynasties (in their date order)

Bruce O'Brien, *God's Peace and King's Peace: The Laws of King Edward the Confessor* (Philadelphia: University of Philadelphia Press, 1999).

Hope Muntz, *The Golden Warrior* (London: Chatto and Windus, 1949), on King Harold.

Don Gillingham, *Richard the Lionheart* (New York: Times Books, 1978).

Kate Norgate, *John Lackland* (London: Macmillan, 1902).

'William Shakespeare', *Richard III* (seventeenth century).

Horace Walpole, *Historic Doubts On the Life and Reign of Richard the Third* (1768, recent edition with introduction by P. W. Hammond: Gloucester: Alan Sutton, 1987).

J. D. Mackie, *The Early Tudors, 1485–1558* (Oxford: Clarendon, 1952).

S. B. Chrimes, *Henry VII* (London: Eyre Methuen, 1972).

Jasper Ridley, *Henry VIII* (London: Constable, 1984).

J. J. Scarisbrick, *Henry VIII* (London: Methuen, 1968).

Giles Tremlett, *Catherine of Aragon, Henry's Spanish Queen: A Biography* (London: Faber & Faber, 2010).

Patrick Williams, *Katharine of Aragon* (Stroud: Amberley, 2013).

Josephine Wilkinson, *The Early Loves of Anne Boleyn*, republished as *Anne Boleyn* (Stroud: Amberley, 2009 and 2011).

Frederick George Lee, *King Edward the Sixth, Supreme Head: An Historical Sketch* (London: Burns and Oates, 1889).

John Edwards, *Mary I: England's Catholic Queen* (New Haven and London: Yale University Press, 2011).

Carolly Erickson, *Bloody Mary* (London: J. M. Dent, 1978).

H. F. M. Prescot, *Mary Tudor* (London: Eyre & Spottiswoode, 1940).

Antonia Fraser, *Mary Queen of Scots* (London: Weidenfeld & Nicolson, 1969).

John Guy, *Tudor England* (Oxford: Oxford University Press, 1988).

_____ *The Children of Henry VIII* (Oxford: Oxford University Press, 2013).

_____ *Elizabeth: the Forgotten Years* (London: Viking, 2016).

Elizabeth Jenkins, *Elizabeth the Great* (London: Victor Gollancz, 1958).

_____ *Elizabeth and Leicester* (London: Victor Gollancz, 1961).

Alison Weir, *Elizabeth the Queen* (London: Vintage, 2009).

Sir Charles Petrie, Bart., *The Stuarts* (London: Eyre & Spottiswoode, 1958).

Glenn Burgess, *Absolute Monarchy and the Stuart Constitution* (New Haven and London: Yale University Press, 1996).

James I (King), *Basilikon Doron, or, King James's Instructions to His Dearest Sonne, Henry the Prince, reprinted by his Majesties Command*, 1682 (Reprinted, Early English Books Online, undated).

Roger Lockyer, *James VI and I* (London: Longman, 1998).

T. Longueville (unnamed on title page), *The Adventures of King James II of England* (London: Longmans, Green, 1904).

Malcolm V. Hay, *Winston Churchill and James II* (London: Harding & Moore, 1934).

Jane Lane, *King James the Last* (London: Andrew Drakes, 1942).

Desmond Gleeson, *The Tragedy of the Stuarts* (London: Cecil Palmer, 1930).

Theo Aronson, *Kings Over the Water: The Saga Of the Stuart Pretenders* (London: Cassell, 1979).

James Lees-Milne, *The Last Stuarts* (London: Chatto & Windus, 1983).

Compton Mackenzie, *Prince Charlie* (London: Dennis Dobson, 1932).

Evelyn Cruikshanks, *The Glorious Revolution* (Basingstoke: Macmillan, 2000).

Jonathan I. Israel (ed.), *The Anglo-Dutch Moment: Essays on the Glorious Revolution and Its World Impact* (Cambridge: Cambridge University Press, 1991).

Agnes Strickland, *Lives of the Queens of England*, vol. XII (on Queen Anne) (London: Henry Cockburn, 1848).

Christopher Hibbert, *George III: A Personal History* (London: Viking, 1998).

Doris Leslie, *The Great Corinthian: A Portrait of the Prince Regent* (London: Eyre & Spottiswoode, 1952).

Christopher Hibbert, *Queen Victoria: A Personal History* (London: Da Capo, 2000).

Sir Alan Lascelles, edited by Duff Hart-Davis, *King's Counsellor: Abdication and War: The Diaries of Sir Alan Lascelles* (London: Weidenfeld & Nicolson, 2006).

Compton Mackenzie, *The Windsor Tapestry: Being a Study of the Life, Heritage, and Education of HRH, the Duke of Windsor, KG* (London: Rich & Cowan, 1938).

~

I do not seek to imply by the relative shortness of this list that there are no other books that are of value. On the contrary, there are many books that can usefully be consulted, especially if – if I may make so bold! – they are read side-by-side, so to speak, with this book so that their readers can take any disagreements between such books and this one into account. What I firmly do maintain, however, is that any book that takes no account of the wonderful scholarship, as to both facts and moral judgements, of the Cobbett–Gasquet–Rogers–Lingard *History of the Protestant Reformation*, whether to accept or to argue against its conclusions, is inevitably defective in that respect. And, despite that book's having consistently enjoyed solid sales ever since its publication, I have never yet come across a book on English monarchs or any individual English monarch written subsequently to it that makes any reference to it.

Acknowledgements

FIRST IN ORDER of my 'indebtednesses' is to Mr. Tom Hodgkinson, of *Idler* renown. He was originally responsible for the idea, the title and the original publication in 2012 of the book, *Gwynne's Grammar*, which launched my new writing career.

Second: Mr. Jake Lingwood, Deputy Managing Director of Ebury Press, and head of its editorial team. He noticed the Idler's original edition of *Gwynne's Grammar*, which was in large-booklet form, and suggested to Mr. Hodgkinson and me that, if I were to expand it and take advantage of the resources that Ebury Press had at its disposal, it could well be popular with the book-buying public, which indeed turned out to be the case, to my great appreciation. Moreover, I cannot imagine a happier author–publisher relationship.

Under this heading, I am also deeply grateful to Miss Laura Horsley, who was most closely responsible, on Ebury's behalf, for seeing this book through its various stages. For the task of editing into its present form the text that I originally submitted, Mr. Lingwood and Miss Horsley appointed Mr. Will Atkins. I am having difficulty in finding words to express sufficiently my appreciation of Mr. Atkins's contribution, which consisted of going through the text in the minutest detail, sometimes correcting, sometimes challenging, sometimes recommending clarifications, sometimes simply playing devil's advocate – always helpfully. Professionalism at its ultimate, it seems to me. Also appreciated is the help of Mr. Ed Pickford in the design of the family tree.

As I have said before and now say for the last time: because of the very large number of facts that need to be included, I think it possible that a book of history covering a long period is about as difficult a book to write as there can be, in terms of avoiding errors big and small. I am deeply grateful to the following people each of whom has painstakingly read the text at different stages, and all of whom, between them, have saved me from many errors, some of them small and some of them extremely serious, and have also suggested items for inclusion, some of them important, which would not otherwise have occurred to me: His Royal Highness the Duke of Kent, Count Nikolai Tolstoy, Mr. Hugh Williams, to whom I am also indebted for having undertaken the difficult task of putting together the family tree, my wife Mrs. N. M. (Frederica) Gwynne and my daughter Miss Chloe Gwynne.

Finally, as formidable, in his competence and painstaking care, as anyone whose help I am acknowledging here has been Mr. Howard Waters, whom Ebury appointed to proofread the final, typeset draft, and who rescued this book from an astonishing number of errors, many of them subtle but all of them significant, that had somehow slipped past the notice of the rest of us.

I thank them all, both for undertaking the considerable labour inevitably involved in the task of working their way through a book of this nature, and for the many improvements they have been responsible for. Being thus thanked should not be taken as implying that any of those mentioned above are in agreement with everything in this book.

These Acknowledgements would not be complete without a mention of my indebtedness to that extraordinary and wonderful institution, the London Library, this appreciation of which by Lord David Cecil (1922–1986) is especially appropriate in a work devoted to kings and queens: 'It has been said that England has produced three institutions at once admirable and unique. I forget what the third is; but the other two are the Monarchy and the London Library.'

Index